Boston Terriers For Dummies®

Questions to Ask Breeders

Before you adopt the Boston Terrier of your dreams, you first need to find a reputable breeder. How do you discern between reputable and disreputable ones? Ask them lots of questions. Here, I've listed a handful of queries to bring when you're interviewing potential Boston breeders. For appropriate answers and more information about finding a breeder, flip to Chapter 4.

- How long have you been breeding Boston Terriers? Do you breed other dogs?
- What dog organizations do you belong to?
- What health problems do you screen for? What congenital defects are present in this breed, and what steps are you taking to decrease those defects?
- What kind of health guarantee do you offer with your dogs?
- Can I visit your facility and meet the dam?
- What are the parents' good and bad points?
- Where were the puppies raised? How have you socialized them?
- How many litters do you have a year?
- When can I take the puppy home?

Questions to Ask Boarding Facilities

Whether you're taking a vacation or traveling for work, you may need to leave your Boston behind. A clean, well-staffed boarding facility makes a wonderful home away from home for your pet. (Chapter 13 lists additional options for boarding your Boston.) Before you drop her off, however, ask the facility owner or manager some questions, including:

- What hours are you open? When can I drop off my dog and pick her up?
- Is the kennel supervised 24 hours a day in case of emergency?
- What vaccinations do you require the dogs to have?
- Are incoming dogs screened for fleas, ticks, and other parasites?
- Is a veterinarian on call in case of emergency?
- What experience do you require your staff to have? Do they know dog first aid?
- How large are the kennels? How often are they cleaned?
- How often are the dogs fed? Watered?
- Can I bring my own food, treats, and toys? Is bedding provided, or can I bring my own?
- Will someone walk my dog every day? Is there a fee for this service?
- Do you offer any grooming services?

For Dummies: Bestselling Book Series for Beginners

BESTSELLING
BOOK SERIES

Boston Terriers
For Dummies®

Cheat Sheet

Questions to Ask Dog Sitters

Some dog owners prefer pet sitters to boarding facilities. As you discover in Chapter 13, you can use a friend, family member, neighbor, or professional dog sitter. If you're hiring a professional pet sitter with whom you're not familiar, be sure to ask her these questions:

- Do you belong to a professional pet-sitting organization, such as the National Association of Professional Pet Sitters?
- Do you have references? If so, can I contact them?
- Are you insured and bonded?
- How long have you been working as a pet sitter? Have you ever dog-sat a Boston?
- What experience do you have with medical care? Do you know canine first aid?
- Will you stay in my home, or will you come by several times a day?
- If you're coming by several times during the day, what times will you come over? How long will you stay?
- What do you charge for your services, both staying at my home and coming over during the day?

Tips for Living with a Boston

- Choose a dog whose age and personality fit with yours.
- Prepare your home by puppy proofing his living area and gathering all the necessary supplies, which are listed in Chapter 5.
- Growing puppies need nutritious food. Feed your dog a healthy diet in the right amounts, and even if he's a good boy, don't overdo the treats!
- Growing puppies also need regular health checks and vaccinations. Meet with your veterinarian regularly during your dog's developing years.
- Educate yourself about common illnesses and breed-specific ailments. Knowing what signs to look for can save your dog's life.
- Keep your Boston looking his best by grooming him on a regular basis. Grooming not only helps him look good, but it's an opportunity to inspect your dog's body and find problems before they turn into emergencies.
- Begin to crate and housetrain your Boston early. Your pup will grow to love his den as his safe place, and you will help him develop good elimination habits as soon as possible.
- Socialize your pup early by introducing him to as many sights, sounds, and smells as possible. The more people and dogs he meets, the better!
- Teach your Boston how to settle, sit, stay, leave it, and heel when he is a puppy. Attend puppy kindergarten and basic training when he is old enough.

Emergency Phone Numbers

Cut these numbers out and keep them by your phone or on the fridge:

Vet's office: _____

Animal hospital/Emergency care: _____

Breeder: _____

Local animal shelter: _____

Animal Poison Control: 888-426-4235 ($50 consultation fee)

For Dummies: Bestselling Book Series for Beginners

Boston Terriers

FOR

DUMMIES®

by Wendy Bedwell-Wilson

BICENTENNIAL
1807
WILEY
2007
BICENTENNIAL

Wiley Publishing, Inc.

Boston Terriers For Dummies®

Published by
Wiley Publishing, Inc.
111 River St.
Hoboken, NJ 07030-5774
www.wiley.com

Copyright © 2007 by Wiley Publishing, Inc., Indianapolis, Indiana

Published simultaneously in Canada

No part of this publication may be reproduced, stored in a retrieval system, or transmitted in any form or by any means, electronic, mechanical, photocopying, recording, scanning, or otherwise, except as permitted under Sections 107 or 108 of the 1976 United States Copyright Act, without either the prior written permission of the Publisher, or authorization through payment of the appropriate per-copy fee to the Copyright Clearance Center, 222 Rosewood Drive, Danvers, MA 01923, 978-750-8400, fax 978-646-8600. Requests to the Publisher for permission should be addressed to the Permissions Department, John Wiley & Sons, Inc., 111 River Street, Hoboken, NJ 07030, 201-748-6011, fax 201-748-6008, or online at http://www.wiley.com/go/permissions.

Trademarks: Wiley, the Wiley Publishing logo, For Dummies, the Dummies Man logo, A Reference for the Rest of Us!, The Dummies Way, Dummies Daily, The Fun and Easy Way, Dummies.com and related trade dress are trademarks or registered trademarks of John Wiley & Sons, Inc. and/or its affiliates in the United States and other countries, and may not be used without written permission. All other trademarks are the property of their respective owners. Wiley Publishing, Inc., is not associated with any product or vendor mentioned in this book.

For general information on our other products and services, please contact our Customer Care Department within the U.S. at 877-762-2974, outside the U.S. at 317-572-3993, or fax 317-572-4002.

For technical support, please visit www.wiley.com/techsupport.

Wiley also publishes its books in a variety of electronic formats. Some content that appears in print may not be available in electronic books.

Library of Congress Control Number: 2007926395

ISBN: 978-0-470-12768-1

Manufactured in the United States of America

10 9 8 7 6 5 4 3 2

WILEY

About the Author

Pets and their quirks have been a part of Wendy Bedwell-Wilson's life for as long as she can remember, but it was through her profession that she grew to truly appreciate them. After working in the publishing industry as a writer and editor for a variety of pet-themed trade, consumer, and online magazines for nearly 15 years, she ventured outside the cubicle and delved into writing professionally about four-legged friends from her home in Hawaii.

Her work has appeared in a range of pet publications, including *Pet Product News, Veterinary Practice News, DogChannel.com, Cat Fancy, Koi World, FAMA, Aquarium Fish, Cats USA, Kittens USA,* and the *Popular Pets* series. She completed one book — *Yorkshire Terriers* for the Animal Planet Pet Care Library series — before tackling *Boston Terriers For Dummies.* Her muses include a rescued Pointer-Hound mutt named Pete and two spoiled cats, Bubba and Benny. They're no Boston Terriers, but they're still little gentlemen.

Dedication

To my mother, Ruth Bedwell, the strongest woman I know.

Author's Acknowledgments

Publishing a book like this requires a team of dedicated individuals, including editors, illustrators, production staff, and breed experts. My thanks goes out to Stacy Kennedy, acquisitions editor; Chrissy Guthrie, project editor; Vicki Adang, copy editor; Patty Kovach, DVM, technical editor; Barbara Frake, illustrator; and the production, printing, and distribution teams who made the book a reality and delivered it to the consumers.

I also owe gratitude to the many Boston Terrier experts I consulted, including dozens of breeders and Boston lovers associated with the Boston Terrier Club of America; trainers Ricko Rask and Ellen Carscadden; Andy Tesene, co-owner of Two Bostons in Naperville, Illinois; Mark Daly, DVM, who answered a host of veterinary questions; the American Kennel Club; the American Veterinary Medical Association; and the countless dog lovers who provided advice, support, and plenty of dog-inspired laughs. Thanks, too, to fellow author Eve Adamson, who helped to guide me to and through the project, and Lee Ann Chearney, my agent and book producer. And I can't forget my patient and loyal husband, Ryan, my family, and our four-legged menagerie that brings unending joy to our lives.

Publisher's Acknowledgments

We're proud of this book; please send us your comments through our Dummies online registration form located at www.dummies.com/register/.

Some of the people who helped bring this book to market include the following:

Acquisitions, Editorial, and Media Development

Senior Project Editor: Christina Guthrie

Acquisitions Editor: Stacy Kennedy

Copy Editor: Vicki Adang

Technical Editor: Patty Kovach, DVM

Editorial Manager: Christine Meloy Beck

Editorial Assistants: Erin Calligan Mooney, Joe Niesen, Leeann Harney

Cover Photo: © ROBERT PEARCY/Animals Animals

Cartoons: Rich Tennant (www.the5thwave.com)

Composition Services

Project Coordinator: Erin Smith

Layout and Graphics: Heather Ryan, Alicia B. South

Special Art: Illustrations by Barbara Frake, color section photos by Jean Fogle (www.jeanfogle.com), Isabelle Francais, and Cathi Winkles

Anniversary Logo Design: Richard Pacifico

Proofreaders: Aptara, Susan Moritz

Indexer: Aptara

Publishing and Editorial for Consumer Dummies

    Diane Graves Steele, Vice President and Publisher, Consumer Dummies

    Joyce Pepple, Acquisitions Director, Consumer Dummies

    Kristin A. Cocks, Product Development Director, Consumer Dummies

    Michael Spring, Vice President and Publisher, Travel

    Kelly Regan, Editorial Director, Travel

Publishing for Technology Dummies

    Andy Cummings, Vice President and Publisher, Dummies Technology/General User

Composition Services

    Gerry Fahey, Vice President of Production Services

    Debbie Stailey, Director of Composition Services

Contents at a Glance

Introduction..*1*

Part I: That Bullish Terrier................................*7*

Chapter 1: Welcome to Boston! 9
Chapter 2: Tracking the Boston Terrier.......................................19
Chapter 3: Committing to a Lifetime of Care 29
Chapter 4: A Match Made in Boston 41

Part II: Caring for Your Boston Terrier................*53*

Chapter 5: Preparing for Your Boston's Homecoming.........................55
Chapter 6: Welcome Home! 75
Chapter 7: Eating Well...89
Chapter 8: Looking Good...101

Part III: Stepping Out......................................*117*

Chapter 9: Housetraining for Bostons 119
Chapter 10: Socializing for Life 129
Chapter 11: Training and Behavior 147
Chapter 12: Taking Training to the Next Level 165
Chapter 13: Traveling with (Or without)Your Boston 179

Part IV: Health and Well-Being........................*195*

Chapter 14: Your Visit to the Veterinarian 197
Chapter 15: Breed-Specific Ailments..217
Chapter 16: First Aid 227
Chapter 17: Caring for the Senior Dog.......................................237

Part V: The Part of Tens..................................*249*

Chapter 18: Ten Trivia Tidbits about Bostons...........................251
Chapter 19: Ten Ways to Make Your Boston's Day..........................255

Index..*259*

Table of Contents

Introduction *1*

About This Book 1
Conventions Used in This Book 2
What You're Not to Read...2
Foolish Assumptions 2
How This Book Is Organized.......................................3
    Part I: That Bullish Terrier................................3
    Part II: Caring for Your Boston Terrier 3
    Part III: Stepping Out 4
    Part IV: Health and Well-Being 4
    Part V: The Part of Tens.................................4
Icons Used In This Book...5
Where to Go From Here...5

Part 1: That Bullish Terrier................................7

Chapter 1: Welcome to Boston! 9

Lovers, Not Fighters 9
    The early days...9
    Personality plus 10
Give Me Shelter — And Food!....................................12
    Feed me!..12
    A home of his own 13
    Time for fun! 15
How to Be a Good Boy...16
    Socializing for life...16
    Listening and obeying 17
Caring for Your Boston's Needs 18

Chapter 2: Tracking the Boston Terrier.............19

Breed Origin and History...19
    The roots of the Boston's build 19
    Stirring in some spunk 20
Building the First Boston 21
    Join the club! 21
    Renewed popularity 22
Developing a Standard 22
    American Kennel Club standards 23
    United Kennel Club standards 27
Personality Aplenty 27

Chapter 3: Committing to a Lifetime of Care 29

Judging Your Compatibility 29
     Considering terrier needs.................................30
     Impatient owners need not apply................................31
     At-home time: It's a necessity 32
Establishing Family Dynamics..32
     Knowing who the main caregiver will be: You 33
     Understanding your children's role 33
     Helping your four-legged friends
       get along with each other 33
Divvying Up Duties 34
     Fitting in regular chores...................................35
     Child-appropriate tasks 38
The Real Costs..39
     One-time and monthly expenses 39
     Unexpected bills 40

Chapter 4: A Match Made in Boston 41

Battle of the Sexes 41
     Mighty males 42
     Attentive females 42
Puppy or Adult? 43
If You Choose a Puppy 44
     Locating a reputable source.............................44
     Recognizing a healthy puppy.............................49
If You Choose an Adult 50
     Working with a breeder................................51
     Connecting with rescues 51
     Recognizing a healthy adult dog.........................52

Part II: Caring for Your Boston Terrier 53

Chapter 5: Preparing for Your
Boston's Homecoming......................... 55

Puppy-Proofing Basics 55
     Stashing stuff inside your home 56
     Minimizing outdoor hazards 57
License and Registration, Please.....................................58
     Making your Boston legal 58
     Registering with the AKC and UKC.......................59
Time to Go Shopping..60
     So many leashes and collars, so little time 60
     Unmistaken identity 62

Fine china or basic bowls 64
Items to keep your Boston contained 65
Cuisine for your canine 68
Bedding for your Boston 69
Playtime! Picking out toys 69
For the fashion-savvy Boston 71
Items for cleanup duty 71
Canine hygiene products 72
Must-haves for your young pup 73

Chapter 6: Welcome Home! 75

Taking the Home Tour 76
The pup's eating and drinking area 76
The den and sleeping area 76
The play areas 77
Meeting Other Members of the Pack 78
Kids, puppy. Puppy, kids 78
Introducing felines, canines, or small pets 80
Surviving the First Night 82
Creating Consistency 83
Establishing a schedule 84
Setting up house rules 86

Chapter 7: Eating Well 89

Feeding a Carnivore: Cost versus Quality 89
Knowing Your Ingredients 90
Pump up the protein 90
Energize with carbohydrates 91
Fats for energy and a shiny coat 91
Take your vitamins, mind your minerals 91
How to Read Pet Food Labels 92
Checking Out Your Commercial Diet Options 93
Crunchy kibble 94
Semi-moist morsels 95
Stew in a can 95
Choosing To Feed a Noncommercial Diet 96
Special Diets for Bostons with Health Issues 97
Come and Get It! Serving Meals 98
Setting up a meal schedule 98
Dishing out the right amount 98
Preventing obesity 99
Supplementing Your Dog's Diet 100
Treating Your Boston 100

Chapter 8: Looking Good **101**

Grooming at Home...101
    Getting ready to groom.................................102
    Caring for healthy skin and coat....................104
    Trimming those nails: A paw-dicure...............106
    Here's to clean ears 108
    Keeping the eyes bright and nose wiped 110
    Tending to those pearly whites 110
Visiting the Groomer or Spa..................................112
    Inspecting the facility...................................113
    Evaluating the staff......................................114
    Considering certification 114
Clothes and Accessories for Your Boston 115
    Sizing clothes for your dog...........................116
    Dressing your Boston....................................116

Part III: Stepping Out **117**

Chapter 9: Housetraining for Bostons **119**

Setting the Stage for Success: Housetraining Basics..........120
    Reinforcing positive behavior.......................120
    Making the trip to the bathroom area............121
    Restricting his freedom.................................122
Training Your Boston...123
Mistakes Will Happen 125
Okay Ways to Go Inside...126
    Read all about it: Paper training 127
    A litter box of his own..................................127

Chapter 10: Socializing for Life **129**

Understanding Your Boston's Developmental Timeline....130
    A brand-new world: The first 6 weeks 130
    Getting to know people: 5 to 12 weeks 130
    Interacting with her environment: 12 to 20 weeks ...131
    Approaching adulthood: 4 months to 3 years 132
Socializing Your Puppy...133
    Keeping her safe, yet social..........................133
    Introducing children — slowly.......................134
    Interacting with four-legged friends..............136
Socializing Your Adult Dog 137
Reading Your Boston's Body Language....................138
    Neutral relaxed..139
    Greeting..140
    Play bow...140
    Arousal 141

Defensive aggression...................................142
Aggressive attack.......................................142
Submission 144
Preventing Fear 144
Being proactive 145
Coping with fear..145

Chapter 11: Training and Behavior 147

School Days 147
Why classes are a good idea 148
The right ages to learn new lessons...........149
Finding the right trainer............................150
Establishing a Commanding Presence 151
Getting started 151
Settle...152
Sit...153
Down 154
Stay...154
Come 156
Leave It and Take It...................................156
Heel...157
Correcting Behavior Gone Bad.........................158
Barking..159
Biting 160
Chewing 160
Digging 161
Jumping up 162
House-soiling..162
Calling in the Professional 163

Chapter 12: Taking Training to the Next Level....... 165

Training for Sport..165
For the well-behaved Boston: Canine
    Good Citizen program 166
Do as I say: Obedience trials 168
Follow that scent: Tracking 169
Boston be nimble, Boston be quick: Agility trials 170
Becoming a Therapy Dog.................................171
Having Some Organized Fun.............................172
Why not try flyball?...................................173
Dancing with the dogs: Canine freestyle 173
Attending a Conformation Trial 174
Being an informed spectator........................175
Understanding the points.............................176
Competition for children and dogs 177

Chapter 13: Traveling with (Or without) Your Boston 179

Preparing for the Journey 180
    Identification, please 180
    The right carrier for the trip 180
    Pack your Boston's bags 182
Hitting the Road 183
    Introducing the car 183
    Driving in style 185
Flying the Skies...187
Leaving Your Boston Behind 188
    Short- and long-term boarding..................189
    Hiring a pet sitter 192

Part IV: Health and Well-Being 195

Chapter 14: Your Visit to the Veterinarian 197

Finding a Vet for Your Pet 197
    Getting referrals from trustworthy sources 198
    Figuring out who's who in the vet world 198
    Knowing what you're looking for...............200
    Interviewing your veterinarian 202
Your Boston's First Vet Visit 203
Vaccinations: Protecting Your Dog
  from Deadly Diseases 204
    Knowing the diseases..................................205
    Following the vaccination schedule..........206
Patrolling for Parasites..207
    Internal parasites: The worms 208
    External parasites: Pesky critters..............210
To Spay or Neuter 213
    Growing up fast: Your Boston's sexual maturity 214
    Understanding the surgical procedures 214
Making Annual Visits 215

Chapter 15: Breed-Specific Ailments 217

With a Snort and Wheeze.....................................217
    Challenged chompers 218
    Upper-airway syndrome 219
    Tracheal hypoplasia....................................220
    Dystocia: Birthing difficulties....................220

What Big Eyes You Have!..221
 Corneal ulcers 221
 Cataracts..222
 Bulging eyeballs 223
 Other eye problems..224
Say What?..225
Trick Knees 226

Chapter 16: First Aid 227

First-Aid Kit Essentials 227
Knowing Normal Vitals..229
 Pulse..229
 Temperature..229
 Mucous membrane color....................................230
 Breathing rate 230
Managing First-Aid Emergencies................................230
 Restraining your Boston.....................................231
 Transporting an injured dog 231
 Administering artificial respiration 232
 Performing heart massage (CPR) 232
 Common canine emergencies 233

Chapter 17: Caring for the Senior Dog. 237

Knowing the Signs of Aging 237
Age-Related Disorders...238
 Arthritis...238
 Cancer 239
 Deafness..240
 Diabetes 240
 Eye disorders 240
 Heart problems 241
 Kidney disease 242
 Obesity..242
 Urinary incontinence 243
Handling Your Senior Boston with Kid Gloves..................243
 Veterinary visits..243
 Nutrition..244
 Exercise...244
 Bedding and sleeping area 245
 Grooming 245
Bidding Adieu to Your Boston....................................245
 How to know when it's time 246
 What to expect...246
 Remembering your beloved Boston....................247

Part V: The Part of Tens..........................249

Chapter 18: Ten Trivia Tidbits about Bostons........251

The Dogfather..251
An American Original 251
What's in a Name?..252
Manly Moniker..252
Top Billing...252
Little Men on Campus 253
Popular beyond Boston 253
The Incredible Shrinking Dog...............................253
State of the Boston 254
Odds 'n' Ends...254

Chapter 19: Ten Ways to Make Your Boston's Day . . . 255

Get the Day Off to a Good Start...........................255
Take a Walk 255
Stroll to the Park 256
Throw a Party...256
Give Your Boston a Bone 256
Take a Spa Day...256
Bake Your Boston Some Cookies 257
Toss a Ball...258
Do Some Homework 258
Enjoy Each Other's Company...............................258

Index 259

Introduction

● ●

*I*f you've picked up this book, you're either considering whether to add a Boston Terrier to your life or you have already. Educating yourself is the first — and most important — step in becoming a responsible pet parent. Kudos to you for furthering your knowledge about the breed!

Learning about Boston Terriers, however, is just the beginning. After you encounter a Boston and get a feel for her good-natured personality, see how intelligent and devoted she is to her owner, understand her diverse and American-bred origins, and experience what a sheer delight she is to be around, you'll be hooked for life.

Making the most of your human-pet relationship involves not only educating yourself about what makes your dog tick, but also realizing how to nurture her and help her develop into the dog she was born to be: a devoted friend, wise companion, and all-around dapper dog.

About This Book

This book serves as a reference guide for life with your Boston Terrier. Its purpose is twofold: First, it'll help you decide whether a Boston is the right breed for you and your family. Some families want a larger breed like a Labrador; others want a fluffy lapdog, like a Bichon Frisé. These pages break down the basics and give you enough practical insight to make an informed decision about whether a Boston will fit into your household.

Second, this book addresses some basic questions about the breed and general dog care. You'll find answers to questions like:

- ✔ Where did the breed originate, and why?
- ✔ What is a Boston's temperament like?
- ✔ How do I prepare my home for her arrival?
- ✔ Will a Boston get along with children and other pets?
- ✔ How do I housetrain my Boston?
- ✔ What are her basic nutritional and grooming requirements?
- ✔ What are some common health concerns associated with the breed?
- ✔ In case of a medical emergency, what do I do?

Conventions Used in This Book

This book contains a lot of information, so to help you navigate through the text, I set up a few stylistic conventions, including:

- ✔ *Italics:* Italic type is used for emphasis and to highlight new words or terms that are defined.
- ✔ **Bold:** Boldfaced text is used to highlight points in a series and bring attention to key concepts.
- ✔ Monofont: Monofont is used for Web sites and e-mail addresses.

You'll notice one other convention, and that's the alternating use of masculine and feminine pronouns. With the help of my astute copy editor, I alternated between male and female, chapter by chapter. I'm not trying to give our four-legged friends human qualities; it just seems much more personable to use "he" and "she" rather than "it."

What You're Not to Read

The information in this book ranges from the absolutely essential — like how to provide adequate nutrition for your Boston — to the not-so-important — like how handlers dress in the dog-show ring. You can find the necessary reading within the body of the book, but you can find the nonessential information in two places:

- ✔ **Sidebars:** The shaded boxes of text that appear throughout the chapters contain supplementary information you can skip or flip through later. It's interesting stuff, but it's not necessary.
- ✔ **Paragraphs highlighted with the Technical Stuff icon:** If you're the type who likes to know why or how, you'll appreciate the technical information contained in these paragraphs. You can, however, skip those nitty-gritty tidbits and still glean what you need to know about Bostons.

Foolish Assumptions

As I wrote this book, I assumed several things about you and the type of information you'd be looking for:

✔ You either have a Boston or you're seriously thinking about adopting one.

✔ You're enamored with the breed and want to know more about its history, distinguishing characteristics, and care requirements.

✔ You've adopted your first Boston and you're not sure what specific things your dog will need.

✔ You have some experience with dogs, but you can use a refresher course in basic care and training.

✔ You're overwhelmed with all those doggy doodads that are out there and you're looking for some guidance.

✔ You're having difficulty with housetraining or obedience, and you're looking for practical advice.

How This Book Is Organized

This book is put together in a logical way that allows you to find information quickly and easily. It contains five parts, each dedicated to a particular topic and broken down into several chapters that go into greater detail.

Part 1: That Bullish Terrier

This first part gives you a general overview of what to expect in this book, and it provides an overview of the breed's history and temperament. It describes where and how the dog originated, what a Boston needs, and what will be required of you and your family.

Ideally, you'll read the chapters in this part before you adopt your puppy so you know what you're getting yourself into! Deciding to add a Boston to your family is an important decision that will take some education. Part I is a great place to start.

Part II: Caring for Your Boston Terrier

After you've decided to welcome a Boston into your life, you'll need to start thinking about how to care for her. This part guides you through how to puppy proof your home and yard, what products you'll absolutely need, how to provide for her nutritional needs, and how to keep her looking her best.

You'll also see the importance of setting up regular schedules for your Boston. Dogs are creatures of habit and like routine in their lives, from eating in the same place to going for walks at the same time every day. Part II will help you through the different routines to set up for your dog and your family.

Part III: Stepping Out

Well-trained and well-behaved dogs are a joy to be around. This part delves into how to mold your dog into a healthy and happy adult who thrives on being around humans and other dogs. You'll find out how to housetrain your dog. You'll understand the importance of proper socialization at all stages of her life. And you'll get an introduction to basic training, competition, and trial events.

Because your Boston will likely shadow you wherever you go — from the grocery store to Grandma's house — you'll want to keep her safe while traveling. Part III also outlines ways to restrain your dog in the car and how to prepare her for an airplane journey. If you can't take her with you, this section also describes how to find a reputable dog sitter or dog daycare center.

Part IV: Health and Well-Being

Perhaps the most important portion of the book, Part IV addresses health and well-being issues through all stages of your Boston's life. It offers guidelines for basic Boston care, including what to expect during your dog's first veterinary visit, breed-specific ailments, first aid, and senior care.

You'll also get an introduction to vaccinations, internal and external parasites, and details about the special needs of *brachycephalic* breeds (dogs with short heads), like your Boston. After reading this section, you'll have plenty to discuss with your veterinarian!

Part V: The Part of Tens

This part contains two chapters that give you fun facts about Boston Terriers. You'll find out ten interesting facts about the breed and discover ten ways to enhance your pet's life.

Icons Used In This Book

A useful feature in the *For Dummies* series, icons draw your attention to — or away from — particular types of information. I use the following icons throughout the book:

This icon appears wherever a bit of advice can save you time, money, hassle, or stress.

This icon points out important information that's worth remembering.

When you see this icon, pay particular attention to the paragraph next to it. It highlights information about dangers that could cause your dog harm.

For those detail-oriented readers, the Technical Stuff icon indicates interesting but unnecessary information that you can skip.

Where to Go From Here

Each chapter and part of this book is self-contained, so you can jump to just about anywhere and find complete information. Though you'll get a more well-rounded understanding of Bostons if you read the book from cover to cover, you don't have to, especially if you're looking for a certain topic, like how to housetrain your dog (Chapter 9), what to expect during your first veterinary visit (Chapter 14), where the breed originated (Chapter 2), or what kennel to purchase (Chapter 5). The Index will guide you to more specific topics.

A logical place to start, of course, is Chapter 1, which is a general overview of the book, and Chapter 2, which details the breed's history, standard, and temperament. Regardless of where you begin, however, you're about to embark on a new adventure — with your Boston!

Part I
That Bullish Terrier

The 5th Wave

By Rich Tennant

"To be fair, the people at the kennel said he liked to play, not that he was playful."

In this part . . .

Before you welcome a dog into your life, one of the first things you'll do is find out all you can about the different breeds. You'll research magazines, Web sites, and books like this one. You'll talk to breeders, dog club representatives, friends, and neighbors. You'll gather as much information as you can so that you will choose the right type of dog for your family.

In this first section of *Boston Terriers For Dummies,* you get an overview of the breed's history and temperament. It prompts you to take a look at your family's lifestyle, leading you to decide whether the Boston Terrier will make a fitting addition to your household. You also understand how to find a reputable breeder and how to identify the perfect pup for you.

You may find, after reading this first section, that a Boston isn't right for your family. Maybe you're looking for a larger breed or a petite lap dog. If that's the case, that's okay! It's better to decide that before you bring the puppy home. But if you breeze through this section and still want to share your life with a Boston, you're on your way to a life-changing experience!

Chapter 1

Welcome to Boston!

. . . .

In This Chapter

▶ Exploring Boston Terriers' ancestors and canine appeal

▶ Understanding a pup's basic needs

▶ Realizing the importance of housetraining and obedience

▶ Knowing how to care for his medical needs

. . . .

*W*hen you think of a Boston Terrier, what picture pops into your mind? Perhaps you think of his unmistakable pug nose and pointy ears, his one-of-a-kind black-and-white tuxedo of a coat, or his endearing snorts and wheezes that trumpet his approach. Bostons pack a lot of personality in their small 15-pound bodies. It's no wonder why you're interested in this dapper little breed!

Before you invite a Boston to share your life, however, you should know a little bit about what makes these dogs tick. In this chapter, I describe why Bostons make such fantastic pets. I also offer pointers for how to care for their basic needs, from food and water to shelter and wellness.

Lovers, Not Fighters

Boston Terriers earned the nickname "American Gentleman" for good reason: They're intelligent, affectionate, classy dogs who make excellent companions. With their amiable demeanor, it's hard to believe that their ancestors were originally bred to be fighters!

The early days

Bostons are a blend of English Bulldogs and white English Terriers (now extinct). The first of these dogs was named Hooper's Judge, owned by Robert C. Hooper of Boston, Massachusetts. He imported the bulldog-terrier blend from his native England around 1870.

Early breeders in the United States admired the dog's look, so they refined and stabilized the breed, selecting for a smaller size, a likeable personality, and large expressive eyes. Eventually, they produced the American original that we know today.

These dogs enjoyed extreme popularity in the early 1900s. Placing first or second on the American Kennel Club's (AKC) list of registered breeds from 1905 through 1934, Boston Terriers were all the rage among fanciers and socialites alike. Over the past century, they've held a prominent position among the AKC's most popular dogs, consistently ranking among the top 20.

Today, Boston Terriers have made themselves at home in a range of households, from small apartments to large farms and everything in between. Though they retain hints of their terrier and bulldog ancestry, Bostons are unique, well-mannered dogs who bring joy to just about any home. To read more about the origins and breed standard of Boston Terriers, flip to Chapter 2.

Personality plus

Ask any Boston owner to describe her dog, and you'll get nothing but praise. Boston owners love their dogs, and for good reason! They're highly intelligent, low maintenance, well-mannered, and ready for anything.

Here are some more reasons to love Bostons:

- ✔ **They're great with kids.** Most Bostons adore children. When children are taught how to behave around dogs, Bostons and kids become fast friends, with the dogs often enduring wrestling matches and playing dress-up without a hitch. Because they have such a solid constitution, these little dogs can handle just about anything that a child can dish out. Jump to Chapter 6 for details about how to introduce your child to a Boston.

- ✔ **They're great with adults.** Integrating well in any household, Bostons make attentive companions for adults and seniors, too. Some Bostons become good *therapy dogs,* well-behaved pups who travel to nursing homes and hospitals to bring joy to patients. Skip to Chapter 12 for details.

- ✔ **They're easy to care for.** A definite perk, Boston Terriers are simple to maintain. They have short coats that can be easily washed and brushed. (See Chapter 8 for more about grooming your Boston.) They don't require a great deal of energy-expending exercise. And they are very intelligent, taking to housetraining and obedience training quickly. (Hop to Chapter 9 and 11 for housetraining and obedience-training details.)

✔ **They're a relatively healthy breed.** Though they do have some difficulties stemming from their shortened snout, or being *brachycephalic,* Boston Terriers are healthy dogs. They often live 12 years, often reaching their 15th birthdays. (Chapter 15 describes some breed-specific ailments to watch for.)

✔ **They fit in just about any home.** Bostons are the perfect size for apartments, townhouses, or single-family homes. Because they don't require a large yard, they make wonderful house pets.

✔ **They get along well with other pets.** Being an easy-going breed, Bostons are happy to share their homes with other dogs, cats, or even a caged hamster or bearded dragon. As long as they are introduced slowly, they'll get along like siblings! (Chapter 6 covers introductions between four-legged friends.)

✔ **They're addictive.** Once you get one, you can't stop, or so many Boston owners attest. Prepare to add a second Boston to your menagerie shortly after you get your first!

Why go purebred?

With all the homeless animals crowding shelters, you may ask yourself, why should I get a purebred dog when I can rescue a mutt? Purebred dogs have their advantages, including:

✔ **You can learn all about the breed before you bring him home.** Unlike a mixed-breed dog, purebred dogs have books like this one dedicated to them. You can read all about Bostons and get an idea of what they're like.

✔ **With a purebred dog, you have a good idea of what you're getting.** After researching about Bostons, you'll know how large the dog will grow to be. You'll be prepared for his playful personality. You'll be aware of any unique medical conditions the breed faces.

✔ **If you adopt your dog from a breeder, you also know the dog's lineage and pedigree.** You can trace the dog's ancestors and learn about her predecessors. You may have a grand champion in your family!

✔ **You'll benefit from breed-specific clubs and organizations dedicated to Boston Terriers.** Often, these clubs offer a forum for discussing health and behavior issues. You can learn about obedience courses and agility trials. Plus, it's a great place to socialize with other Boston lovers!

If you feel strongly about adopting a puppy or adult rescue, consider opening your home to a rescued Boston. Organizations across the country continually look for loving homes for special-needs or abandoned Boston Terriers, including: the Boston Terrier Club of America (http://bostonterrierclubofamerica.org/rescue.html), Boston Terrier Rescue (www.btrescue.org), Boston Terrier Rescue Net (www.bostonrescue.net), and Nationwide Boston Terrier Rescue Inc. (www.nationwidebostonrescue.org).

Give Me Shelter — And Food!

Like any pet, Boston Terriers require food and water, shelter, stimulation, and lots of love to thrive. The following sections touch on your pet's basic needs and how you can fill them.

Feed me!

Because they're considered small dogs, Bostons don't require copious amounts of food, unlike their giant-breed cousins who can eat up to 5 cups of chow a day or more!

Bostons eat a lesser amount, so quality matters when feeding your dog. You need to provide a delicious diet that meets his nutritional needs, which include digestible protein, carbohydrates, fats, vitamins, and minerals. Luckily, pet stores and veterinary offices offer more variety than ever before — from dry kibble and canned foods to holistic and prescription diets. You'll find a formula that you and your dog are happy with.

Chapter 7 gives you more-detailed nutrition know-how, but for now, here's a rundown of the different diets you can feed your Boston:

- ✔ **Dried kibble:** These crunchy little morsels are formulated to contain all the nutrition your Boston needs. They come in a wide range of flavors and formulas, and contain a variety of nutrition sources. Whatever you choose, make sure that it's a quality recipe that derives its protein, carbohydrates, and fats from easily digestible sources.

- ✔ **Semi-moist:** With a texture resembling moist clay, semi-moist foods also contain balanced nutrition. They contain higher water content than the dried kibble, but because of the higher sugar content, semi-moist foods can cause plaque and tartar buildup on a dog's teeth, which can lead to tooth decay. Semi-moist food is best served as a treat rather than daily.

- ✔ **Canned:** What dog doesn't love a meaty stew? Canned diets closely resemble "real" food. They're often packed with carrots, potatoes, chunks of meat, and lots of gravy. Canned diets provide complete nutrition, a good amount of water, and a tempting meal for finicky eaters.

- ✔ **Natural or organic:** Very popular diets to feed dogs, many natural formulas derive their ingredients from organic farms and often claim to contain "human-quality" ingredients. These foods can be excellent choices for your Boston, but only buy them from reputable sources.

✔ **Raw:** Raw diets are just that: raw meat to feed to your pet. The prepackaged meals can be found in your pet store's freezer case. If you choose to feed your Boston a raw diet, first consult with your veterinarian. These diets lack the vitamins and minerals found in plant-based foods, so you'll need to supplement your pup's meals to provide adequate nutrition.

✔ **Homemade:** Rather than purchase a premade dog food from the grocery store, some people prefer to make their dog's meals from scratch. There are quite a few dog food cookbooks on the market that contain mouth-watering recipes for your pup. To ensure your Boston is getting all of his nutritional requirements, however, consult with your veterinarian before offering this type of diet to your dog.

✔ **Prescription:** Purchased through veterinary offices, prescription diets are for dogs who may have allergies or special nutritional requirements. Your veterinarian can prescribe the best brand to ease your Boston's condition.

Besides offering your pup a quality diet, you also need to feed him the right amount of food. A 15- to 20-pound dog, like your Boston, typically eats about a ½ cup per meal, twice a day. If you feed him treats, you should decrease that amount to account for the extra calories. You don't want a bulging Boston!

Food is important, but clean water is even more so! All dogs require access to fresh clean water to keep their bodies functioning normally. Fill his bowl daily and put one wherever your Boston roams — including outside and near his food bowl.

A home of his own

Just like you, your Boston needs his own space — a safe, comfortable environment to call home. That home includes his own crate or kennel, and his larger home — yours!

Creating his own space

Dogs are *denning* animals, which means that they like to have a dark, enclosed cave where they can feel safe and secure. Their den is where they can sleep, take a nap, or just enjoy some private time with their favorite toy.

A crate or kennel makes a perfect den. Available at your local pet specialty retailer, crates or kennels are typically made from plastic, powder-coated metal, or durable canvas. No matter what type you choose, make sure that it's easy to clean and sized appropriately — not too big and not too small. Jump to Chapter 5 for more information about kennels.

Crates are also a tool to help you housetrain your Boston. When you *housetrain* your dog, you teach him to hold his bladder and bowels until he's in an approved bathroom area. Dogs rarely defecate in the same place they sleep, so when you confine him to his den, he'll learn to wait to go to the bathroom. Chapter 9 gives you step-by-step instructions for how to housetrain your Boston.

Adapting your space

Though he'll have his own den, he'll consider your home an extension of his domain. To keep him out of trouble, you need to dog-proof your home, just as you would childproof a home. Get on all fours — your hands and knees — and investigate each room from your dog's perspective:

- ✔ **Kitchen:** With all the smells to investigate and cabinets to explore, the kitchen is a tempting place for a Boston. Install childproof latches on all the cabinets and drawers, and keep a secure lid on the garbage can.

- ✔ **Bathroom:** The bathroom can be a dangerous place for your pup. Cosmetics, medications, razors, and dangling cords look like playthings to your Boston. Keep them out of his reach. Your dog could ingest a stray cotton swab or bar of soap — which could mean a trip to the emergency room!

- ✔ **Living room:** A busy area of the house, the living room contains a range of temptations, from houseplants and electronics to strewn shoes and books. Secure loose cords behind furniture, and keep houseplants and other important objects out of your Boston's reach.

- ✔ **Bedroom:** If an item of clothing smells like you, it's fair game for your dog! To protect your belongings, keep your clothing and shoes in a closed closet. Secure loose cords, position plants out of your Boston's reach, and keep the area tidy.

- ✔ **Garage:** Keep all those car fluids, yard tools, fertilizers, and poisons behind closed and locked cabinets. Antifreeze is a particular danger because it tastes sweet to animals, yet just a small amount can be toxic.

- ✔ **In the yard:** Rat poisons, snail bait, and fertilizer can be deadly to your dog, and gardening tools look like fun toys to a playful pup. While your Boston is in his exploring stages, avoid using poisons and put away your tools to prevent bumps, cuts, and other injuries. It's better to be safe than sorry!

Chapter 5 has more details about protecting your Boston from dangers in your home.

Time for fun!

Your Boston also needs some things to keep his little mind stimulated. From balls and toys to interactive games and playtime with you, you can offer your curious Boston all sorts of diversions.

Bostons in Toyland

Toys and games for your Boston include squeaky toys, plush animals, bouncy balls, and treat-dispensing Kongs. Your Boston will choose his favorite and adopt it as his own!

Pet stores stock a variety of toys. Choose those that are sized appropriately for your small Boston. Toys that are too small can be a choking risk; too large may mean your dog won't play with them.

 To keep things interesting for your dog, rotate his toys. Instead of giving him a dozen new toys at once, pull them out sporadically or offer him a new one when the old one wears out. You'll want to buy him a fun new trinket every time you visit the pet store, but resist the temptation to give it to him right away.

Get out and play

With their ceaseless energy — especially when they're puppies — Bostons love to get out and explore. Here are some fun things you can do with your dog:

- ✔ **Take a walk.** Outfit your pup in a harness, attach a leash, grab some pickup bags and go for a walk. Your Boston will explore everything he comes into contact with! If you take your puppy on dusty trails, however, keep the journey short. His prominent eyes are prone to scratches and irritation. Stick to walks through a grassy park or around the neighborhood where he's less likely to irritate his eyes.

- ✔ **Visit your local dog park.** As pet popularity continues to skyrocket, more dog parks are opening up. These fenced-in areas allow you to let your Boston run free! Before you visit one of these places, however, make sure he's up to date on all his vaccinations.

- ✔ **Play a game of fetch.** A great way to expend pent-up energy, a rousing game of fetch challenges your Boston to retrieve and return a ball, disc, or any other quarry. Some dogs enjoy this fun for hours and hours!

- ✔ **Get involved in organized sports.** Enroll your Boston in competitive sports like agility, tracking, or flyball. *Agility* requires your dog to run through obstacles in a timed race, *tracking* challenges him to follow a scent over a distance through various terrains, and *flyball* pits him against other dogs to jump over hurdles to catch a flying tennis ball. Organizers of these activities can be found through your local dog breed club. Chapter 12 describes these fun sports in detail.

✔ **Plan a party.** Who doesn't love a party? Gather your dog-owning friends and host a dog social. Make a cake — for the dogs, of course — plan games and activities for the dogs, and have a fun time! The dogs will love to interact and socialize, and you will enjoy spending time with other dog owners.

How to Be a Good Boy

Besides providing food, shelter, and toys for your dog, you also want to train him to be a well-behaved member of society. Here are some things to consider:

Socializing for life

Socializing your Boston is when you teach him how to interact with his world. When your Boston is a puppy, he needs to experience as many sights and sounds as possible. He needs to meet many different people and be introduced to many different situations. When you teach him these things, he'll be on track for becoming a well-mannered pooch.

Here are some milestones you should be aware of. (Chapter 10 contains additional pointers for bringing up a polite Boston.)

Part of the litter

From birth to about 6 weeks of age, puppies get their social stimuli from their mother and littermates. They learn how to interact with one another, begin to understand the social hierarchy, and start to develop their own personalities. Because your puppy will likely still be with his mother (and breeder) during these first formative weeks, you won't see too much of this developmental phase.

The human connection

Dogs begin to interact with humans when they reach 5 to 12 weeks of age. They learn — hopefully — that people bring positive things, like food, shelter, and lots of love. It's critical at this phase to introduce your Boston to as many people as possible. They should hold your dog, pet him, and handle him. They should let the puppy sniff them and get to know what humans are like.

At about 8 weeks old, puppies enter their first fear phase. At this age, he becomes aware of the world around him — and sometimes, it can be frightening! Most breeders won't let puppies go to their new homes until after they pass through this fear phase.

The wide, wild world

By the time your Boston reaches his 3-month birthday, he'll be ready to explore the world. From about 12 weeks to 20 weeks old, your Boston should experience as many different environments as possible. He'll want to inspect and sniff everything he sees. Take your dog with you wherever you go (if possible) to open his eyes to the world. The more things he experiences, the better.

Listening and obeying

Obedience is more than teaching your dog fun parlor tricks. *Obedience* is when your dog learns to obey commands like "come" or "stay" — edicts that may be very important if he is in a life-or-death situation, like running into oncoming traffic!

When you're teaching your Boston basic commands, always use positive reinforcement rather than negative correction techniques. *Positive reinforcement* recognizes the pup's positive behaviors, rewarding him with treats and praise for a job well done.

Puppy kindergarten is a great place to begin to teach your puppy obedience. Often offered through veterinary clinics, pet specialty stores, or humane societies, puppy kindergarten teaches you tools for training your Boston. You learn basic commands, including the following (which are also detailed in Chapter 11):

- ✔ **Settle:** This command puts your dog in a submissive position. Your pup is calm and relaxed, with soft eyes, ears back, belly up, and tail tucked. He is essentially relinquishing control.

- ✔ **Sit:** Sit is when you command your dog to stay in place, waiting for your instruction. The starting point for most other commands, Sit requires your pup to look to you for guidance.

- ✔ **Stay:** Paired with Sit, Stay is when your dog holds his position until you tell him otherwise. It's a posture that can save his life.

- ✔ **Come:** Another life-saving command, Come tells your dog to return immediately to you. It's one of the most important commands your dog will learn.

- ✔ **Heel:** When you walk with your Boston, you want him to walk beside you and not pull on the leash. This is especially important for Bostons because some can have narrow windpipes, which make it difficult to breathe.

Caring for Your Boston's Needs

To keep your Boston healthy and happy until his 12th or 15th birthday (or longer!), you need to care for his medical needs. That includes establishing a good relationship with a veterinarian, keeping a canine first-aid kit handy, and being aware of your dog's unique medical needs. Here are some things to consider:

- **Veterinary visits are fun!** Besides you and your family, your dog's veterinarian will be his best friend. Your vet will offer preventive advice, emergency service, annual checkups, and general advice about dog care. Teach your Boston early that visits to the veterinarian are something to look forward to! Chapter 14 describes qualities to look for in veterinarians and what to expect during your pup's vet visits.

- **Know your Boston's special medical needs.** Bostons are a *brachycephalic* breed, which means that their shortened snouts can create respiratory challenges. That snorting and wheezing may be endearing, but it can be a sign of a debilitating medical condition. See Chapter 15 for details.

- **Be prepared.** Gather canine first-aid supplies and keep them near your human first-aid kit. In case of emergency, those tools can help to stabilize your Boston until you can get him to an emergency clinic. The essentials are listed in Chapter 16.

- **Check him while grooming.** Your Boston can't tell you when something hurts, but you can watch his reactions when you inspect his body while grooming or petting him. Look for unusual lumps, bumps, or sore spots. If you see something new, consult with your veterinarian.

- **Aging Bostons have special needs, too.** Elderly dogs have their own set of medical conditions, including age-related disorders and dietary changes, that warrant your attention. Chapter 17 goes through them in detail.

Chapter 2

Tracking the Boston Terrier

. . . .

In This Chapter

▶ Looking at the Boston Terrier's lineage and history

▶ Meeting the first Boston Terrier and her offspring

▶ Developing a standard for the breed

▶ Getting to know the Terrier's temperament and personality

. . . .

*B*oston Terriers enjoy a rich and well-documented history that reaches back to the mid-19th century. They represent one of a handful of breeds that claim the United States as their home turf.

You can learn a lot about your Boston by understanding the different breeds that make her up. In this chapter, you discover the origins and history of the Boston Terrier, how and why the dog was developed, her various breed standards as defined by the country's top registries, and the Boston's spunky yet gentle temperament and personality.

Breed Origin and History

Boston Terriers, nicknamed the "American Gentlemen," owe their compact physique and exuberant charm to their forefathers: English Bulldogs (commonly known as Bulldogs) and white English Terriers (now extinct). They are two very distinct breeds, but they blended together to create the stout, lovable dog you know today.

The roots of the Boston's build

Early Bulldogs, known as *Molossers,* descended from ferocious Mastiff-type dogs who were bred to fight in Roman arenas. These same litters produced guard dogs, protectors, and draft dogs. They were known as *Alains* or *Alaunts* until the Middle Ages.

Large, solidly built dogs with heavy bones, muscular necks, and short muzzles, Molossers comprise a group of early canines known for their strength and courage. They were the predecessors of the Mastiff, Great Dane, Newfoundland, Rottweiler, and other large- and giant-breed dogs who tip the scales at 100 pounds or more. Embodying vigor and bravery, early generations of these massive dogs guarded shepherds' homes and flocks with their sheer might and guttural barks.

In England, these vicious dogs were known as *Bandogs* because they required bands, ropes, and chains to contain them. Those who weren't cut out for the fight ring assisted butchers in controlling savage bulls awaiting slaughter. (In those days, people believed that when the dogs harassed the bulls before butchering, the bulls yielded a more tender and nutritious meat compared to those that were immediately killed!)

Breeders developed these dogs with short legs and a stout body to keep them safe from the bull's piercing horns. Eventually, these dogs were bred to participate in a sport that pitted the dog against a tethered bull. Known as *bull-baiting,* the dog clenched the bull's nose with its strong undershot jaw with the goal of taking down the restrained beast by suffocating or bleeding it to death.

The English Parliament banned the sport in 1835, but the dog's tenacious temperament and formidable traits remained in subse- quent generations. Its physical characteristics — the undershot jaw, its heavy body weight, and low center of gravity — became the standard by which the dog was bred.

You can see many of these qualities in the Boston Terrier. It cer- tainly is no longer a fighter, but its stocky build, square and blocky shape, and slightly undershot jaw are now hallmarks of the breed.

Stirring in some spunk

Energetic and spirited, terriers descend from working dogs bred to hunt and kill vermin. Known as *ratters,* the dogs performed specific jobs for their owners that required speed, agility, and a rapid response.

When the British wanted to breed spunk and agility into their dogs, they turned to the terrier. They chose the white English Terrier, a small, white working dog who eventually evolved into Fox Terriers and Jack Russell Terriers. The white English Terrier became extinct in the 1870s, but it has been linked to several bulldog-terrier crosses, including the English Bullterrier, American Pit Bull Terrier, and the Boston Terrier.

As a group recognized by the various dog registries, terriers range in size from the smaller West Highland White Terrier (14 to 21 pounds) to the large Airedale Terrier (43 to 60 pounds). Though their sizes differ, they all exhibit the feisty, energetic nature that made them such adept vermin catchers.

You can see the terrier's traits in your Boston, too. (And not just in her name!) She is a very intelligent and lively breed who always wants a job to do, whether it's playing a game or chewing on a piece of rawhide.

Building the First Boston

The Boston Terrier you fell in love with traces her ancestry to a dog named Judge, who was owned by Robert C. Hooper. A resident of Boston, Massachusetts, Hooper purchased an imported bulldog-terrier crossbreed from his native England around 1870.

More resembling a bulldog than a terrier, Judge weighed 32 pounds and displayed a stocky build with a short *brindle coat* (a coat pattern speckled with varying shades of gray, brown, and tan fur) and a white collar.

Edward Burnett of Southborough, Massachusetts, admired Hooper's dog and bred his 20-pound *bitch* (female dog), Gyp, with Judge. Gyp displayed similar blocky characteristics to Judge, but she was all white and shorter. Their mating produced only one offspring: Well's Eph. Described as an unattractive dog, Well's Eph produced eye-catching offspring, including a male named Barnard's Tom. Tom exhibited the characteristics embodied by Bostons today, but most acknowledge Judge as the breed's Adam.

Early breeders continued to refine the dog, selecting for compact size, distinct look, and gentlemanly temperament. The Boston Terrier took on the positive characteristics of both its bulldog and terrier ancestors: lap dog, vermin chaser, watchdog, and down-to-earth scrapper.

Join the club!

In 1889, Charles F. Leland, a Harvard University student and breed fancier, located 40 others in the Boston area who shared his love of the dog. He invited them to form a club called the American Bull Terrier Club. They showed dogs under the name Round Heads or Bull Terriers.

Gaining acceptance in the American Kennel Club, however, would not come easy. Bull Terrier and Bulldog fanciers objected to the new breed, claiming that it was distinctly different and protesting the similarity of the breeds' names.

Relentless, the new breed's supporters pressed on, eventually establishing the Boston Terrier Club of America (BTCA) in 1891, taking on the name of the city where the dog originated. They wrote a standard that still influences the breed standard today (see the "Developing a Standard" section later in this chapter).

By 1893, the AKC admitted Hector, the first Boston Terrier stud, into its registry.

The Boston Terrier Club of America exists to this day, maintaining the original breed standards through a network of breeders and fanciers. To join the BTCA, you must submit an application with two letters of recommendation from BTCA club members in good standing, and be voted in by the board of directors. Once accepted, you must agree to abide by the club's constitution and bylaws. Visit www.bostonterrierclubofamerica.org for more information.

Renewed popularity

During the Boston's early days, it enjoyed extreme popularity, consistently holding the number-one or number-two spot among AKC registered breeds from 1905 to 1935.

Its popularity has waxed and waned since then, but another peak may be on the horizon. In 1995 and 1996, the breed ranked number 23 and number 21 respectively in the AKC registry, and by 2006, the organization listed it as the 15th most popular registered breed. In their namesake Boston, Massachusetts, Boston Terriers' popularity has risen even higher — they're listed as the area's 11th most popular dog. (Flip to Chapter 18 for more trivia tidbits about Bostons.)

They may never reach the number-one spot again, but as companion dogs, Boston Terriers are hard to beat.

Developing a Standard

You already know what your Boston looks like. She has those adoring dark eyes, short black- or brindle-and-white coat, those perpetually perked-up ears, and a stance that could scare off the brashest bull (well, at least the neighborhood cat!).

Someone had to come up with the unmistakable "look," or the Boston's *breed standard,* and that's where breed clubs come into play.

In order for a breed to be recognized by a country's presiding kennel club (in the United States, it's the AKC), that breed's fanciers must organize and provide documentation certifying that their dogs had bred true to form and free from *out-crosses* (introduction of other breeds) for at least five generations.

The breed club develops a written description of what the dog looks like in her most ideal form. It details things like her eyes, ears, nose, jaw, head, body, tail, forequarters, hindquarters, and demeanor with humans.

Judges use breed standards to judge dogs during competitive events, but many people use breed standards, too, to decide what type of dog to introduce into their home. By reading the various breed descriptions, prospective dog owners will know what to expect from a particular breed; you can find out everything from its adult height and weight to its care requirements and personality. If you're looking for a lap dog, you certainly wouldn't want to adopt a Great Dane!

You can read a paraphrased version of the Boston Terrier's AKC breed standard in the following section and compare the descriptions to your Boston (or, if you want, you can consult the AKC Web site for the exact information and wording). The standard has been revised since Charles F. Leland and the original Boston Terrier Club wrote it in 1891, but it still retains many of the original characteristics that made the dogs so endearing more than 100 years ago.

The standard is only a guideline for the ideal Boston Terrier. If your dog doesn't meet up to these marks, don't worry, unless you plan to show her, of course!

American Kennel Club standards

The American Kennel Club is the most well-known and recognized dog registry in the United States. It was founded in 1884 with the mission of "upholding its registry and promoting the sport of purebred dogs and breeding for type and function." It advocates purebred dogs as family companions, and canine health and well-being. It also stands up for the rights of all dog owners and promotes responsible dog ownership.

The AKC was the first registry to recognize the Boston Terrier as a unique breed in 1893 when it admitted the dog into its stud books. The registry classifies Boston Terriers under the *Non-sporting Group*, which is a catchall for dogs who don't fit into other categories.

The following sections outline the breed standard for the Boston. You can also check out Figure 2-1.

Figure 2-1: An "ideal" Boston wears a distinctive black- or brindle-and-white coat, has a well-balanced and compact body with a short head, and exudes grace and strength.

A matter of size and proportion

The breed standard divides the Boston Terrier class into three sub-categories: under 15 pounds, 15 to 19 pounds, and 20 to 25 pounds.

No matter her size, a Boston Terrier looks compact and sturdy but not blocky, chunky, or spindly. Ideal examples of Bostons appear well-balanced, meaning the dog's body is proportionate to her legs, neck, and head. Her back and muscles must also be in proportion and enhance the dog's weight and structure.

A square head

A Boston Terrier's square-looking head is flat on top and wrinkle free, reminiscent of that bulldog look. Her cheeks are flat, and her brow is short and sloped. Her large, dark eyes, which are set wide, and her small, erect ears, standing up on the corners of her skull, give the dog her alert and kind expression.

The dog's *muzzle* (made up of the nose, mouth, and jaws) is wide, short, and square and has no wrinkles. The muzzle is no longer than one-third the length of the skull and parallels the top of the skull. The Boston's black nose has a well-defined line between its nostrils.

Grouping the breeds

Dog registries categorize the dogs into *groups,* which are collections of dog breeds that exhibit similar traits, temperaments, or purposes.

The AKC divides dogs into eight groups:

✔ **Sporting:** This active and alert group of dogs includes Pointers, Retrievers, Setters, and Spaniels. They are generally the dogs who participate in hunting and field activities, so they require regular exercise — and lots of it — to expend their endless supply of energy.

✔ **Hound:** These are the hunting dogs of the pack, using their keen eyesight, sensitive noses, and stamina while tracking down prey. But their similarity stops there because this group comprises a range of breeds, from Afghans and Beagles to Dachshunds and Whippets.

✔ **Working:** Bred to guard property, pull sleds, and perform water rescues, dogs in the Working Group are highly loyal and intelligent. They are large and strong, so they don't make suitable pets for most households. This group includes dogs like the Doberman Pinscher, Saint Bernard, and Mastiff.

✔ **Terrier:** The terrier personality precedes itself. Lively and energetic, terriers entertain their humans for hours on end. They were bred to hunt vermin, so they still enjoy a good dig in the backyard now and then. Terriers range in size from the small Westie (formally known as the West Highland White Terrier) to the large Airedale.

✔ **Toy:** Dogs in the Toy Group have one job in life: to embody pure joy and delight. Bred as companions, these diminutive dogs make ideal pets for people who live in apartments or small spaces. Examples of dogs in the Toy Group include the Chihuahua, Maltese, Pug, and Yorkshire Terrier.

✔ **Non-sporting:** Boston Terriers fall into this group, which also includes the Bichon Frise, the Poodle, and the Bulldog. It's a catchall category for dogs who aren't bred for a particular sport or job.

✔ **Herding:** Members of the Herding Group have the ability to control the movement of other animals — including humans! Though many dogs in the Herding Group no longer rustle up cattle or steer sheep into their pen, they still herd their owners. Examples of dogs in the Herding Group include the Australian Shepherd, Collie, and the German Shepherd Dog.

✔ **Miscellaneous:** Dogs in the Miscellaneous Group are on their way to becoming recognized AKC breeds. When breed fanciers show that an interest in the breed exists and steps are being taken to have it recognized as a breed, the AKC places them in this category. Once listed among the Miscellaneous Group, the Beauceron and the Swedish Vallhund, for example, have recently become eligible for AKC registration and competition in the Herding Group shows.

A stocky body

Carrying that square head, the Boston's neck, back, and body should be proportionate to and balance the overall appearance of the dog.

Her slightly arched neck carries her head proudly, and her level back is parallel to the floor and runs perpendicular to her legs. Her chest is deep and extends back to her loins.

The Boston's short and tapering tail sits low on her rump. The tail can be straight or curly, but it shouldn't be too long.

She's got legs

A Boston's *forequarters* include her shoulders, which are sloping and well laid back; and her elbows, which point straight back. Her forelegs sit well apart and are lined up with the shoulder blades. They're straight with short, strong *pasterns,* or bones above her feet.

Her hindquarters feature strong, muscular thighs. She should have a bend at her *stifles,* or knee joint, and it should be aligned vertically with no bowing. Her *hock,* or ankle joint, should be well-defined, and her *hocks,* or lower legs, should be straight and short to her feet.

At the base of her muscular legs, small sturdy feet support her body. They should fall straight, and have well-arched toes and trimmed nails.

Walk this way

The Boston Terrier walks like a graceful, sure-footed, powerful dog. Moving with confidence and ease, her legs should move in a perpendicular line with the ground below; she should not cross one foot in front of the other or turn her feet outward.

Coat of three colors

A Boston's short, smooth coat comes in three colors, each with white markings: *brindle* (a mixture of colors), *seal* (black with a red cast), or black.

The Boston's distinctive tuxedo-like coat pattern — a white streak across her muzzle, a white shot from her forehead to her nose, a white chest, and white boots on her feet — give her that unmistakable look.

Temperament

Described as intelligent, friendly, lively, affectionate, loving, and loyal, the Boston Terrier's amiable personality makes her an easy best buddy. The dog truly deserves her nickname, "American Gentleman."

Other registries

The AKC and the UKC are recognized dog registries in the United States. Other countries have registries, too, and they each have their own breeds and groups that make up their stud books.

Other registries in English-speaking countries include:

- Canadian Kennel Club

- Australian National Kennel Council

- The Kennel Club (United Kingdom)

- Kennel Club of India

- Kennel Union of Southern Africa

The Fédération Cynologique Internationale, or the World Canine Organization, is an international kennel club based in Belgium. The FCI claims 80 member countries and recognizes 335 dog breeds.

United Kennel Club standards

Established in 1898, the United Kennel Club is the largest all-breed performance-dog registry in the world. Listing dogs from the United States as well as 25 foreign countries, the UKC distinguishes itself by focusing on the "total dog package," recognizing a breed's hunting ability and training instinct, as well as its looks.

The UKC first recognized Boston Terriers in 1914. Listed within its Companion Dog Group, the UKC standard is virtually identical to the AKC's, with only one exception: The AKC recognizes three weight subcategories while the UKC recognizes two, which are under 15 pounds, and up to and including 25 pounds.

Personality Aplenty

With a nickname like "American Gentleman," you can expect your Boston Terrier to be good-natured, intelligent, and polite with a sense of humor. But like many American gentlemen, they embody a little bit of spunk and spirit that makes them unique.

Breeders and fanciers describe Bostons as gentle, alert, and well-mannered. The dogs can be rambunctious, harkening back to their terrier ancestors. But that same energy can be redirected into rousing games of fetch, flyball, or agility. (Check out Chapter 12 for fun things to do with your Boston.)

Not known to be barkers, Boston Terriers don't make the best guard dogs — especially because they're too friendly to strangers! They adore children and senior citizens, making a properly social-ized Boston an ideal pet for a young family or an empty-nester.

Bostons get along splendidly with other canine and feline pets. They enjoy having one another for companionship. If you've ever seen a pack of Bostons playing together, you know how much fun they can have!

Despite the Boston's charming characteristics, you should con-sider these challenges that come with this canine "gentleman:"

- ✔ **Unstable temperament:** Bostons bred by unethical and inexperienced breeders may not exhibit stable demeanors. Obedience instructors and veterinary behaviorists counsel many clients whose Bostons display neurotic behavior, such as ceaseless barking, hyperactivity, and aggression. Purchase your dog from a reputable breeder who knows how to select for stable temperaments. (Flip to Chapter 4 for advice on find-ing a breeder and choosing a healthy puppy.)

- ✔ **Housetraining difficulties:** Drawing on that terrier stubborn-ness, Bostons can be difficult to housetrain. Plan to spend at least six months training your dog before you see results. (You can help your Boston master housetraining basics with Chapter 9.)

- ✔ **Snorts and snores:** Because of their shortened muzzles, Bostons tend to snort, wheeze, grunt, and snore loudly. Some Boston owners find these little noises endearing, but they drive others crazy! In some cases, the noises can indicate breathing difficulties, and your veterinarian can diagnose and treat any problem or potential problems. (For more details about Boston Terrier–specific health issues, turn to Chapter 15.)

Chapter 3

Committing to a Lifetime of Care

In This Chapter

▶ Determining whether a Boston Terrier is the right dog for you

▶ Understanding how your Boston will fit into the family

▶ Delegating responsibility to family members

▶ Analyzing the real costs of dog ownership

*A*n exuberant Boston draws smiles from virtually everyone he meets, but choosing to spend the next 15 years or so caring for the living creature is a commitment that you should not take lightly. Do you think you're ready for a Boston Terrier? More importantly, are you ready to welcome an energetic, intelligent, well-mannered dog into your home?

High-spirited dogs, like a Boston, require even more tolerance and understanding. Boston Terriers are intelligent pets, and they develop many interests and need challenging activities to keep their busy minds occupied. When you're choosing a type of dog to bring into your home, you should consider not only the dog's needs, but your needs, too. Your family's expectations and lifestyle should match what needs the dog may have.

You can discover more about the responsibilities involved in raising a Boston Terrier in the pages that follow. This chapter is really all about what you and your family can expect when you commit to care for your Boston.

Judging Your Compatibility

Truly an American Gentleman, your Boston Terrier will complement your household. Gentle and kind, entertaining and comical, he will make you laugh with his antics and personality.

Boston Terriers make wonderful pets, especially for young, active families or empty-nesters looking to add a dog to their home. Bostons do very well with children; mature Bostons have been known to stoically take almost any teasing or roughhousing that a child can dole out! And because the dogs are so gentle and well-mannered, they make ideal companions for seniors who may not physically be able to vigorously exercise their pet.

If you and your family can commit to providing the dog what he needs to thrive, like devoted training time, a regular schedule, patience and understanding, near constant companionship, and lots of love and attention, then you may have found a match made in Boston! Here, you can read more about these traits that your Boston needs to succeed.

Considering terrier needs

Though your Boston is a terrier, he's not as rambunctious as some breeds. He is lively and curious, but he's far from his vermin-chaser roots. (See Chapter 2 for more details about the Boston personality.)

To thrive in your household, he'll need some boundaries to keep him safe and content:

- ✔ **Security:** Bostons don't make very vicious guard dogs. Your Boston will rarely bark, unless he's trying to communicate with you. He'll welcome strangers with a playful lick and wag, and would happily go home with just about anyone — as long as treats and attention are involved. For this reason, your Boston must be kept in a fenced or enclosed yard. And when you walk with him, he must always be on a leash.

- ✔ **Training:** A very intelligent dog, your Boston will benefit greatly from puppy kindergarten and basic training classes. He may choose to chase a butterfly or play with his class-mates because he is easily distracted, but patience is para-mount. If you're diligent with his training, it will pay off in the long-run. For more info on training, flip to Chapter 11.

- ✔ **Indoor living:** Because of your Boston's short coat and short, flat nose, your dog will spend much of his time inside with you. He won't tolerate extreme temperatures or weather well. When he is outside during the summer, you'll need to provide a cool, shady area for your pup; during the winter, you'll want to bundle him up before braving the elements.

- ✔ **Regular schedule:** Your Boston will also need to be welcomed and loved by your entire family. Each person should dedicate him- or herself to caring and nurturing the puppy or adult dog. Establish chores for each person, agree to use the same train-ing tools, and remember that this dog is part of the family.

Are you ready for a Boston?

You are ultimately responsible for the health and well-being of your Boston. Does your household embody these characteristics?

✔ Patient and tolerant of mistakes

✔ Willing to devote much of your time to training and socializing your Boston

✔ Interest by the entire family in raising and nurturing your dog

✔ Concern for the dog's welfare

✔ Active, with time to exercise the dog at least twice a day

✔ Open to modifying your entire routine and home to accommodate the Boston

If so, get ready to welcome a Boston into your family!

Impatient owners need not apply

In general, dog owners need to be patient and dedicated, and for owners of a Boston Terrier, this statement couldn't be more true. Because he has terrier blood coursing through his veins, he will be rambunctious and willful at times, pushing boundaries and testing your tolerance. He is also very intelligent, which makes training easy, but when that wit combines with a willful attitude, you may need to out-think your dog.

You can expect to teach your dog everything from housetraining to behaving properly around other dogs. He'll look to you for guidance in any given circumstance, so you'll need to be prepared to lead your pup in a loving, tolerant way.

Accidents and trials will happen, and you will need to endure them as any parent would. A male may mark his territory. Your dog may use your favorite shoes as chew toys. Dog proofing your home may detract from its décor. At the same time, your dog will absolutely adore you, and your health will benefit from sharing your home with a pet. After you welcome a dog into your home, your life will never be the same again!

If you're willing to devote energy to raising your Boston, he'll reward you with lifelong love and companionship. A patient and understanding pet owner will raise a well-mannered pup. It just takes time and dedication.

At-home time: It's a necessity

If you have the time to dedicate to raising a dog, a Boston makes a wonderful companion in virtually any household.

Boston Terriers love to spend time with their human caretakers. Through decades of selecting for specific traits, breeders have fostered characteristics that make these dogs companion animals. Because they're extroverts, Bostons thrive on contact with their family and suffer if left alone for long periods of time.

An ideal home for a Boston is one that buzzes with activity all day long. Bostons aren't happy being alone and often benefit from having a Boston brother or sister. When properly socialized and trained, they get along splendidly with children and other pets, both canine and non-canine.

Your Boston will want to spend all his time with you and your family. If you travel frequently, work long hours, or are otherwise committed to tasks that require you to be away from home for long periods of time, you should think twice about adding this dog to your home. And if you're experiencing major life changes, such as changing jobs, expecting a baby, mourning a death, or coping with a serious illness, you may want to hold off on purchasing a puppy.

Establishing Family Dynamics

When you choose to adopt a Boston Terrier, he will become an integral part of your family. He is still a dog, but many of the decisions you make about travel, hobbies, purchases, décor, and lifestyle will require you to consider your family pet.

Because of this new ball of fur, the dynamics of your family will change when your Boston comes home. Each individual — from the adults to the children — will have new responsibilities. As a family, you will need to communicate more with each other, making sure that each person is on the same page when it comes to training and discipline. It will be a learning experience for all of you.

If you have other pets, their roles will shift as well, especially as the animals establish their dominance order. Dogs are pack animals, so as soon as your Boston comes home, he'll naturally discern his place in your household ranking system. Just as your family will adjust to the duties and responsibilities of owning a new pet, your Boston will need to adjust to his new surroundings, too.

Knowing who the main caregiver will be: You

If children are part of your family, it's likely that your son or daughter is prompting the purchase of your puppy.

New and novel in her young world, your child will insist that she will care for the dog, feed him, clean up after him, and bathe him. And she just might — for a time. She'll be happy to take your Boston on walks and play fetch, but when it comes to getting up at 6 a.m. and taking him to the bathroom, or cleaning up an accident in the middle of the living room floor, she'll likely balk.

The reality is that you — the adult — will ultimately do most of the work in raising and caring for the dog. You'll be the one taking him to the bathroom in the middle of the night. You'll be the one who makes sure he has the right amounts of food and water. You'll be the one who structures his playtime and makes sure that he socializes with other animals and humans.

Understanding your children's role

Most children love dogs. They'll play together from sunup to sundown, becoming constant companions and quick best friends.

Children, and even teenagers, however, can't be expected to be the sole caregivers of a pet. Soccer games, schoolwork, and social engagements often interfere with the day-to-day responsibilities associated with raising and caring for a dog.

You can, however, delegate specific tasks to your children. If you have more than one child, consider rotating chores to broaden their experiences. Later in the chapter, you'll find a list of duties suitable for children of any age.

Helping your four-legged friends get along with each other

Most Boston Terriers are courteous and laid back enough to get along with other pets, both canine and non-canine varieties. When raised from puppyhood in a home filled with other animals, Bostons will learn to fit in without a hitch. With time and training, adult Bostons, too, can be trained to bunk with other pets.

Keep in mind, however, that Bostons retain their terrier roots and may try to chase down a pocket pet, like a guinea pig or rat. Cautiously introduce them to each other in a safe, neutral environment, gradually giving each more freedom to sniff out the other. Even if they do get along, supervise them. You don't want your Boston making a toy out of your beloved bunny!

If you care for an easily spooked or alpha cat, you can minimize the hissing and flying fur by following these steps:

1. **Leave your Boston in his crate during the first few introductions.**

   Carefully hold the cat and sit next to the kennel containing your dog. Let them smell each other through the kennel walls or bars, and watch their reactions. If your cat hisses and bears her claws, or if your puppy whimpers, back away slowly and try again the next day, gradually increasing the time they spend together. Give both animals lots of praise when they can tolerate each other's company.

2. **After your cat shows signs of being comfortable with your Boston, let your cat walk freely around the kennel until she grows accustomed to the new smell.**

   As soon as she sniffs his kennel and approves of his presence, she'll ignore the kennel and likely perch somewhere, watching your new little dog and keeping a keen eye on every move he makes.

3. **In time, you'll be able to leave your dog's kennel door open, and they'll freely interact.**

   When you can give them this freedom depends on your cat's tolerance of the dog and your Boston's exuberance level. An uptight cat may become annoyed by a playful pup, whereas a docile dog won't cause a ruckus at all. Watch your animals closely until you're absolutely confident that they'll get along. Ideally, they'll be best friends before long, sharing the same cushy bed.

Chapter 10 contains more advice on making sure your Boston behaves like a gentleman around other animals (and people).

Divvying Up Duties

Who knew that welcoming a dog into your household could open up so many job opportunities! Each family member will have some sort of daily doggy duty to perform. Because humans have welcomed dogs into the domestic setting, your Boston can't care for himself as he would in the wild, so you'll need to provide fresh food and water for him, exercise him, take him to the bathroom, and teach him basic manners, among myriad other tasks.

Besides the daily chores, you'll also need to plan for weekly, monthly, and yearly duties, such as attending basic training courses, giving him a bath, feeding him heartworm medication, and taking him to the veterinarian for his annual checkup.

Fitting in regular chores

To help with your planning efforts, you can follow the rough guidelines shown in Figure 3-1 for the daily, weekly, monthly, and yearly chores required to keep your pup happy and healthy.

Of course, the schedule for each household will differ, but these are intended to be a starting point for your life with your Boston.

Daily duties

These tasks will need to be performed every day, sometimes more than once a day.

- ✔ **Feeding:** When your Boston is a puppy, he'll need to be fed up to four times a day; when he's an adult, he'll need two meals a day. You should feed your dog on a regular schedule, such as at 9 a.m. and 6 p.m., so he knows exactly what to expect.

  Also keep in mind that just as you would wash your own dishes, your Boston's bowls need to be thoroughly washed with soap and water after every meal. You'll also want to keep an eye on his eating habits and note any irregular behavior, like a poor appetite or vomiting (see Chapter 7 for more on feeding).

- ✔ **Keeping fresh water available:** Often paired with the feeding regimen, this is an ongoing job that requires you to check your Boston's water bowl and refill it with clean water when necessary. Plan to wash the bowl on a daily basis.

- ✔ **Bathroom responsibilities:** A young Boston will require frequent bathroom visits while you housetrain him (see Chapter 9) — at least every two hours, if not more often. As he gets older and learns how to ask to go outside, you'll need to supervise him while he does his business, eventually letting him go by himself when he's an adult. Every day, you'll need to clean up his bathroom area, scooping up his feces and spraying down the area with water, if necessary. When you take him for walks, you'll want to carry plastic bags to clean up the presents he leaves behind.

✔ **Exercise:** Being the energetic dogs that they are, Bostons require daily exercise. You can take yours for an hour-long walk, play fetch for 20 minutes, or enjoy a fun session of flyball (see Chapter 12). The more exercise, the better, because it will allow your Boston — and you — to get a good night's sleep.

✔ **Grooming:** They don't require rigorous coat care like some breeds, but Bostons do need a daily brushing to keep their shedding under control. Plan to spend 10 minutes or so for the day-to-day grooming regime.

✔ **Training:** When your Boston is old enough for training and behavior classes (about 10 to 12 weeks old), you can plan to spend about 20 minutes each day practicing what you've learned (see Chapter 11). It's important to reinforce his learning every day because basic training forms the building blocks for more advanced tricks later on.

Weekly chores

Though not as extensive as the care your Boston requires daily, these weekly tasks are necessary and vary in each household.

✔ **Socializing:** Once a week, take your Boston to the local dog park or dog-friendly shopping center where people and their pets congregate. Let them greet your dog. It's important that your puppy experience as many people, smells, and experiences as possible to grow into a healthy, well-adjusted adult (see Chapter 10 for more info). Adults need ongoing socialization, too, but it's not as critical as when your Boston is a pup.

✔ **Training classes:** Typically held once a week, puppy kindergarten and basic training classes get your Boston off to a great start in proper obedience and behavior. If you've adopted an adult Boston, he can learn new tricks, too! Obedience classes will teach you and your dog the basic training skills introduced in puppy kindergarten.

✔ **Agility training or other sporting activity:** After your dog passes puppy kindergarten and basic training, enroll him in some agility or flyball classes (see Chapter 12). They will focus his energy into a positive outlet — and you'll meet other dog people who love their pets as much as you love yours!

✔ **Brushing his teeth:** Plan to brush your Boston's teeth at least once a week, though once a day would be ideal (but maybe not realistic!). Good oral hygiene will keep your dog's pearly whites clean and tartar-free. (Chapter 8 tells you how.)

✔ **Eye check:** Because Bostons have such prominent eyes, check them at least once a week for discharge, dryness, or other irregularities (see Chapter 8). Consult your veterinarian right away if you suspect a problem.

Today

☑ *7 a.m.: Wake up Buster and take him outside to bathroom area. Clean up after him.*

☑ *8 a.m.: Wash Buster's food and water dishes.*

☑ *9 a.m.: Feed Buster and fill his water bowl.*

☐ *9:30 a.m.: Take Buster outside again and play fetch for a bit. Clean up after him.*

☐ *10 a.m.: Naptime.*

☐ *Noon: Right when he wakes up from his nap, take Buster outside to the bathroom area. Clean up after him.*

☐ *2 p.m.: Play with Buster. Take him outside again. Practice lessons learned in puppy kindergarten. Clean up after him.*

☐ *2:30 p.m.: Naptime.*

☐ *4 p.m.: Take Buster outside when he wakes up and clean up after him again.*

☐ *6 p.m.: Feed Buster his dinner and refill his water dish.*

☐ *6:30 p.m.: Take Buster outside again. Clean up after him.*

☐ *7 p.m.: Grooming time! Brush his coat and give him a quick massage.*

☐ *7:30 p.m.: Take Buster outside one more time. Clean up after him.*

☐ *8 p.m.: Bedtime for Buster. Put him in his kennel.*

This week

☐ *Monday: Dog birthday party at Heather's house.*

☐ *Tuesday: Puppy kindergarten, 8–10 a.m.*

☐ *Wednesday: Brush Buster's teeth after grooming him and check his eyes.*

☐ *Thursday: Go to the dog park for an hour or two.*

☐ *Friday: Invite new dog friends over for a play date.*

☐ *Saturday: Spend the day with Buster.*

☐ *Sunday: Go on a long walk with the family.*

This month

☑ *Give Buster his heartworm medicine.*

☐ *Apply Buster's flea and tick prevention.*

☐ *Trim Buster's nails, clean his ears, and give him a bubbly bath.*

☐ *Check Buster's body for lumps, bumps, or other abnormalities.*

☐ *Call veterinarian and schedule a follow-up appointment.*

Figure 3-1: Caring for your Boston requires daily, weekly, and monthly chores.

Monthly musts

Mostly related to health, these chores are best done around the
same time each month, such as within the first week.

- ✔ **Giving heartworm medication and flea-and-tick prevention:**
  During routine exams, your veterinarian will prescribe heartworm and flea-and-tick prevention for your Boston (see
  Chapter 14). To keep him parasite-free, give your Boston the
  medication once a month.

- ✔ **Grooming:** Bathing, nail clipping, and ear cleaning should be
  done once a month. Plan to spend a good hour at least giving
  your Boston a bath, clipping or grinding down his nails, cleaning his ears, and making him handsome. (Flip to Chapter 8 for
  pointers on sprucing up your Boston.)

- ✔ **Overall health check:** While you're doing your monthly
  grooming ritual, inspect your dog's body. Look at his coat and
  skin, checking for scrapes and lumps. Check his eyes, nose,
  and mouth for signs of redness or irritation. Inspect his paws,
  checking his pads for cuts. If you see anything out of the ordinary, consult your veterinarian.

Annual checkups

You can plan to take your Boston to the veterinarian once a year
for his annual checkup. During that visit, your veterinarian will
weigh him, check his heart and lungs, look in his eyes and ears,
and perform an overall assessment of your dog's health. The
annual checkup is the ideal time to bring up any questions about
your dog's health or behavior. (Chapter 14 explains the details of
what to expect when you and your Boston visit the vet.)

Child-appropriate tasks

To ease the day-to-day chores that you need to do for your Boston,
enlist your children's help. Under your supervision, of course, you
can involve them by assigning tasks such as these:

- ✔ **Cleanup duty:** Ask your child to accompany you when you take
  your Boston to the bathroom. She can grab a plastic bag and
  clean up the bathroom area after the dog does his business.
  Make sure she washes her hands when she comes back inside.

- ✔ **Feeding time:** Make it your child's job to remind you when it's
  time to feed your pup. If she's old enough, ask her to measure
  and pour the food into the dog's bowl.

- ✔ **Refilling the water bowl:** Assign your child the chore of
  making sure the water bowl is always full of fresh, clean water.

✔ **Cleaning out his kennel:** You can ask your child to shake out her pet's blanket, straighten up the kennel, and gather strewn doggy toys.

✔ **Brushing and grooming:** Daily grooming tasks give your child a chance to bond with your Boston. Involve her as much as possible with washing and brushing tasks.

✔ **Training and behavior practice:** Ask your child to attend puppy kindergarten with you and practice simple commands, like Sit and Stay, with your dog. You can also enlist your child's help when selecting reference and training materials.

The Real Costs

Dog ownership isn't cheap. Though it's common knowledge that you'll have to pay for dog food, supplies, veterinary bills, and cleaning supplies, have you ever calculated the monthly costs?

In 2004, the American Kennel Club (AKC) surveyed more than 1,000 visitors to its Web site to determine what pet owners pay to care for their pooches. In addition, the American Pet Products Manufacturers Association Inc. (APPMA), a nonprofit trade organization that serves the pet products industry, conducts a pet owners' survey every two years that tracks pet-product purchasing behavior of its respondents.

Between these two organizations' reports, you can see in this section that owning a dog has its costs (although most owners would agree that it's worth it!).

One-time and monthly expenses

When you purchase a car, you expect to pay the one-time costs of the car itself, the taxes, and the warranty. You also expect to pay the ongoing costs of gas, insurance, and maintenance. In the same way, you can expect to pay one-time and ongoing expenses when you bring your Boston home.

✔ **One-time, major expenses:** The APPMA's 2005–2006 survey reports that pet owners spent an average of $655 purchasing a small purebred dog, like your Boston Terrier. The AKC's numbers mirror the APPMA's numbers at $646. So you can expect to pay about $650 for your Boston, depending on where you live.

Adopting a Boston from a shelter or rescue can cut this cost significantly, depending on the organization. Several rescues, such as Wonderdog Rescue in San Francisco, California, offer purebred adult dogs for $300 or less, and that price includes spay or neuter surgery and vaccinations.

You'll also need to have your dog spayed or neutered, a cost that runs $160 according to the AKC. Plan to spend another $350 on training fees and supplies, the organization reports, and an additional $350 on nonconsumable pet products, like bowls, leashes, and a crate.

✔ **Ongoing (and in some cases, fun) expenses:** You'll also need to budget for routine expenses and consumable items, like food, treats, leashes, and medication. The AKC reports that survey participants spend an average of $2,489 per year in food, veterinary visits, travel, grooming, boarding, toys and treats, ongoing training, and dog events. Costs will, of course, vary depending on where you live.

Unexpected bills

One expense you can't plan for is an emergency. The AKC reports that an emergency veterinary visit will cost $631; the APPMA says that number is $594. If your Boston requires emergency veterinary care, you can expect to pay a pretty penny to keep your dog healthy.

To cushion the cost of emergency veterinary care, you can purchase health insurance for your Boston. It may seem like an extravagant expense — about $300 to $400 per year — but it can save you thousands of dollars if your Boston ever requires critical care.

You can find pet health insurance companies through a variety of sources, including the AKC, your breeder, your veterinarian, or a quick online search. You can also ask members of your local Boston Terrier Club for referrals.

Like human health insurance, pet health insurance requires you to pay a premium every month. In exchange, the policy covers annual exams, prescription flea prevention, heartworm protection, vaccinations, hospitalization, accidents, radiology, surgeries, and even cancer treatments. After you meet your deductible, the insurance company pays a percentage of the medical costs.

Pet health insurance differs from human health insurance in that, in most cases, you pay for the veterinary bill up front (no co-pay), submit a claim form, and get reimbursed for a percentage (or all) of the medical costs. This feature allows you to take your pet to virtually any licensed veterinarian without worrying about whether the clinic will accept your insurance.

Different policies offer different benefits, so look at all your options before choosing one for your Boston. It'll be worth it!

If you decide to forgo pet health insurance, squirrel some money away — at least several hundred dollars — for medical emergencies, just in case.

Chapter 4

A Match Made in Boston

In This Chapter

▶ Deciding what gender of Boston to adopt

▶ Choosing between a puppy or an adult

▶ Finding the Boston of your dreams

▶ Identifying a healthy dog

*I*t's easy — and common — to follow your emotions when selecting a new dog. You fall in love with that adorable puppy in the window, so you bring her home on a whim, only to find that you're not prepared or you don't have time to share your life with a puppy.

You can approach the adoption process with greater success if you decide in advance what breed, gender, and age suit you and your family's lifestyle. You've already chosen your breed — a Boston Terrier — so now it's time to decide whether you want a male or a female dog, and whether you want a puppy or an adult.

This chapter explores the personalities of both the male and the female Boston, as well as compares the qualities of a puppy and an adult. By educating yourself, you can make an informed decision about what Boston Terrier is right for you.

After you've decided the age and the gender of your Boston, you must go about finding one. This chapter also leads you through the different sources for finding a dog, including breeders, rescues, pet stores, and even newspaper advertisements.

Battle of the Sexes

Like humans, male and female Bostons embody distinct characteristics that make them unique. You can see these behavioral differences readily when the dog is not spayed or neutered. Males are loyal and devoted companions, but they will mark their territory. Females, on the other hand, don't lift their leg, but they come into heat twice a year, requiring you to guard them from male suitors.

If you decide to neuter or spay your Boston, many of his or her gender traits will diminish, but his or her personality won't change. (See Chapter 14 for details on spaying and neutering your Boston.)

Physiologically, Boston males are slightly larger than females. Other than that, the two genders look identical. Ultimately, your personal preference dictates which gender to choose.

Mighty males

Males make loving and devoted companions. True gentlemen, males are playful and entertaining. They tend to maintain a constant mood, though they can be rowdy and raucous depending on the individual's personality.

As such, males will search for females in heat, so they are prone to running off and sowing their canine oats. Adolescent males may also challenge and disobey your commands, especially if a female is in the vicinity, so you'll need to add an extra dose of patience during training sessions.

Unaltered males (those who can reproduce because they haven't been neutered) tend lift their legs to mark their territory, letting other dogs know that your home and yard are his turf. Male dogs do this regardless of whether they are housetrained, so you'll need to have some odor-busting cleaning products on hand. (See Chapter 9 for more on housetraining.)

In altered males, however, these problems are virtually eliminated. They will be less likely to roam, mark their territory, be aggressive, and rebel against your authority. Unless you're planning to breed or show your Boston, you should definitely plan to have your male Boston neutered.

Attentive females

Female Bostons make sweet and loyal companions, too. With her mother-like instincts, she dotes on her human family just as she would her canine family.

Unlike their male counterparts, however, *unspayed* female Bostons (those who can have baby Bostons) can be moody and temperamental, especially when they come into *heat* (their fertile period) twice a year. When this happens, you'll need to isolate her from ready and willing male suitors. You'll also need to clean up her bloody discharge during that time or outfit her in a pair of absorbent pet pants.

After your female Boston is spayed, however, her bossy tendencies will cease (for the most part!), and she'll settle into a more emotionally constant temperament.

Puppy or Adult?

There's nothing quite like a puppy. They're cute and cuddly, and the gaze from a Boston puppy's big, round eyes can melt any heart. She'll rely on you completely to care for her every need. You'll teach her how to act, where to sleep, and what to play with. As she grows up, you'll help mold her personality and behavior.

An adult dog, however, can be a delight, too. She has graduated from that awkward puppy stage into adulthood, rendering her more manageable and independent. Depending on her history and training skills, you won't have to send her to basic obedience classes or housetrain her. She's simply ready to be your constant companion.

Choosing between a puppy and adult can be a challenging task for any dog lover. Each has its benefits and drawbacks. Before making a decision, ask yourself these questions:

- ✔ **Do you have the time to dedicate to raising and training a puppy?** If you work at home or have some flexibility with your schedule, a puppy is for you! If not, consider an adult dog who has been housetrained and is relatively independent.

- ✔ **Is your lifestyle conducive to raising a dog?** Pet owners who prefer to stay at home rather than go out are a step ahead when it comes to raising a puppy. If you enjoy going out, an adult who is already trained would suit you better.

- ✔ **Do you want to breed your dog?** If so, you need to find a breeder who is willing to adopt out a breeding young-adult female dog who has already begun to display her adult conformation and temperament.

- ✔ **Is it important that you raise the dog yourself?** If so, definitely choose a puppy who you can watch grow up. An adult dog has already established her personality, and she may have some behavior issues left over from the previous owner.

- ✔ **Do you have children?** Older children can help with the chores associated with raising a puppy; younger children may not be ready for such responsibility. An adult Boston who has been raised around kids will be tolerant of playful children, though she should be supervised at all times.

- ✔ **Is cost an issue?** The purchase price of a purebred puppy is often more than that of adults or rescues. If price is an issue, consider adopting an adult.

> ✔ **Is it important for you to help a retired show dog or rescue?** If so, then open your home to an adult Boston. Many Boston breeders will place a retired show dog or a female after she is past the breeding age of 5 years old.

These questions are only a few that you should ask yourself and your family before deciding on an adult or a puppy. Also consider your experience in raising a puppy, the current — and future — makeup of your family, and the activity level of your household. Keep in mind that although puppies are adorable, many adult Bostons are looking for homes, too.

If You Choose a Puppy . . .

Get ready for some fun! Raising a puppy to adulthood is one of the most rewarding experiences you can imagine. Not only will you watch your pup grow and develop into a healthy adult, but she'll also be adaptable and easy to train. You can look forward to a lifetime of companionship and adoration from your Boston baby.

You can also expect long hours training and socializing your puppy. You'll need to feed her at regular times throughout the day, take her to the bathroom, and spend lots of time bonding with her. The patterns and behaviors that you develop in her now will be with her for her entire life, so you will need to be aware of your actions and how they will affect her later.

But before all that, you'll need to find your puppy first!

Locating a reputable source

You can find purebred puppies from breeders, online, at your local pet store, and through sources listed in consumer magazines. You can even find purebred puppies listed in the newspaper.

But how do you know if the breeder or dealer is reputable? How can you be sure that the dog you're getting is healthy, is bred from quality parents, and has begun to be socialized? How do you know that your Boston will be of sound temperament?

You need to look for upstanding breeders and dealers who are experts at selecting, breeding, and preparing dogs for loving homes. These breeders sell the animals through a variety of outlets, from individual placements by the breeders themselves to offering them through responsible pet stores.

Breeders

A *reputable dog breeder* is someone who seeks to preserve and improve the breed that they love. Often, a breeder sticks to rearing one type of dog. She is actively involved in the dog fancy and shows her dogs at kennel club competitions. Her goal is to perfect the traits that make the breed unique.

What makes a breeder reputable?

- ✔ She chooses her breeding stock very carefully, with the goal of improving and preserving the breed. She uses the breed standard as a guide to produce the best puppies she can.

- ✔ She tests her puppies for congenital defects and illnesses, and she tries to eliminate unhealthy dogs from her breeding program.

- ✔ She supplies Boston buyers with a proof of health screening, a sales contract, and plenty of references.

- ✔ Though she may list her name among other breeders in national magazines, she typically doesn't sell her puppies through local or regional newspapers advertisements. She doesn't need to because she often has a waiting list for her healthy, well-mannered puppies.

- ✔ She will ask you about your home, your lifestyle, your experience with dogs, and your goals with the puppy. She may even ask you to complete an application.

- ✔ She willingly opens her home so you can inspect her facilities. She introduces you to the dam and her litter, and she'll show you photos, pedigrees, and health certificates from the litter's sire.

- ✔ She will take back a dog from her breeding program if you can no longer care for the puppy.

You can find breeders listed in one of the many dog breed magazines or from an online search, but your best bet is to locate your regional kennel club or breed club and ask for a list of recommendations. The Boston Terrier Club of America (www.bostonterrier clubofamerica.org), for example, maintains a breeder referral list of members who have signed a code of ethics and conduct.

Dog shows offer another opportunity to locate Boston breeders. After watching the dogs compete, talk to some of the people showing their dogs. Ask them about their breeding program or where they got their dogs.

When you find a breeder with whom you feel comfortable, ask her some questions. She'll be expecting you to do so! (*Note:* If she seems put out or taken aback by your questions, that should be a red flag.)

✔ **How long have you been breeding?** The more experience, the better.

✔ **How long have you been breeding Boston Terriers? Do you breed other dogs?** People who breed one particular type of dog are truly dedicated to bettering the breed. People who breed based on the latest fad or those who breed several different types of dogs should raise a red flag.

✔ **What dog organizations do you belong to?** Reputable breeders should belong to some membership-based club or organization, like the Boston Terrier Club of America, with the goal of continuing their education in the breed.

✔ **What are the parents' strengths? What shortcomings do they have?** Though most breeders will boast about the quality of the dam and sire, question her to learn about any behavioral or temperament problems, like possible aggression or poor socialization skills.

✔ **Can I visit your facility and meet the dam?** The answer to this question should always be, "Of course." Even if the breeder has no puppies at the time, she should welcome you into her facility so you can see the dogs in her breeding program.

✔ **Where do you raise your puppies? How have you socialized them?** Ideally, the breeder has raised the puppies in her home around the sounds of normal daily activities. You want to find out whether the pups are getting used to being around people.

✔ **What health problems do you screen for? What congenital defects are common in Boston Terriers, and what are you doing to decrease those defects?** If the breeder says, "None," or "My dogs are perfect," run the other way! All breeds have the potential for some sort of genetic defect, so your breeder should be upfront about health problems that may present themselves. If possible, know the correct answer to this question in advance. (Chapter 15 covers common Boston ailments.)

✔ **What kind of health guarantee do you offer with your dogs?** At the very least, the breeder should guarantee against any debilitating health problems and congenital defects.

✔ **How many litters do you raise a year?** Breeders who produce more than three litters per year may not be paying enough attention to the dogs' health. Avoid breeders who always have puppies because that can be a sign of irresponsible breeding practices.

✔ **When can I take the puppy home?** A reputable breeder will let her puppies go home when they're 9 to 12 weeks old.

Backyard breeders and puppy mills

These terms are packed with negative connotations, and for good reason. Some backyard breeders and puppy mills breed and raise purebred puppies as a commodity, with little or no interest in the dogs' well-being.

A *backyard breeder* is often a person who breeds her dogs to make some extra money. She knows little or nothing about selecting for specific genetic traits or preventing congenital malformations.

A *puppy mill* is just as it sounds: a facility that churns out puppies purely to make money. Disreputable puppy mills are often on a farm or in a residence, and they keep their animals in filthy, inhumane conditions. The dogs being used to produce the puppies aren't taken care of properly and are usually bred each season with no chance to recuperate.

There are, however, reputable *hobby breeders* who are learning from an experienced mentor. Similarly, *puppy distributors* raise puppies en masse, but the dogs are cared for by a veterinarian, raised in pristine facilities, and socialized on-site by staff members who adore the dogs.

Before pooh-poohing a novice breeder or puppy distributor, do your homework and get the facts. It may not be as bad as you think.

Pet stores

When it comes to selling purebred puppies, pet stores often have a bad reputation. Criticized as smelly shops that display their puppies in cramped, dirty kennels, some pet stores have earned this reputation, to be sure.

Some pet store owners, however, do an excellent job at visiting puppy breeders, scrutinizing puppy distribution centers, and finding loving homes for puppies who they sell through their retail shop. They keep the dogs in sanitized play areas and socialize them with other puppies and people. They question potential buyers, screening them and requiring them to fill out applications. They act as a liaison between the breeder and the buyer.

The owners of one pet store in Southern California, for example, regularly visit each breeder with whom they work. They take in only as many puppies as their retail facility can handle, and they keep them in an open play area during the day so the puppies can interact with each other. Three designated employees are specially trained to care for the puppies and check potential buyers. The store owners recognize the need in the community for purebred puppies from a reputable source, and they have filled that need with healthy, well-cared-for puppies.

Unfortunately, that shop is not the norm, but you can find responsible pet stores that sell purebred puppies. You just need to know what questions to ask.

First, arrange to meet with the pet store owner. If he isn't available or doesn't have time to talk to you, run away! How could he have time to care for the puppies if he doesn't have time to talk to you!

Next, prepare to ask the shopkeeper these questions:

- ✔ **Do you have a source for Boston Terrier puppies?** Depending on where you live, a Boston may be hard to find in a pet store. Ask the shop owner whether he can get one, and if his answer is yes, ask how involved you can be in selecting the puppy.

- ✔ **What kind of background do you have on the puppies?** While many pet store owners won't have the detailed information and pedigrees that are available from a breeder, he should have the dogs' medical history, including shots and wormings that have been done; whether the dogs can be registered, and with what registry; the age of the puppies; and a list of medical problems, if any.

- ✔ **Where did the puppies come from? Have you inspected the facility yourself?** The shop owner should know exactly where the puppies came from, and ideally, he should have inspected the facility at least once. He should be keeping tabs on the breeder or distributor, knowing as much as possible about the facility, the breeding practices, and the care the animals receive.

- ✔ **Do you work with a veterinarian?** Puppies sold through pet stores should be under the care of a veterinarian who oversees their health and well-being.

- ✔ **How do you socialize the puppies?** To grow up to be healthy adults, puppies need to interact with other dogs, be handled by humans, and introduced to a variety of sounds and smells. Pet store owners should be able to describe how their puppies are being socialized.

- ✔ **Can I inspect the puppies?** Look at the puppies to make sure their eyes are clear and bright, that there are no signs of external parasites, that their skin and coats look healthy, and that they show no signs of *hot spots* (surface skin infections that look like festering sores) on their backs or legs. The puppies should be energetic and full of life.

- ✔ **Can I inspect the facility?** Look at the play area and kennels where the puppies are housed. Is the area clean and sanitized? Is the air cleaned through air purifiers? You should smell no odor at all, and you should see no feces or urine in the kennels. The facility should be as pristine as possible.

✔ **What kind of guarantee do you offer?** The pet shop should offer a health guarantee in case the puppy becomes ill after you take her home. A *health guarantee* ensures that you can return the puppy within a specific time period (typically several days, depending on the contract) if your veterinarian sees any signs of health problems or congenital defects.

✔ **What information do you need from me?** To determine whether your home is fit for a puppy, a reputable pet store owner should ask you about your experience in keeping a dog. He should ask if you live in a home or an apartment, and whether you have a yard or outdoor area to exercise your pet. If the shopkeeper doesn't question your ability to care for the animal, he's not acting responsibly.

That puppy in the pet store window may tug at your heartstrings, but don't rush in and buy it just to rescue it from the retailer. Though some pet stores offer healthy pups, many don't, and that expensive impulse purchase may lead to unanticipated veterinary bills. Besides, by buying a pup from a disreputable pet store, you're supporting the production of puppy mill dogs.

Magazine advertisements

Perusing the classified section in dog magazines is another way to find a purebred puppy. Many of these sources, however, don't screen the breeders, so if you choose to find your Boston this way, do so with caution.

Call the breeders in the advertisements and ask them the same questions that you would ask a breeder who was referred to you by another Boston owner or kennel club. Just keep in mind that cold calling breeders is the riskiest way to find a pet.

Recognizing a healthy puppy

Regardless of where you get your pup, she should be as healthy as possible when you bring her home. You want your Boston to begin her life with you as a sound, well-adjusted pet without obvious physical or behavioral flaws.

Physical characteristics

You can begin this puppy health-check while the dog is at the breeder's facility or in the pet store. If the puppy is still with her littermates, look at the entire group. They should all be active and playful. There should be no sick or weak puppies in the bunch; if one is sick, the others will likely come down with the same illness.

The pups should all have clear, bright eyes with no redness or discharge; cold, damp noses; and clean ears with no signs of ear mites. None should be shaking her head or scratching at her ears, because this behavior can indicate an infection. Similarly, there should be no odor around the dogs' ears. Their gums should also be pink and healthy.

Their coats should be shiny and clean, and their skin should appear pink and healthy with no hot spots or sores. Their bodies should appear full, firm, and muscular. Their bellies should not be bloated, which could be a sign of worms.

If you see signs of any physical malady, point it out to the breeder or shopkeeper right away. But if the Boston puppy you have your eye on checks out, take a closer look at her behavior among her littermates. Get to know their personalities.

Behavioral characteristics

 You want an alert Boston who leaps up to see you, wagging her little tail in sheer ecstasy. You don't, however, want a pup who appears overly aggressive or domineering, charging over her litter-mates to get close to you. That little pup is a discipline problem waiting to happen!

At the other end of the spectrum, you don't want a shy, submissive pup who hides in the corner or appears listless. Stick with a dog who falls in the middle: excited but not giddy, laid back but not listless.

If the breeder okays it, take the puppy into an area where she hasn't been before. Put her down and watch her reaction. If she follows you, she's eager to please. If she chooses to explore her surroundings, she's a curious pup who may still have a short attention span. All the different reactions point to the pup's personality.

If You Choose an Adult . . .

An adult Boston makes an excellent choice for a family that wants a dog but doesn't want to endure trying puppy behaviors, like housetraining, obedience training, and chewing. Hundreds of healthy adult Bostons who are looking for a family to love are available across the country.

You can find adult Bostons through kennel clubs and breeders. Often, after the dogs are past their reproductive stages, breeders place Bostons in loving homes so they can enjoy the rest of their lives being spoiled by loving owners. You can also find adult Bostons through breed-rescue organizations that specialize in finding homes for dogs whose owners can't care for them anymore.

Rescuing a Boston

If you choose to adopt an adult Boston Terrier, one of these national rescue organizations can help. They have hundreds of healthy Bostons who are looking for loving "forever" homes. They even have special-needs dogs who require a little extra care and nurturing.

✔ Boston Terrier Club of America (`www.bostonterrierclubofamerica.org/rescue.html`)

✔ Boston Terrier Rescue (`www.btrescue.org`)

✔ Nationwide Boston Terrier Rescue (`www.nationwidebostonrescue.org`)

✔ The Boston Site (`www.thebostonsite.com`)

✔ The Boston Terrier Rescue Net (`www.bostonrescue.net`)

When you adopt an adult dog, remember that you're saving a Boston's life. Most people gravitate toward puppies, but the adults need homes, too, and you can feel good about giving the dog a second chance.

Working with a breeder

Boston breeders can be an excellent source for finding an adoptable adult dog. Many times, they have adult males or females who they no longer use for breeding or who have developed flaws that no longer allow them to compete in conformation shows. They may also have an adult dog who was returned to them because the owner was no longer able to care for her. These dogs make fine companions, and you can be sure that they have been well cared for.

You can find a reputable breeder by attending a dog show, contacting your regional kennel club, searching through periodicals, or asking your veterinarian or pet store owner for a referral. Assess the breeder just as you would if you were buying a puppy: Ask questions, visit the facility, and check references whenever possible. (See the "Breeders" section earlier in this chapter for more info.)

Connecting with rescues

Purebred dog rescue has become quite popular over the past ten years as the number of purebred dogs being euthanized in shelters has increased. Sponsored by breed clubs and independent organizations, these rescue groups have formed to save these animals and find new homes for them.

You can find a Boston rescue group in your area by contacting a national group, or you can check with your regional humane society, animal control facility, veterinarian, or even pet store for breed rescue information. Many of them track rescues and can provide whatever contact information you need.

Most rescues require that you complete an application and conduct an interview with the organization's representative. He will ask you questions similar to those a breeder would ask. When you're approved for an adoption, you'll be placed on a waiting list or told if there are dogs available.

You won't likely be able to get as much information about the dog as you would if she were a puppy from a breeder, but you can find out if the dog is healthy and housetrained.

After the dog moves in with you, the organization will likely follow up to be sure the dog is settling in okay. The group doesn't want the dog back in rescue again, so it takes every care to make sure that the adoption will work out.

Recognizing a healthy adult dog

A healthy adult dog has the same characteristics as a healthy puppy. It should be lively and energetic, happy to see you, and willing to approach you without fear.

In addition, look for the following features:

- Clear, bright eyes with no redness, discharge, or injuries
- A cold, wet nose with no discharge of any kind
- Clean, erect ears with no signs of ear mites or infection
- Clean and bright teeth with little tartar
- A smooth, clean coat free from external parasites, including fleas, ticks, and mange
- Healthy, pink skin with no sores
- An overall sound structure with healthy legs, paws, and body
- No signs of coughing, congestion, or diarrhea
- Free and easy movement with no difficultly moving about
- Well-socialized, appearing confident and not afraid of sudden sounds or movements
- Up to date on her shots and vaccinations

Part II
Caring for Your Boston Terrier

The 5th Wave
By Rich Tennant

"Okay, before I let the new puppy out, let's remember to be real still so we don't startle him."

In this part . . .

You've decided to welcome a Boston into your life. So now what? Is your home prepared for the new arrival? What supplies do you absolutely need? How do you schedule and delegate all the chores associated with your new pet?

This second section of *Boston Terriers For Dummies* answers these questions and more. You figure out how to puppy proof your home and yard. You discover the range of pet products available, and decide which ones you need and which ones you want! You also explore how to provide for your Boston's nutritional needs and keep her looking her best.

Chapter 5

Preparing for Your Boston's Homecoming

. . . .

In This Chapter

▶ Preparing your home and yard for your new arrival

▶ Licensing and registering your Boston

▶ Creating a shopping list of basic Boston necessities

. . . .

*Y*our Boston is coming home and will want to explore his new surroundings. His arrival, however, requires some careful planning to ensure his safety, health, and happiness. From putting away puppy temptations to buying the most nutritious food, your dog relies on you for his well-being and survival.

This chapter explains how to puppy-proof or dog-proof your home and yard, describes how to properly license and register your dog, and gives you a shopping list of essential equipment you need in anticipation of his homecoming.

Puppy-Proofing Basics

Preparing your home and yard for a new puppy is similar to doing so for a curious toddler. Look at the world from your Boston Terrier's perspective — about 2 feet off the ground! Your pup will want to investigate every electrical cord, every closet, and every rut in the yard, and he won't distinguish between your favorite pair of shoes and his chew toy.

The following sections point out common puppy temptations that you'll find both inside and outside. By removing the temptations before he comes home, you'll set up your Boston to succeed.

These suggestions are intended to be an overview of what your Boston may come across in his new home. Thoroughly inspect your home and yard before your pup comes home, and continue to do so daily. If your dog swallows something that may be harmful or injures himself in any way, contact your veterinarian immediately.

Stashing stuff inside your home

From the kitchen to the office, temptations abound inside the home. Small items that resemble playthings are easy prey for your pup. Look at the surroundings from your dog's point of view — best done by getting down on all fours — and pay particular attention to the following areas.

Kitchen

The kitchen contains all sorts of interesting drawers, cabinets, and cords, not to mention smells and tastes. If he can get into a cabinet or drawer, your Boston will explore everything inside. Childproof latches, which can be found at your local hardware store, prevent curious pups from investigating off-limit areas and keep potentially dangerous foods and cleaning supplies out of reach.

Power cords look like fun chew toys to a teething Boston. Tucking them out of reach, blocking them, or enclosing them in a chew-proof PVC tube will divert your dog's attention.

Tempting smells entice Bostons, too. Be diligent about putting left-overs away rather than leaving them on the counter. And secure the garbage can with a locking lid or store it behind a latched cabinet door to keep the rubbish inside the can — not all over the kitchen floor (or inside your Boston's belly)!

Bathroom

The bathroom can be a dangerous place for a Boston. Razors, pills, cotton swabs, and soap left within your dog's reach can be easily chewed and ingested — which can mean an emergency visit to your veterinarian. Family members need to be conscientious about cleaning up after themselves in the bathroom. Put shampoos, soap, tissues, and accessories out of reach or inside a cabinet or drawer.

Especially while your Boston is young, keep the toilet lid down at all times, or keep the bathroom door closed. A curious pup can jump into the bowl and drown.

As with the kitchen, use a trash can with a locking lid, or stash it under the sink. Also install childproof latches on the drawers and cabinets, and be sure to tuck dangling cords away.

Bedroom

Dogs are scent oriented, so they gravitate toward anything that smells like you. Shoes, slippers, and clothing will quickly become toys if you don't safeguard such items behind a closed closet door. Keep clothing picked up, store shoes out of reach, and put laundry in a tall, closed hamper.

Store jewelry, hair ties, coins, and other small ingestible items in containers or drawers, and secure any exposed cords or wires. Many dogs like to den under the bed or wedge themselves behind furniture, so put up temporary blockades to prevent your Boston from hiding where he shouldn't.

Office

Your Boston may be drawn by all sorts of temptations in your office: papers, magazines, cords, wires, paperclips, rubber bands, and staples. These items may be fun to play with, but they can be fatal if chewed or swallowed. As with the rest of the house, pick up strewn office supplies, secure or enclose cords and wires, and keep decorative items well out of your Boston's reach.

Plants attract dogs, too, so place them on a shelf or counter if possible. If not, consider putting them in a spare room and keeping the door closed until your Boston has graduated from his curious puppy stage.

Minimizing outdoor hazards

When you look around your garage and yard, you'll see many obvious and not-so-obvious dangers to your Boston. Just as you inspected and puppy-proofed the inside of your home from your dog's perspective, do the same with the outside of your home.

Poisons and chemicals

Paint, cleaners, insecticides, fertilizers, antifreeze, and gasoline represent a handful of poisons and chemicals that you may have in your garage or outdoor shed. Antifreeze, for example, has a sweet taste that attracts animals, but it can be deadly if ingested, even in small amounts. Secure all bottles, boxes, and containers of these substances behind a locked cabinet door, or store them on high shelves that your pup can't reach.

Rat poisons, snail bait, and ant traps can look like toys or tasty treats to your pet, but they, too, should be put away when your Boston comes home.

Plants

Bostons are curious dogs, and they'll investigate — and possibly dig up — many of the plants in your yard if left unattended. Some plants, such as daffodils, foxglove, Bird of Paradise, and lupine, can be poisonous to your dog and cause varied reactions, ranging from a rash to vomiting and diarrhea. You can find a list of the most commonly encountered toxic plants at the American Society for the Prevention of Cruelty to Animal's Animal Poison Control Center Web site: www.apcc.aspca.org.

Protect your pup — and your foliage — by fencing in plants and delineating where he is allowed and where he isn't.

Tools and gardening equipment

Though they may be too unwieldy for a Boston pup to wrangle, power tools, cords, and gardening equipment should also be kept out of his reach. Sniffing a sharp blade could cut his delicate nose, or tugging on a cord may cause a heavy saw to fall and break one of his bones, or worse.

License and Registration, Please

In most counties and states, licensing your Boston Terrier is the law. You will need to apply for and obtain a dog license from your local animal control agency soon after you bring your pup home.

Registering him with one of the national or international dog registries is voluntary. This process begins with the breeder, who first registers her dog's litter. When you take ownership of the puppy, the breeder gives you a dog registration application, which you must complete and mail to the registering organization. You can do this before or after you bring your Boston home, but it must be done before the pup reaches his first birthday.

Making your Boston legal

Depending on where you live, county or state laws require that your dog be licensed. A *dog license* gives you permission to legally own the animal. The dog-licensing agency issues an identification number along with a dog tag bearing the number that your Boston wears at all times.

The licensing laws are in place to protect your dog and other animals against rabies, which can threaten their lives. Licensing your Boston also ensures that he will be returned to you if he wanders away from home and is picked up by animal control. The fees you pay for licenses go toward returning thousands of animals to their homes each year, finding homes for thousands more, and contributing to spay/neuter programs in your area.

To apply for a dog license, contact your local animal control agency. They will send you a form that will ask for your name, address, and phone number, as well as your pet's name, breed, sex, age, microchip number (if applicable), and whether your Boston has been spayed or neutered. The agency may also require a copy of your pup's rabies vaccination and sterilization certificates.

Upon approval of your documentation, you will receive a licensing tag with a unique number that you need to attach to your dog's collar and make sure he wears it at all times. If your Boston makes a run for it, chances are good that he will be picked up and returned to you if he is wearing his collar and tag.

Licensing fees vary from area to area, but generally, unaltered animals cost more to license than spayed or neutered animals. Renewal forms are sent annually.

Registering with the AKC and UKC

The American Kennel Club (AKC) and the United Kennel Club (UKC), the two most well-known dog registries in the United States, record purebred dogs and issue them an AKC or UKC registration number.

Dog registries have specific requirements for eligibility. For example, to be eligible for registration, your Boston's parents, the *sire* (the papa dog) and the *dam* (the mama dog), and their litter must also have been registered by their owners and the breeder. You can check with the individual registries for additional requirements.

Benefits of registering your Boston include

- ✔ Permanently recording him in the AKC or UKC registry

- ✔ Obtaining a certificate of registry

- ✔ Gaining access to various ancillary benefits. For example, the AKC offers a free pet healthcare trial, a certificate for a free veterinary visit, a new puppy handbook, and eligibility to participate in competitive AKC-sanctioned events.

To register your Boston, you need to fill out the application jointly with the litter's owner. She provides the dog's sex, color and markings, whether the registration is standard or *limited* (meaning a single dog whose litter won't be eligible for registration), transfer date, your name and address, and her signature.

You provide the dog's name, payment information, registration options, and your signature. Both registries charge a nominal, non-refundable fee. When the application and fees are approved, you receive an official certificate of registry.

To delve further into choosing and buying a Boston from a registered breeder, turn to Chapter 4.

Time to Go Shopping

Shopping for your Boston, which is like shopping for a furry member of the family, can be intimidating! Walk through any pet boutique, big-box retailer, or local department store, like Target or Wal-Mart, and you'll see aisles of premium diets and treats, plush beds, toys of every shape and size, and even haute doggy couture.

It's temping to splurge on your new dog. Don't worry: You'll have plenty of time to do that. To begin with, however, you can pick up a few items to make your Boston Terrier's homecoming smooth. Brands, quality, and costs run the gamut. Shop around, but don't sacrifice quality for price.

So many leashes and collars, so little time

Your Boston will need a collar, leash, and possibly a harness soon after you bring him home. This section gives you the scoop. Also check out Figure 5-1 for an assortment of popular choices.

Collars

A collar makes more than a fashion statement; it also holds the dog's licensing tag and *ID tag,* which lists your contact information should he ever get lost. The collar also attaches to the leash, which you need to walk your Boston.

For your dog's first few collars, pick up an adjustable nylon type with a buckle. These collars come in a variety of colors and styles to fit your Boston's personality. To find the right size, either measure the diameter of your Boston's neck and add 2 inches for some growing room, or take your dog to the pet store and try some on him. Plan to buy several collars as your pup grows.

After your Boston is fully grown, decorative collar choices are endless. You can buy a diamond-encrusted leather collar, a colorful vinyl collar, or even a studded motorcycle-dog collar! You can even buy collars to match outfits or to celebrate seasons.

Figure 5-1: Collars, leashes, and harnesses come in many varieties.

Whatever collar you choose, be sure that it's sized and weighted appropriately for your Boston. Big heavy collars can catch on objects and choke your dog; small cat collars can be too restrictive.

Other collars designed for training purposes, such as *slip chain* or *choke collars,* can be purchased after your Boston's a little older and you've consulted with your veterinarian or a professional trainer on how to use them correctly.

Leashes

The leash, which attaches to the collar, gives you control during walks or obedience training. You can coordinate the leash and collar so they match. When you purchase a leash, make sure the attachment won't break or unhook from the collar, and choose one with a strong and comfortable loop for your hand.

Like collars, leash choices include an array of lengths, styles, and materials, including nylon, hemp, cotton, leather, and vinyl. For your Boston's first few leashes, a 4-foot nylon, cotton webbing, or leather variety is all you need. As you begin obedience training, you'll need longer leashes, including 6-foot and 15-foot lengths.

Harnesses

You can also choose a harness for your Boston. Rather than loop around your dog's neck, a *harness* loops around his shoulders and torso (see Figure 5-1 for an example). The dog steps into it, and you simply snap or buckle it closed. The leash attaches to the back of the harness instead of the collar, putting the pressure around his body instead of his neck.

You can use a harness and collar interchangeably, but a harness is especially suitable for Bostons who pull when walking. A harness doesn't give you as much control as a collar, but it does prevent the dog from gasping or choking if he leads you on excursions.

Unmistaken identity

Your Boston will require some identification, and you can choose from several options: ID tags, tattoos, and microchips. They each have their benefits and drawbacks, so the best option is to use a combination of at least two.

- ✔ **ID tags:** Readily visible on your dog's collar, ID tags list information about your dog and you, such as your Boston's name and your name, address, and telephone number. At the very least, list your name and the best way to contact you, whether it be a cellphone, office phone, or home phone. (If you're wondering how an ID tag is different from a license tag, the answer is simple: The license tag usually lists the dog's license number and the animal control agency's phone number. It generally doesn't list all of the personal information included on an ID tag.)

  ID tag styles include plastic, engraved metal, and reflective tags in all shapes, sizes, and colors. You can order them from your veterinarian or purchase them at your local pet store. These tags are the most common form of identification, and they are often used to reunite a lost dog and owner. If you have several collars for your Boston, be sure each one has an ID tag.

ID tags can fall off the collar, and sometimes the engraving wears off, the imprint fades, or the tag becomes too worn to read. So regularly check the ID tag to make sure it's still attached to the collar and is readable. And if you move to a new home, make sure the tag has your current information on it.

✔ **Tattoos:** Tattoos are another identification option (and I'm not talking about an image of a fire hydrant permanently painted on his foreleg). An authorized tattooer, generally recommended by your veterinarian or breeder, tattoos a unique number on your Boston's skin, typically on his belly or inner thigh. A virtually painless procedure, the tattoo is done with no anesthetic and takes only minutes to do. First, the dog is placed on his side, and you hold his head and front paws while an assistant holds his back paws. Then, the area is shaved and disinfected. The tattoo is applied, the area is washed thoroughly, and a light coating of petroleum jelly is applied over the top. The area heals completely in several days, leaving behind a permanent identification number.

The number can be virtually any sequence you choose: the dog's AKC or UKC number, a random number selected by the tattoo registry, or even your Social Security number, which, historically, has been the number of choice. The number is then listed with one of several national tattoo databases. When your dog is found, the shelter contacts the various registries and matches the tattoo number to you.

This ID method is a less reliable way to guarantee that your dog will be returned to you. The person who finds your dog may not know to look for a tattoo, and if she does, she may not know what it signifies or how to access the national database. If you decide to tattoo your Boston, use a secondary form of identification, like an ID tag, that lists your contact information.

✔ **Microchips:** A rice-sized microchip is another method of identifying your Boston. Injected by your veterinarian between your dog's shoulder blades, this microchip contains a code that is stored in a database with your contact information. When your dog is found, a staff member at the shelter uses a handheld scanner to read the code in the microchip. The code is then entered into the database, which tells the shelter your name and phone number, so you and your dog can be reunited.

If you have your dog microchipped, take the time to register your contact information and keep it up to date. The microchip won't do any good if there's no name or phone number associated with it, or if the information is incorrect! Similarly, if you move, change your phone number, or sell your dog, notify the registry and update it as necessary.

Fine china or basic bowls

Your Boston will need food and water bowls when he comes home. These doggy dishes vary as much as dinnerware patterns for people. From custom-painted ceramic ware and hand-thrown pottery to sleek stainless steel bowls and durable plastic dishes, place settings for your pooch have as much personality as the Bostons themselves. Elevated racks adorned with wrought iron or carved wood add elegance to the food and water bowls (see Figure 5-2).

Figure 5-2: You can go as low- or high-end with food bowls as you like.

Each material has its benefits and drawbacks:

- ✔ **Plastic bowls are lightweight and inexpensive, but they retain residue and harbor bacteria as they break down.** Your Boston may chew on his bowl and swallow the little plastic pieces. Then you may be making an unplanned trip to the vet. If you choose plastic, purchase a harder, dishwasher-safe plastic and replace it at the first signs of wear.

- ✔ **Custom ceramic pieces weigh more than plastic dishes, so they're not likely to tip over or be turned into a toy.** However, these dishes are more expensive and breakable, and if they're made overseas, they may contain lead, which can be harmful to your Boston. Make sure any piece you choose is sturdy, lead-free, and dishwasher safe. You can find beautiful bowls in designs to match virtually any décor.

✔ **Stainless steel bowls, though generally the most expensive, clean and sanitize easily.** They're heavy enough that your dog won't wander off with one, and they're virtually indestructible. Some designs include rubber bases to keep them from sliding across the floor as your Boston scarfs down dinner.

Your Boston will need at least two sets of bowls (two for food and two for water) that you can rotate so you can wash them regularly. Because your Boston will grow to only 25 pounds, a 16- or 24-ounce, standard-depth bowl will suffice.

Items to keep your Boston contained

A must for any puppy owner, containment devices keep your Boston in a confined area where you can monitor and housetrain him. You will need a dog crate or carrier, and an X-pen, playpen, or gate when you bring your Boston home.

Carriers come in three categories:

✔ **The crate or travel carrier,** which doubles as a den and can be used in the home, the car, or on an airplane

✔ **The around-town tote,** which transports a pup into dog-friendly establishments

✔ **The pet purse,** which looks like a handbag and takes the pet into taboo places, like restaurants and theaters

X-pens, playpens, and baby gates corral curious puppies. If you are unable to keep your eyes on your Boston, pens and gates offer an excellent short-term solution.

You can find a full range of carriers at your local pet store or pet specialty boutique; look for the X-pens, playpens, and baby gates in the baby section of most major department stores.

Quality matters when selecting crates, carriers, and containment devices. Choose the highest quality that you can afford to keep your Boston safe while he's contained.

Crates and travel carriers

Crates and travel carriers not only provide for your Boston's easy transport to and from the veterinarian's office, but they also serve as a housetraining tool, a cozy dog den, and a place for him to hide when strangers come to visit.

Crates and kennels come in a wide variety of sizes and materials, including plastic, nylon, powder-coated wire, and stainless steel (see Figure 5-3). The hard-sided plastic and fiberglass models, which are generally lighter and more portable, frequently double as airline-approved carriers (check with your airline to be certain). They also keep your Boston warmer in the winter. The wire and stainless steel varieties allow for more air flow during hot summers, but they don't provide the privacy your Boston may want.

Figure 5-3: Choose crates and carriers according to your needs.

Your dog should be able to stand up, turn around, lie down, and stretch out in his kennel. Bostons enjoy a cozy den-like area rather than a wide-open space. Though you may want to give your Boston an entire room of his own, he prefers to feel enclosed in his crate.

When you bring the crate home, put it together and make sure the pieces fit together properly, the door latches correctly, and the handle works as it should. Also check for any sharp spots that may cut your Boston. Lay down a washable fleece lining or blanket to create a comfy space for your pup.

Soft-sided carriers and pet purses

In addition to a crate, many small-dog owners purchase a portable soft-sided carrier (see Figure 5-4). These about-town totes resemble trendy purses or shoulder bags, and they feature a range of accoutrements, such as a cellphone holder and pockets for keys, your wallet, dog treats, and plastic bags. Some of these carriers are also airline approved, so you can take your Boston with you wherever you go. If you're ready to hit the road with your Boston, read Chapter 12 first.

Figure 5-4: Soft carriers and totes are for portability, not safety.

The smaller pet purses and totes allow you to take your Boston with you when you attend meetings, shop, or dine. You and your pooch will look fashionable when motoring about town, but don't think that these small bags will provide much protection when your dog travels in a car or airplane. Unlike the soft-sided carriers, the purses lack the structural integrity required by airline regulations.

Designer carriers in fashionable designs and materials often come with a removable fleece liner (for easy cleaning and comfort), as well as matching collars, leads, and food bowls, creating a coordinated look for your Boston. There's no reason why you and your dog can't be cosmopolitan!

Depending on his final adult weight, your Boston will likely outgrow his portable doggy bag as he matures. When he gets too big to sling over your shoulder, outfit him with a fashionable collar-leash combo and let him strut his stuff.

X-pens, playpens, and gates

X-pens are a set of portable wire panels that confine your pup to a specific area. You can adjust them to fit any space. After you have assembled the pen, you can enclose your pup, his crate, food and water bowls, and toys inside the space. Playpens, much like those for human babies, serve a similar purpose. You can take both the X-pen and the playpen outside so your Boston can enjoy a little sunshine, though always under your watchful eye.

Baby gates will give your Boston a little more freedom inside the house. They confine your pup to one room or one part of the house, keeping the rest off limits. They easily attach to door frames, and you can remove them whenever you want. For more about establishing off-limit areas, turn to Chapter 6.

Both X-pens and baby gates are safe ways to keep your Boston confined to a particular area. Never leave him alone for too long, however. Puppies need bathroom breaks and stimulation, and rambunctious adolescents could knock the barrier down!

Cuisine for your canine

When it comes to food and treats for your Boston, you can choose from countless diets and menus. From crunchy fortified kibble and canned stews to organic blends fit for human consumption, pet food manufacturers roll out hundreds of healthy diets and treats for dogs.

Diet

As a puppy, your Boston requires food formulated for growth and development. It contains more essential nutrients, such as protein and carbohydrates, that encourage the growth of healthy bones and muscles. When he's an adult, he can eat food designed for maintenance. These diets pack less of a punch than the puppy formula, but they still provide everything your Boston needs to be healthy. (See Chapter 7 for more on choosing the best diet.)

Selecting the right food can be daunting. You can feed the same diet that the breeder fed your Boston to prevent an upset stomach, or you can talk with your veterinarian about the right diet for your dog. Keep in mind, however, that your Boston will do much of the choosing; if he doesn't like the taste, he'll let you know!

Treats

Treats vary almost as much as diets. You can give your Boston the traditional biscuit. You can tantalize him with freeze-dried meat. You can visit your downtown doggy bakery and order him some freshly baked cookies. You can even make your own treats!

When purchasing treats, note the ingredients and nutrition information so you know what you're feeding your pup. Though you'll be tempted to treat your Boston often, remember that these are treats, not meals. Too many goodies can spoil your pup's appetite or lead to a weight issue.

In addition, many treats are not intended for puppies, so check the label for feeding instructions.

Bedding for your Boston

Everyone loves a comfy bed, and Bostons are no exception. The first night your pup comes home, you'll want to give him a warm cozy place of his own to lay his head — inside his crate, of course. Besides possibly suffocating your puppy or ruining your sofa, sharing your bed with your dog or letting him sleep wherever he pleases can lead to dominant behavior issues down the road.

While you're housetraining your Boston, you may have him sleep in his crate or kennel. Smaller beds and bumper beds covered in fleece or sheepskin are designed just for this purpose. They keep the dog warm and cozy while he's sleeping the night — or day — away.

After your Boston is housetrained and graduates from his crate to a real dog bed, you can choose from all shapes and sizes: round beds, square beds, basket-style beds filled with cushions, and even beds that look like mattresses. The beds are often stuffed with cotton, poly-blends, or memory foam, along with cedar chips for odor and insect control. Most beds have removable, washable covers.

As with the other Boston essentials, purchase a bed that is sized appropriately for your dog. You want him to feel cozy and safe, and your pup won't get that feeling from a giant bed.

 If your pup tends to chew on his bedding and ingest some of the foam or stuffing, remove it from his crate or take it away from him to prevent possible intestinal blockage. Offer him a blanket or towel to sleep on until he gets over his chewing phase.

Playtime! Picking out toys

Bostons love their toys. They wrestle with them, carry them from room to room, and chew them until they're unrecognizable. The highly intelligent Boston needs the stimulation that toys provide.

Like every other section in the pet store, the toy choices seem endless. From squeaky balls and figurines shaped like your favorite politician to colorful ropes, stuffed animals, and stuffable hard rubber balls, there's a toy for any dog's taste.

Despite all the choices, you should only offer your Boston toys that are sized appropriately for him. Imagine your 20-pound Boston wielding a Great Dane–sized toy or accidentally swallowing a tiny Yorkshire Terrier–sized bone! An increasing number of companies manufacture small- to medium-size dog toys, like small tennis balls, stuffed animals, and rope toys, so ask for them when you visit your local pet store.

Choose toys that are durable and well-made. When you bring the toys home, check for potential hazards, such as small pieces that can fall off and be swallowed. Your Boston won't destroy toys like some dogs can, but you still want to ensure your pet's safety.

If your dog does destroy a squeaky toy and exposes the noise-maker, replace the toy. Also replace or repair toys whose stuffing is falling out, or whose rope strands are overly frayed. You don't want your Boston eating anything he shouldn't!

Tug toy throwdown

In years past, tug toys endured their share of criticism. The popular wisdom was that the tugging action encouraged aggressive behavior in dogs.

The wisdom is changing.

Trainers now say that tugging is a natural behavior that can be used in positive reinforcement training. If the human always wins the tug of war, the dog will realize that his place in the pack is secondary to the human.

Likewise, in multiple-dog settings, such as dog-friendly workplaces or daycare facilities, the dogs tug among themselves, determining the pack order. This innate behavior can be easily translated to a domestic setting.

When you and your Boston play tug of war with one of his new toys, make sure you win every time. Safely tug back until you are the top dog in the pack, no matter how long he fights. If you don't, you may find yourself butting heads with your dog!

A cautionary note: Bostons with dominance issues should steer clear of tug toys. The play can encourage confrontational behavior regardless of who wins the battle, so if your dog thinks he's the king of the castle, play fetch instead.

Bostons are intelligent dogs, and toys that require them to work or think will keep them busy for hours. Treat-filled hard rubber toys are perfect for this task. They will also give your Boston an alternative to chewing your favorite pair of slippers.

Toys are fun, and you'll be tempted to give your Boston all the toys at once, but don't give in! Keep a secret stash of toys and dole them out as your dog destroys them.

For the fashion-savvy Boston

Your Boston may look like tough little fighter, but he can look stunning in some dandy doggy duds.

In most pet specialty stores today, you can find a range of clothing designed especially for dogs. From T-shirts and costumes to designer jackets and booties, your Boston can wear just about any outfit to fit his mood.

Bostons typically wear a size small or medium, depending on the dog and the design. When you're considering a piece of clothing for your dog, take a look at the cut of the attire. It should look like it would fit a dog. Clothing for dogs is not miniaturized clothing for people. Their arm (well, foreleg) holes are in the front, not on the sides. Also take a look at how it fits. The outfit should be adjustable and give in areas around the neck and legs.

Some dog clothing is functional. If it's raining, a slicker keeps your dog warm and dry. If you're going boating with your Boston, a floatation device ensures your dog is both safe and fashionable. If you're going to a costume party, that bumble bee outfit will certainly create a buzz. Some clothing is purely for the dog owner's benefit. You can decide whether you'll dress your Boston in trendy fashions or functional favorites.

Items for cleanup duty

Cleaning up after your dog is one of the necessary evils of pet ownership. When your Boston is a puppy, you'll need to clean up indoor potty accidents. When your dog is an adult, you'll need to clean up his bathroom area outside.

Luckily, many different products cater specifically to this dirty job. You can find a variety of cleaners, including those formulated to neutralize pet odors, in most pet specialty stores.

Eliminating all traces of accidents is critical because if the odor isn't removed, your Boston will continue to choose that same place to relieve himself. So look for a product that not only cleans up the accident, but neutralizes it as well.

Pooper scoopers, a cleanup necessity for picking up your pup's poop, range from gadget-filled devices to the simple shovel and rake. You can also find cleanup bags in various sizes, shapes, and materials, including biodegradable varieties. Keep a good supply of those on hand for long walks in the park or through the neighborhood. (Ready to know more about housetraining your Boston? Read Chapter 9.)

Canine hygiene products

Your Boston's coat requires regular washing, brushing, and clipping. Your Boston also needs his toenails trimmed, his ears cleaned, and his teeth brushed.

Before your Boston comes home, have your primping products ready. The sooner you can introduce your dog to the grooming routine (see Chapter 8), the better.

Store the following items in a tote or container for easy access. You'll also want to designate a specific area in your home for grooming so your Boston will learn what to expect:

- ✔ **Brush and comb:** You need a pin brush and a comb to smooth your Boston's smooth coat. A *pin brush* is a rubber-backed brush with fine pins that may have small rubber balls on the ends. Choose a metal or stainless steel comb with narrow teeth on one end and wider teeth on the other.

- ✔ **Shampoo and conditioner:** You can choose from many shampoo and conditioner options. Some contain botanicals and aroma-therapeutic ingredients, while others have oatmeal, fruit essences, and aloe vera. Coat conditioning sprays beautify the coat in between washings.

   Don't share your hair products with your Boston; they're too harsh for his skin. Instead, use formulas designed especially for dogs.

- ✔ **Toenail clippers:** You'll need clippers to keep your Boston's nails trim and dull. You can choose from two versions: a *guillotine style* that cuts the nail in one motion, or a *scissor style* that snips through the nail. Use the type that you're most comfortable with.

✔ **Small scissors:** A small pair of scissors comes in handy when you're trimming the hair inside your Boston's ears or around his paw pads. Choose a quality stainless steel pair that feels comfortable in your hands.

✔ **Blow-dryer:** You likely already have one of these for yourself or someone in your household, but it should be part of your Boston's grooming arsenal, too.

✔ **Cotton swabs and cotton balls:** You'll use these items to clean your Boston's ears and eyes.

✔ **Toothbrush and toothpaste:** As soon as your Boston's permanent teeth come in (around 4 to 6 months old), you'll need to brush his teeth several times a week with a child's toothbrush and dog toothpaste — not human toothpaste — to clean bacteria, plaque, and tartar from his mouth. Poor dental hygiene has been linked to heart and kidney disease in Bostons. Get him used to the ritual early by brushing his baby teeth once a week so he gets used to you working in his mouth.

The grooming regimen may seem like a lot of work, but with regular maintenance, you'll soon look forward to spending some quality primping time with your pet!

Must-haves for your young pup

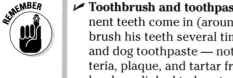

Puppy owners have their own shopping list. Besides a crate, toys, food, and other essential items listed in the previous sections, puppy owners need some specific items to help them through this fascinating time of development.

✔ **Housebreaking pads:** Housebreaking pads are absorbent sheets lined with plastic, and they prevent mistakes from soiling your floor. Often used to line the area inside an X-pen, a package or two of these makes cleanup easy.

✔ **Bumper pad or bed:** A bumper pad fits inside the crate, giving your baby Boston a comfortable place to rest. You may instead choose a small bed to use inside or outside the crate. Whichever you purchase, make sure the pad or the bed's cover is removable and machine washable because accidents will inevitably happen.

✔ **Toys:** Because adult toys are too big for small pups, you need small plush or rope toys sized just for them. Pick toys that don't have sharp edges or removable parts that can be swallowed. If the stuffing starts falling out of a toy, throw it away and offer your Boston a new one.

Chew toys, often covered with knobs or bumps, are designed to soothe sore gums and encourage the pup to cut his teeth. Some can be frozen, and others are edible.

✔ **Chewing deterrents:** Puppies will chew; it's to be expected. If your Boston develops a penchant for the corner of your couch, you can spray chewing deterrents, like Bitter Apple Spray, on the area to discourage the behavior. Before using this type of product on furniture or fabric, spot-check it in an inconspicuous place to make sure it won't ruin the item.

During your Boston's chewing stage, keep a constant eye on him even if you do use a spray deterrent. When you can't supervise him, put him in his kennel to keep him out of trouble.

✔ **Gentle shampoo:** A puppy's coat and skin can be sensitive, so you'll also want to pick up a shampoo and conditioner formulated just for him. They often contain soothing ingredients, such as oatmeal or aloe vera.

Chapter 6

Welcome Home!

In This Chapter

▶ Creating consistency for your Boston

▶ Establishing household rules and a set schedule

▶ Determining safe areas for your puppy

▶ Introducing your Boston to your other pets

*I*t's time for your Boston to come home! You've shopped for supplies and puppy-proofed the house. You've planned for her every need, from buying the perfect crate to indulging in the newest leash-collar combo. Now the fun really begins!

When you welcome a puppy — or adult dog — into your home, the antics never seem to stop. Your intelligent little Boston will entertain you, challenge you, and push your limits from the moment she walks through the door. To keep your relationship thriving, you need to set up some household rules that dictate where she's allowed to be, what she's allowed to do, and how she's expected to act.

Similarly, you should set up some rules for the humans in the household. By following regular routines and consistent training techniques, you and your family can teach your Boston how to become an integral part of your family.

A new home can be an intimidating scene for your new puppy, making even the boldest Boston quiver. In this chapter, you discover some ways to make the environment welcoming for your new dog, including how to introduce her to her new surroundings, introduce her to other pets, set up a schedule for eating, relieving, and sleeping, and establish rules for her and other members of your household to follow.

 If you work Monday through Friday, try to bring your puppy home on a Friday afternoon or Saturday morning. You'll have two full days to spend with your new Boston. You'll be able to establish a routine for feeding, going to the bathroom, and playing. You'll also be able to take much-needed naps when your puppy does!

Taking the Home Tour

The first thing to do when you bring your Boston home is show her around the house, focusing on the places that are going to be most important to her: her eating and drinking place, her sleeping space, her play area, and her bathroom spot outside.

While your Boston is a puppy, limit the number of rooms she has access to. Doing so helps your Boston feel safe and secure, and it teaches her boundaries. After she matures, you can expand her universe to include other areas of the home and let her roam around the house, following you from room to room.

Before entering the home, give your pup a chance to relieve herself out in the yard. That way, you can have peace of mind that she won't have an accident while she sniffs and explores her new digs.

The pup's eating and drinking area

The area where your Boston chows down and fills her belly will be one of her favorite spots.

A logical place to put your dog's food and water bowls is in the kitchen, but some people prefer to put it in the laundry room, garage, or other out-of-the-way spot in the house, particularly if the kitchen is very small.

Wherever you decide to serve your pup's meals, let everyone in the family know that the area is your Boston's designated dining room. Introduce the area to your dog when she comes home, using lots of praise and enthusiasm. If she feels like taking a few bites, let her. If not, that's fine too. She's likely too nervous and excited right now.

The den and sleeping area

A crate acts as your Boston's den and sleeping area. Typically made of hard plastic or powder-coated metal, this kennel is like your dog's cave: It's her safe place where she can enjoy some "me" time.

During the day, you will place your Boston in the crate with the door closed while you train her to hold her bladder. Dogs typically won't relieve themselves where they sleep, so this teaches your dog to wait until you take her outside.

With the door open, the crate serves as your dog's personal space. She'll use it as a hideaway when she feels like a nap and as a safe place when strangers come over. At night, you will put her to bed in the crate until she's old enough to sleep on a traditional dog bed.

If you're using a different crate than the one you brought her home in, show her where it's kept. If you're using the same crate, set it up in its spot in the house, and then show her where she can find it. Toss a treat into the crate to encourage her to go in and take a look around. (For more on how to introduce your pup to her crate, flip to Chapter 9.)

Not sure where to keep the crate? Consider these questions:

- ✔ **Where do you spend the most time?** Where will your Boston get the most opportunities to socialize and get familiar with new smells, sights, and sounds? Your Boston will want to feel like she's part of the pack, and she won't feel like that if she's isolated in a room away from you and your family.

- ✔ **Will you have another crate in the bedroom?** If so, purchase a second crate and line it with training pads. When she's older and can spend all night in her crate without messing it, throw in a cushy pillow and warm blanket.

- ✔ **Are there any drafts in the area?** Keep the kennel away from fireplaces, open windows, or heating or air conditioning vents so your Boston doesn't become overheated or chilled. Keep the kennel out of direct sunlight, especially during the summer and in warmer climates.

- ✔ **Is the area easy to clean?** Will you be able to clean up an accident quickly? Don't put the crate on an expensive rug or near heirloom furniture! Put it on an easy-to-clean surface and, if necessary, lay down sheets of newspaper just in case.

The play areas

Bostons love to play, so you also need to create an area that is safe and fun for your pup to play in. When your Boston is a puppy, she doesn't need much space: Keeping her in an X-pen or playpen will do. But as she grows and needs more room to play, expand the area to one or two rooms, such as the living room and the bedroom.

To help your Boston understand what area is her play area, keep her toys there, and when you introduce her to that space, take a few minutes to let her play with some of those toys in that space.

When deciding what areas of the house are suitable for your dog to freely romp in, make sure the area is easy to clean, doesn't contain expensive furniture or harmful plants, and is a place where the family often gathers. Her crate should also be in or near that area.

Meeting Other Members of the Pack

Part of welcoming your Boston into your home is to introduce her to other members of the pack — including the children and other pets. With training and discipline, most Boston Terriers integrate into a household without a hitch. This section explores how to bring your new family together.

Kids, puppy. Puppy, kids.

If you have children or if kids frequent your home, they're probably more excited about your Boston than you are! Most kids adore puppies, but a young person's exuberant behavior can be a bit much for your new dog. Children who are awkward or inexperienced around animals may hurt the puppy by mistake. To prevent overstimulation or accidental injury (on the part of the kids or the dog!), here are two sets of guidelines: one for young children and one for grade-schoolers.

Children who haven't been exposed to dogs need some extra hand-holding during the first few introductions. Instruct them to never approach a strange dog, especially when adults aren't present. If they know the dog, tell them to never put their face close to a dog's face or tease the animal. Don't frighten the child, but let him know that dogs are animals and can behave unexpectedly.

Teaching the tiny tots

Younger children, including toddlers and preschool-age kids, will likely see your Boston pup as another one of their fuzzy stuffed animals! It's easy to see why: The cuddly dog is a living, interactive plaything who delivers hours of entertainment. However adorable they are, Bostons aren't toys. With improper handling, a pup can be seriously injured. Her prominent eyes can be damaged, or she can get overly excited and hurt herself.

When you introduce your children to your Boston, use these steps:

1. **Sit on the floor or in a chair and hold the puppy in your arms. Ask the child to slowly approach, not moving too quickly.**

   Make sure that the child understands that he should not toddle up to or play with the puppy without you (or another adult) around.

2. **Invite the child to pet the puppy. Show him how to handle a dog carefully and gently, modeling the behavior for the child and allowing him to mimic you.**

Point out the puppy's eyes, nose, and mouth. Let him know that these are sensitive off-limit areas on the dog's body.

3. **When the child asks to hold the puppy, have him sit on the floor and gently place the Boston in his lap. Tell him to handle and touch the puppy gently, not holding on too tight.**

   Stay nearby and supervise the pair.

4. **Watch the dog's — and the child's — body language. If either starts to squirm or cry, playtime is over.**

   Place your puppy back in her kennel or playpen (after you take her to her bathroom area, just in case!). You want the experience to be a positive one for everyone involved, and if one or the other becomes uncomfortable, that can ruin the fun for everyone.

5. **After your child and puppy have met, go over the rules with your child.**

   Make sure he understands that the dog is not a toy, that she requires special handling, and that you (or another adult) must be present when he wants to play with her.

Advising preadolescents

Little balls of energy, most grade school–age kids will want to immediately run and play with the puppy. When your Boston is older, those active games are okay (with supervision, of course!). But when your child is meeting the puppy for the first time, all that excitement will be too much for her to handle.

For the first few interactions, ask your older child to follow these rules with the puppy:

- ✔ **Sit and wait:** Ask the child to sit quietly on the floor and bring the puppy into the room. The child may be tempted to turn toward the dog and pick her up, but tell him not to. Have him wait until the puppy comes to him.

- ✔ **Explore and sniff:** Let the dog approach the child and sniff him. The pup will run her cold little nose all over the child, getting to know his scent. The child can have a toy or a treat in his lap to lure the pup over.

- ✔ **Doggy handshake:** After the pup sniffs the child, have him extend a hand for the pup to smell. Teach the child that this is the appropriate way for a person to introduce himself to a dog.

- ✔ **Supervised play:** When the dog is comfortable with the child, the child can then gently pet and play with the puppy. Don't let him pick up the puppy without your permission, and remind him not to play too rough or exuberantly.

> ✔ **Use caution:** Instruct the child that a Boston's eyes, nose, and mouth are off-limit areas that are prone to injury. Teach him to handle the puppy with extreme care, never poking at her, pulling her ears or tail, or pinching her.

Training the teens

You can use the techniques in the "Advising preadolescents" section with adolescents and teenagers, too, modifying them depending on child's maturity level. A responsible preteen may be able to handle holding the puppy and brushing her, whereas an active youth may need to tone down his excitement before hanging out with the Boston. You know your child's limitations, so use common sense when allowing them to interact.

Introducing felines, canines, or small pets

Easygoing, affectionate, and highly adaptable, your pup will, after some supervised introductions and training, get along well with other pets in your home. Her size isn't so large that cats will be overly intimidated, yet she still commands a presence that the other animals will respect.

Your pup and the other animals' temperaments will determine whether they'll become best friends or roommates who tolerate each other. Though she's not a true terrier, your Boston does retain her terrier roots, and she may feel the urge to chase or play tag with your cat, other dog, or small animal. Similarly, some pets can be aloof and territorial toward new beasts.

Introducing the animals is another part of setting boundaries for your Boston and teaching her the household rules. If your dog knows that it's against the rules to chase the cat, for example, she'll be less inclined to do so, especially if she knows that there are consequences to her actions.

You can make the introductions easier by organizing structured and controlled visits to let the animals sniff each other and get used to each other. After the animals are comfortable with each other, you can let them have supervised visits.

Structured sniffs

Being driven by their noses, animals like to meet each other by sniffing their unique scents. Before your dog even meets the other animals in the household, she'll smell them on your clothes, and she'll know that she'll be among other pack members.

Introducing your pets face to face can be very easy or very difficult. It all depends on the personalities and temperaments of the animals. To play it safe, kennel the puppy and bring her to the other pet. Let them look at each other and sniff each other. Watch their body language. Is the cat hissing or curious? Is the dog growling or wagging her tail? If the pup or other animal shows no interest in the other, don't force them together; they'll interact when they're ready.

If they seem to get along well, let the animal out of the kennel and see what both pets do, being very watchful in case a fight breaks out. The two will sniff each other some more, check each other out, and nudge each other with their noses. If you're lucky, they'll start playing and become fast friends!

When you bring two dogs together, the current dog may see your puppy as a threat to his place in the pack, depending on his temperament and personality. Introduce them in a neutral environment, like a park or someplace other than your house (the current dog's "turf"). Watch their behavior, and if the current dog begins to display dominant or aggressive behavior, separate them and try again later. They'll eventually learn to live with each other.

Don't worry if your pets don't get along like loving siblings the first time they meet. Becoming buddies takes time. Make the introduction ritual part of your daily routine, and remember to give both animals all the positive reinforcement you can by praising them while they bond. You're sure to see results.

When you're introducing your Boston to your cat (who will likely be a little aloof and possibly defensive), be especially cautious of the cat's claws and your pup's eyes. If a fight breaks out, your cat can scratch your Boston's delicate eyes, which will require an emergency call to your veterinarian.

Supervised playtime, protected alone time

After your pets begin to get along, let them play together — always supervised, of course! Sit back and watch them as they romp on the floor, play with toys, or just snuggle for a nap. After the animals recognize that their new roommate isn't a threat, they'll share the same space, becoming part of the pack.

Just because they get along, however, doesn't mean you can leave them alone together while you're gone. It will take a while for them to grow accustomed to each other, so plan to put them in separate rooms or leave your puppy in her crate if you run to the market. If you must leave them alone together, make sure that the cat has easy access to a high counter, or your pup has access to her kennel. If you have another dog, let him do as he normally does, but secure the puppy in her crate until you return.

Birds and bunnies and bearded dragons, oh my!

Other pets, including birds, small animals, and reptiles, can coexist with your Boston, too. Introduce them in the same way you would cats and other dogs: First, let them smell each other through your Boston's crate or the other critter's cage, and then let them meet face to face while you carefully hold the critter or bird.

Unlike cats, small animals or reptiles should not, under most circumstances, be allowed to play with your Boston. No matter how well-behaved your Boston is, a free-roaming rodent looks too much like a tempting treat or toy. Some reptiles can pass *salmonella* (a bacterium that causes diarrhea) to your dog if she licks him or ingests his feces. Birds, however, if they're caged, or allowed to fly in the home and perch on a play gym, will do just fine with your Boston, as long as they have a safe spot out of your dog's reach!

Sectioning off areas of your home

If all else fails and your pets just don't get along, you may need to section off areas of your home to keep the household peace. Some Siamese just don't want the Boston around. Some Bostons can be too playful for a 9-year-old Persian. Sometimes, it just doesn't work out. So what do you do?

Most homes can be divided to allow the cat to have his space and the dog to have her space. The easiest way to do this is by putting up a baby gate between the two areas. The cat can explore the dog's space and still escape in case of a squabble. It may inconvenience you and your family, but if means keeping the peace, it's worth it!

Surviving the First Night

After a day filled with exploring her new home and meeting her new family, your pup will be pooped. You'll be ready for a long night's sleep, too, after picking up your new puppy, introducing her to her new home, and getting used to this new arrival. But the truth is that the first night with your Boston will be a long one for both of you.

Instead of cuddling with her mama and littermates like she's done her entire life, your pup will be bunking in a new bed. She'll be confined to an unfamiliar crate, and surrounded by strange smells and sounds. She'll be scared, and rightfully so! As a brand-new puppy parent, you can expect to be up all night tending to her needs.

Here's what you can expect the first night:

✔ **Lots of potty breaks.** Your Boston has not yet learned to control her bladder or bowels, so you'll take her to the bathroom area at least every two hours. After she eats her final meal of the day, take her outside to use the bathroom. If she doesn't go right away, take her back inside and try again in 30 minutes or so. Put her to bed after she eliminates, and then set your alarm (mental or manual) for two hours. When you take her outside throughout the night, don't make a big deal of it and don't get the pup excited. Let her know that you mean business — and that she should do her business!

✔ **Lots of cleanup.** Even though you'll take your pup to the bathroom every couple of hours, she may accidentally soil her kennel. Line her crate with absorbent pads to soak up any messes that may happen, and arm yourself with a pet-safe cleanser and several rolls of paper towels.

✔ **Lots of whimpering.** Your pup will be lonely. All her life, she's been surrounded by sights and smells she knows, like her littermates and her mama. Now, she's confined to a strange kennel with no one around, so of course she's going to whimper! As difficult as it will be, do not take her out of the kennel to comfort her. If you do, you teach her that she gets her way when she cries — and that's a hard habit to break!

✔ **Lots of comforting.** Though you should not take the pup out of her kennel throughout the night (except for bathroom breaks), you can comfort her by speaking softly to her, consoling her when she cries. This works particularly well if you kennel your pup in your bedroom. If you kennel her in the living room or other area of the house, however, plan to get up to comfort her when she cries.

By the time the sun rises the next day, you'll be exhausted, but you will have survived the first night. This will become a regular routine for several months until your Boston becomes housetrained and trustworthy. Don't worry: It will get easier, especially as your pup grows accustomed to the routine.

Creating Consistency

Dogs like consistency. From puppyhood to adulthood, dogs like to follow a regular routine of sleeping, hunting, eating, and playing. This need for routine reaches back to dogs' wild days when their pack leader dictated their schedule of resting, scavenging or hunting, eating, and socializing with other dogs in their pack.

Modern-day dogs are no different. They prefer a regular schedule of sleeping, eating, and playing — and sleeping and playing some more! They don't need to do it for survival as their ancestors did, but they still have an innate need for consistency.

Dogs also want to know the rules. They look to the leader for direction on what to do next. When a pack member falls out of line, the leader puts her back in her place. This sets up a consistent pattern of what the leader and other pack members expect.

In your Boston's life, you are the pack leader, and providing your Boston with regular schedules and rules sets her up for success. Instead of letting her do whatever she wants and run the household, you should establish her routine as soon as she comes home. It's all about shaping her behavior so she integrates with her new pack.

Establishing a schedule

As soon as you carry your puppy across your threshold, you will set up schedules for her. You will feed her three to four times a day at regular intervals. You will take her to her bathroom area after mealtime, playtime, naptime, and every couple of hours in between. You will also put her to bed at the same time every night. By doing these things, you create consistency for your Boston, and help her develop habits that will last her lifetime.

These schedules also help you as you train your Boston. They set her up to successfully integrate into your household. Housetraining her, for example, will be much easier if your dog is eating at the same time every day because you can expect her to use the bathroom at regular times after she eats.

To help your puppy plan her day, feed her at regular times each day, take her to her bathroom area on schedule, put her to bed at the same time each night, and give her plenty of exercise to help her burn off extra energy.

Regular meals

Your Boston puppy requires at least three to four meals a day. (See Chapter 7 for details about what to feed your pup.) You need to feed your puppy right when she wakes up in the morning, late morning, early afternoon, and dinnertime — about every three to four hours or so. Whatever times you decide, stick to them.

Adolescent and adult dogs require two meals a day. Feed her in the morning and in the early evening, at the same times every day.

By doing so, before long you'll be able to predict when your Boston needs to take a trip to her bathroom area!

Regular bathroom breaks

Regular trips to the bathroom area are essential in housetraining your dog. (Skip to Chapter 9 for tips on housetraining.) Your Boston puppy, while she's learning to control her bladder, won't know to ask to go outside to use the bathroom. It will take her several months before she learns to hold it until she goes outside.

To help train the puppy, take her on regular bathroom breaks throughout the day, including when she wakes up in the morning, after a nap, after she eats, after she plays, and every couple of hours in between, depending on her age and maturity level.

When your Boston gets older and learns bladder control, you still want to take her to the bathroom area or let her out to the yard on a regular basis. Only when your dog knows how to tell you she needs to go can you let her dictate when to go to the bathroom.

Regular bedtime

Regular bedtime also teaches your dog routine. Your pup's growing body requires lots of sleep at night, despite all the naps she takes during the day! To teach her to crash at the same time every night, put her to bed at the same time. Say, "Time for bed," in a positive, soothing voice, put her in her crate, and turn off the lights. Before long, she'll know when it's time for bed and head to her crate.

An older Boston will fall right into the habit, especially if she's had a routine since birth. She may pace and wander occasionally, trying to get settled, but when you tell her it's time for bed, she'll fall fast asleep in no time.

Regular exercise

Puppies need exercise to burn off excess energy and stretch their growing muscles. Your Boston puppy will want to play with her toys and roll around as you tickle her belly. She'll look forward to the time spent with you.

Your adult Boston also needs exercise to burn off steam. In an enclosed yard, she'll run around and patrol the territory, hunt for imaginary intruders, and chase them away. She'll enjoy long walks with you, too, through your neighborhood, to the park, or on a trail through the forest.

Get out and move with your Boston at least once a day. The activity not only helps her sleep at night, but it also helps her focus and be a well-behaved member of your family.

Setting up house rules

As pack leader, you dictate what rules your Boston should follow. You tell her where she's allowed and where she's not. You tell her where she sleeps, eats, and plays. Begin teaching your Boston these rules immediately because it is much easier to teach her the right way first instead of having to break bad habits later on.

It isn't just the pup who has to learn the ropes. The other pack members — the humans — have rules to follow, too. To raise a happy, healthy Boston, each family member needs to tend to puppy-related chores, and use consistent training and teaching methods.

Here are some points to ponder when establishing rules for everyone in the home.

For the dog . . .

Dogs are creatures of habit. After your Boston figures out the routine, she'll do the same thing all the time. When you set up household rules and enforce them (with love and positive reinforcement, of course!), your Boston will fall into line.

As you and your family discuss how your Boston will be treated and cared for, consider the following questions:

- ✔ **How do you want your Boston to behave?** Begin training your puppy to act the way you want your adult Boston to act. Though those cute puppy behaviors may be endearing at first, they can be the beginning of bad habits. Discuss with your family how they think an ideal Boston should behave, and work together toward those goals.

- ✔ **What area will your pup use for housetraining?** Select an outdoor bathroom area and use it consistently with your Boston. Choose an area that's easy to access, that doesn't get muddy when it rains, and that's easy to clean. Also decide whether you will use an indoor bathroom area, such as a dog litter box, if you live in an apartment or townhouse. (See Chapter 9 for more hints on housetraining.)

- ✔ **Which rooms will your Boston have access to?** You want to limit your Boston's environment to one or two rooms where the family spends the majority of their time. These rooms shouldn't have expensive rugs or heirloom furniture, and they may need to be blocked off with baby gates. If you can't watch the puppy, she needs to be confined to her crate or X-pen. When your Boston is an adult, she can have access to the rest of the house.

✔ **Where will your Boston sleep?** If your answer is "In bed with me," you may want to rethink your strategy. Your puppy can fall off the bed during the night and injure her leg or back, or you may inadvertently roll over and crush her. Instead, let her sleep in a crate in your bedroom so she feels close to you. You'll be able to hear her if she cries in the middle of the night. Another behavior issue to consider is if you and your Boston share a sleeping area, she will think that you and she are equals — and you essentially relinquish your post as pack leader.

✔ **Will your pup be allowed on the furniture?** That's up to you and your family. Because your Boston won't exceed 25 pounds or so, she'll fit quite nicely on the chair next to you or on your lap while you enjoy some television or a good book. At the same time, if you allow her access to the couch during her first days at home, it will be very hard — and confusing for her — to restrict it later on.

✔ **Where will you feed your Boston?** Are you okay with feeding your dog in the kitchen? That's the most logical place to set up your dog's food and water station. She'll quickly learn where her next meal will be served. Keep the water bowl in an area where you can see when it gets low. You should empty, clean, and refill her water bowl at least once a day.

✔ **Will you give your Boston table scraps?** Besides encouraging a lifelong habit of begging, feeding your dog table scraps can cause her to forgo her dog food for people food, or she could eat both and put on unwanted pounds. People food can also increase the likelihood of bladder stones, diabetes, and pancreatitis. Instead, offer her treats like cheese, cooked chicken or beef, or crunchy vegetables (in small amounts) in her food bowl on special occasions. Your Boston will appreciate them a lot more than food thrown from the table on a daily basis!

✔ **What training method should you use?** Many training methods exist, so do your homework and choose a humane approach that includes positive reinforcement. Make sure that your entire family — and friends — follows the same training regime.

✔ **Where will your Boston stay while you're away?** If you're running out to the market for a few hours, your puppy will be content in her crate. But if you're going to be gone longer, consider a dog daycare (if your pup is old enough), or restrict her to her X-pen lined with newspaper.

 Come up with rules for your Boston before you bring her home, and begin enforcing the rules right away, being as consistent as possible. She is an intelligent dog and will pick up on these rules quickly, but practice patience and diligence in your training. It'll be worth it!

From the pack to the family

By nature, dogs are highly social. This behavior reflects back on their ancestors — wolves — who lived in closely knit packs with a social structure built around a dominance hierarchy.

When dogs became part of human families, they viewed people as part of their pack structure and interacted with us using the same behavioral patterns they would for canine members of their pack.

Dogs happily accept a subordinate role to people who assume a dominant position toward them. The degree to which they do depends on the breed, gender, and individual differences. Females, for example, more readily accept dominance from humans than males.

Modern-day dogs love socialization, and they'll do almost anything for praise and affection — especially for a dominant member of their family! When you assert your role as pack leader early, you'll raise a healthy and well-integrated canine member of your family.

For the rest of the pack . . .

You need to set up household rules for the other members of your family, including the children, adults, and other pets. Consistency is key to raising a well-trained pup, so all the parties involved have to follow the same routines and use the same training commands to ensure that your pup doesn't get conflicting messages.

The rest of the family will also have some new chores, too, with regard to routine care of the puppy. Unless you're a one-person household, or one (responsible) person chooses to be responsible for everything, give everyone who is old enough or capable enough a chore to do to help raise your Boston puppy. Some jobs aren't as glamorous as others, but they're all necessary to raise a happy, healthy dog. To keep it fun, consider rotating job duties or encourage various family members to become experts at their specific chore. (Flip back to Chapter 3 for a refresher of what duties you can delegate.)

 Small children should be supervised by an adult while doing their puppy-care chores. And you should check on older children to make sure they're doing their dog duties. A responsible overseeing adult can make sure that everything gets done and can be on the lookout for health problems that may arise.

Chapter 7

Eating Well

. . . .

In This Chapter

▶ Discovering what nutrients your Boston needs

▶ Deciphering pet food labels

▶ Deciding what kind of diet to feed your Boston

▶ Knowing how much and how often to feed your Boston

▶ Rewarding — and spoiling — with treats

. . . .

*Y*our Boston's diet gives him the gusto he needs to get through the day. These bully dogs with their hearty appetites require a healthy diet that gives them the right amount of protein, carbohydrates, fats, vitamins, and minerals per serving. With so many dining choices available from your local pet store, how do you choose?

This chapter explores generic and premium brands that vary in price and size, as well as dry kibble formulas and canned concoctions in hearty rich gravy. You can even make your Boston's diet from scratch, if you really want to. Besides helping you figure out what diet is right for your Boston, this chapter can help you establish an eating schedule based on his age. A proper diet will help your Boston grow to his full potential.

Feeding a Carnivore: Cost versus Quality

Before they became the domesticated pets that we know today, dogs scavenged and preyed on small animals. They also foraged for food, eating berries, grains, and other plant matter when necessary. This diet gave them the protein, fat, carbohydrates, vitamins, and minerals they needed for a complete, healthy diet.

As a house pet, your Boston still requires these basic nutrients. Depending on his age, each dog has different requirements. Young pups need a diet formulated for growth; adults need a diet formulated for maintenance.

Price varies dramatically between brands of dog food. Though all dog food manufacturers must follow basic guidelines, the more expensive, or *premium,* varieties often exceed those specifications and, therefore, cost more. The ingredients are higher grade, come from whole-food sources, and contain fewer fillers.

The premium brands frequently contain added nutrients, too, such as antioxidants and vitamin supplements, which benefit senior dogs, overweight dogs, or specific breeds like your Boston.

Generally speaking, you get what you pay for when it comes to dog food — but don't presume expensive is better. Your veterinarian can help you choose a diet that's right for your Boston.

Knowing Your Ingredients

Dogs require certain amounts of protein, carbohydrates, fat, vitamins, and minerals to support their normal bodily functions. This section takes a closer look at each type of required food source and how it keeps your Boston healthy and happy.

Pump up the protein

Your Boston uses protein for growing and developing hair and skin, producing hormones, building muscle mass, regulating metabolism, and healing damaged tissue.

In many premium brands of dog food, protein is the first ingredient listed. Beef, chicken, turkey, lamb, or duck are the proteins most often used. Other sources include fish, fish meal, liver, eggs, milk, and milk products.

Some grains and beans, such as rice, wheat, corn, barley, and soy, also contain protein. They're not complete sources of protein like animal protein, but when combined with other types of food, they can provide many of the amino acids dogs require.

Boston puppies thrive on foods that contain about 28 percent protein; adult Bostons typically maintain on foods that contain 22 percent protein.

When you choose a diet for your Boston, don't pick one based on the formula's protein percentage alone; the protein source matters, too. In general, the lower-priced foods use a lesser-grade protein that's harder for your dog to digest.

Energize with carbohydrates

Carbohydrates, which are sugars and starches found in plant foods, provide the quick energy Bostons need to exercise and play. Making up about 50 percent of your dog's diet, carbohydrates also provide fiber, which is essential for proper bowel function. Common sources of fiber are rice, grains, peas, pasta, and even potatoes.

Carbohydrates, however, are also used as fillers. They're cheaper than protein, so manufacturers use corn and rice to bulk up the foods sold at a lower price. Premium foods often contain high-quality complex carbohydrates to give the dog fiber and sustained energy.

Too many cereal grains can result in a hyped-up Boston. If your dog is bouncing off the walls, take a look at how many and what types of carbohydrates are in his diet, and limit them, if possible. The fillers also cause your dog to eliminate more often, which means more trips to the bathroom.

Fats for energy and a shiny coat

Fats and oils do more than make foods taste good. They provide energy and help your Boston feel satisfied. Fats are needed to break down certain vitamins, such as vitamins A, D, K, and E. Unsaturated fatty acids, such as oleic and linoleic acids, also support skin and coat health. They make your Boston's short coat shimmer and shine.

Boston diets may contain anywhere from 8 percent to 18 percent fat, depending on the manufacturer. If your Boston's coat is looking dull, consider a food that has a higher percentage of unsaturated fats. If he's looking a little overweight, switch to a low-fat diet after talking with your veterinarian.

Take your vitamins, mind your minerals

In addition to proteins, carbohydrates, and fats, Bostons require vitamins, which help the body fight disease, absorb minerals, regulate metabolism, and grow and function normally. Plant and animal foods naturally contain vitamins.

The body maintains and stores fat-soluble vitamins in the body's liver and fatty tissues, and water-soluble vitamins, such as vitamins B and C, are flushed out daily and must be replaced. The right balance of vitamins is crucial to your Boston's health.

Minerals, such as calcium, iron, phosphorous, and nitrate, are elements and inorganic compounds the body needs for proper growth and function. Dogs require seven major minerals and 15 trace minerals, including copper and potassium. Minerals help maintain the salt levels in the bloodstream, and build bones and teeth. Like vitamins, minerals must be balanced for good health.

Most commercial and premium diets already contain all the vitamins and minerals that your dog needs. Your veterinarian may recommend some supplements for specific needs, such as glucosamine for a senior dog suffering from arthritis, or vitamins for a dog who's eating a homemade diet. (Check the "Supplementing Your Dog's Diet" section below for more reasons to add extras to your pup's meals.) Always follow your veterinarian's advice and consult her before adding supplements.

How to Read Pet Food Labels

No doubt you read the labels on foods you eat. The labels contain basic information about the item, including its calories, nutrient content, and ingredients. Dog food labels are no different.

Pet foods are regulated by the Food and Drug Administration's Center for Veterinary Medicine and must contain certain information on their labels. Following is a breakdown of that info:

- **Feeding instructions:** The feeding instructions give guidelines for how much to feed your Boston based on his weight. If the diet is formulated for puppies, it will give feeding instructions based on age, too. Sometimes it will include information about when and how often you should feed your dog.

- **Guaranteed analysis:** The guaranteed analysis breaks down by percentage what nutrients are in the food. It lists minimum levels of crude protein and crude fat, and maximum levels of crude fiber and moisture. It also includes percentages or measurements of additives, vitamins, and minerals.

- **Ingredients:** The ingredients are listed in descending order by amount. Often, a form of protein appears first in line, followed by grains, fats, additives, and preservatives.

✔ **Nutritional adequacy statement:** The nutritional adequacy statement says whether the food provides complete balanced nutrition for a dog based on nutritional levels established by the Association of American Feed Control Officials (AAFCO). The statement also provides a life-stage claim, which states the *life stage* (growth/lactation, maintenance, or all life stages) for which the food is intended.

AAFCO has developed two nutrient profiles for dogs: growth/lactation and maintenance. All foods must meet at least one of these profiles. Some labels claim the food is intended for all life stages. Those foods provide enough nutrients for an animal's growth and reproduction, as well as for maintaining a healthy adult.

✔ **Manufacturer's contact information:** A name and address of the manufacturer, packer, or distributor are required; some- times manufacturers include a toll-free phone number or Web site address, but these aren't mandatory.

Armed with this information and the nutrient recommendations from the previous section, you can now examine your Boston's food label with confidence. Call the manufacturer or talk to your vet if you have questions.

Checking Out Your Commercial Diet Options

After you understand the importance of the ingredients in your Boston's food (see the "Knowing Your Ingredients" section), you can evaluate the different meal options available at the market. Three commercial types are sold at most grocery and pet stores:

✔ Dry food

✔ Semi-moist food

✔ Canned food

No matter the form, each morsel of food for Bostons should be packed with nutrients. Because they have smaller mouths and stomachs, Bostons require smaller pieces of food than larger dogs. Those smaller pieces must contain all the nutrients and calories they need to keep them going. Dog food companies know this, so when they develop diets for smaller dogs, they put as much nutri- tion as possible in each bite.

Crunchy kibble

It may not look too appetizing to humans, but *kibble* (or dry food) is delicious to dogs. The kibble's shape, size, texture, smell, and taste have been researched and tested by scientists and veterinary nutritionists. These folks develop recipes, conduct feeding trials, and check for complete nutrition to ensure each kibble meets the FDA's standards.

Bostons digest dry food easily. Made by cooking the ingredients together in big batches, forming it into kibble-size bites, and baking it, dry food is often the least expensive food on the shelf. Because it is baked, dry food can be left out in your Boston's bowl all day without spoiling. And the kibble's crunch helps keep your dog's teeth tartar-free.

You can add variety to your Boston's dry food diet by feeding semi-moist or canned food periodically, or offering a mix of wet and dry food at mealtime.

Going natural: Is it really better?

In addition to the common commercial brands of foods, most pet specialty stores also carry dry and canned or jarred foods in "organic" or "natural" varieties, or those that may be "fit for human consumption." What does this mean?

The organic and natural trend has moved into the pet market. Popular with human foods, organically grown meats, produce, and grains are grown without the use of pesticides, chemicals, or other such means. Many dog owners believe that feeding their pets a diet free from those additives will benefit and extend their pet's lives. As in the human market, organic pet foods need to meet certain criteria to prove that the ingredients are grown organically before they can bear the label.

Food intended for human consumption meets different standards than food intended for animal consumption. More and more, pet owners want to know that the quality of their pet's food is just as good as their own. They like the fact that they could sit down and eat the same food their pet eats. Some pet owners go the extra step and make their own food for their dogs. But these human-quality foods are an easy alternative to homemade.

Organic or human-grade foods are generally more expensive. They cost more to make, and they're often made by smaller companies that don't produce the same quantities as larger manufacturers.

Whether they're formulating an organic diet or a grocery store brand, manufacturers are required to follow strict guidelines for making quality pet food. Rest assured that the majority of over-the-counter diets will meet your pet's basic dietary requirements.

For Bostons who have dental problems, are recovering from surgery, or are just finicky, however, dry food poses a challenge. They can't bite into or digest the hard pieces of food, or the dried morsels aren't appealing enough for a picky dog's discriminating taste. These dogs may require semi-moist or canned food instead.

Semi-moist morsels

Semi-moist foods are soft to the bite with a texture resembling Play-Doh. They come in all shapes and sizes, from kibble-size morsels and patties to whimsical shapes that look more like treats than food. They often come in resealable bags to keep the moisture locked in.

Like the dry foods, semi-moist foods are formulated to serve the nutritional needs of the dog. The benefit of semi-moist compared to kibble is the water content, which makes it easier for elderly dogs or those with dental problems to chew. The food also smells more appetizing to finicky dogs.

To give the semi-moist food its look and texture, however, manufacturers often add chemicals, artificial sweeteners, and colors. Be sure to read the label and check the food's nutritional content before feeding. A high amount of corn syrup or artificial sweetener can be harmful to your Boston's metabolism, causing him to gain weight. Semi-moist food can also lead to tartar buildup on teeth.

Stew in a can

Big chunks of meat in hearty rich gravy look good not only to dogs, but to their owners, too, who may want to give their pets something that resembles "real" food. Available in myriad flavors, combinations, and recipes, canned foods combine the protein, carbohydrates, fats, and water in a way that caters to many dogs' taste buds. It may not smell good to humans, but many dogs like it.

Canned food is up to 70 percent water by weight, which supplies the Boston with much-needed water. Its taste attracts finicky eaters, it's easier to bite and chew than kibble, and it comes in small quantities for small diets. Canned food has a long shelf life and works well for dogs traveling to shows or obedience trials.

Despite its benefits, canned food generally costs more. You can't leave it out like dry food because it can spoil, and you have to refrigerate leftovers. Some Boston owners worry about what animal parts are used in the canned food, not to mention the additives and preservatives. Also, it can cause diarrhea in some dogs and cause tartar to build up on their teeth.

Choosing To Feed a Noncommercial Diet

Although commercial diets contain everything the dog needs to thrive, some people prefer to prepare their dogs' meals themselves. Raw diets and homemade diets allow Boston owners to have more control over what they feed their pets.

✔ **Raw diets:** You can think of these meals as dog-style sushi. Raw diets consist of raw meat and bones that you feed to your dog. Proponents and opponents each have their varying opinions on this type of diet. Some believe the diet improves their pets' skin, coat, and teeth, and increases their stamina and vitality. Others caution against *E. coli,* parasites, and other risks associated with raw meats. These diets are often supplemented by some source of fiber and vitamins.

Some manufacturers have begun selling raw diets at pet stores. Often found in a freezer, these diets are individually packaged to make feeding simple.

✔ **Homemade diets:** Homemade diets are meals made from scratch, just like Mom used to make. Often fed to finicky dogs or those with food allergies, these diets incorporate whole foods, such as potatoes or rice, and protein sources, such as cooked chicken or beef, that aren't packed full of preservatives. Bostons don't eat a lot, so preparing homemade meals can be relatively simple as long as you include all the nutrients that your Boston needs.

Your Boston will tolerate diet changes, but to protect your dog's health, consult a veterinarian before introducing him to raw or homemade meals.

Before feeding your Boston a raw or homemade diet, consider these factors:

✔ **Do you have the time to prepare the diet?** Preparing a homemade or raw diet is just like cooking for another member of the family. The food should be prepared every few days to ensure freshness.

✔ **Do you have the space to store the raw meat or meals?** Because these foods don't have preservatives, they need to be stored in the refrigerator or the freezer.

✔ **Do you travel a lot?** If so, a diet like this may not be appropriate. Dog sitters or boarding centers may not be able to make dinner for your dog every night. And if the dog travels with you, you may not have access to the foods or a kitchen.

✔ **Do you have access to organic meats, or is there a reliable butcher near you?** If not, a homemade diet may require that you cut your own meat or search out organic meat sources.

✔ **Do you know enough about dog nutrition to ensure your Boston is getting all the vitamins and minerals he requires?** You can research and learn about dog nutrition, or you can meet with a veterinary nutritionist to outline meals and supplements for your Boston.

 If you're going to feed your Boston a raw or homemade diet, first and foremost, visit a veterinarian. You can consult a board-certified veterinary nutritionist to help you develop a diet for your Boston. You may even want to talk to a conventional veterinarian and a holistic vet to hear their opinions.

Special Diets for Bostons with Health Issues

Prescription diets are specially formulated meals sold through your veterinarian. Using different combinations of nutrients, these diets are designed to address specific health needs, such as bladder stones, diabetes, obesity, renal disease, or food allergies. The foods come in dry and canned forms, similar to commercial diets.

Your veterinarian will prescribe a special diet if she believes your dog requires it. Before you start feeding your Boston the prescription diet, ask your vet these questions:

✔ **Why do I need to feed my Boston this diet?** Your vet will explain why this particular diet will benefit your pup's health, as well as any other lifestyle changes that you need to make.

✔ **How often and how much do I feed?** Feeding instructions will be listed on the label, but your vet may alter the recommendations depending on your pup's diagnosis. Follow her instructions for maximum benefit.

✔ **Will I need to feed this diet to my dog indefinitely?** The answer will depend on the dog's condition. If your Boston is obese, for example, you may only have to feed him a "diet" food until he reaches his goal weight. If he's diabetic, however, he may be on the special formula for life.

Prescription diets cost more than commercial diets, but the health benefits far outweigh the additional money you'll spend. Because these formulas are packed with nutrition, it's likely that you'll feed your Boston less quantity while providing more nutrients. Plus, you'll have the peace of mind knowing that you're offering your pup the very best.

Come and Get It! Serving Meals

Boston puppies and adults have different feeding requirements. Puppies eat foods formulated for *growth,* which means the foods contain more digestible nutrients, like protein and carbohydrates, to help them build strong muscles and bones. Adults eat foods formulated for *maintenance,* which means the foods contain the right amount of nutrients to maintain their current size and weight. Puppies and adults also have different eating habits. Puppies eat up to four meals a day, whereas adults require two.

In the next sections, I outline a feeding schedule and portions for Boston puppies and adults.

Setting up a meal schedule

Young puppies need to eat up to four meals throughout the day to stimulate growth, keep their metabolisms fueled, and prevent *hypoglycemia,* or low blood sugar. Some experts recommend *free feeding* puppies, which means leaving dry food out all day and allowing the pup to eat whenever he feels like it. The free feeding is then supplemented by regularly scheduled mealtimes:

- ✔ **Puppies up to 12 weeks old:** Feed four times a day in addition to providing dry food.
- ✔ **From week 13 to week 24:** Feed the pup three times a day.
- ✔ **From six months on:** Feed your Boston twice a day.

As the pup's body figures out how to use the nutrients in his meals appropriately, you should stop free feeding and stick with the twice-a-day routine. If the food is out all day, the adult Boston will eat it, and if he's not getting enough exercise, the sturdy dog will quickly pack on the pounds.

Dishing out the right amount

The amount of food you feed your Boston depends on the individual dog's growth stage, activity level, and external factors, like temperature or stress. At first, offer your puppy small amounts of food formulated for growth, but gradually increase how much food you give him as he grows (as you'll see below). When he becomes an adult and you switch his diet to food formulated for maintenance, feed him the same amount each mealtime. Active dogs or those enduring stress, like moving or welcoming a new addition to the household, may require more food, depending on the circumstance.

Refer to the feeding instructions printed on the label or consult your vet for advice. Adjust the amounts by how the dog looks. If your Boston has a bulging belly, decrease the portion a bit.

Generally, feed the following amounts at each mealtime:

- ✔ **Puppies up to 12 weeks old** (feeding a diet formulated for growth): ¼ to ⅓ cup, four times a day

- ✔ **From week 13 to week 24** (feeding a diet formulated for growth): ½ to ⅔ cup, three times a day

- ✔ **From six months to one year** (feeding a diet formulated for growth): ¾ to 1 ¼ cup, two times per day

- ✔ **Adulthood** (feeding a diet formulated for maintenance): ⅓ to ½ cup, two times per day

If you decide to free-feed your puppy, remember to keep the bowl of kibble filled all day. Gradually decrease the amount as he ages.

Preventing obesity

More pets than ever are obese, and Bostons are no exception. A high-calorie intake and a sedentary lifestyle result in an overweight pup. Adult Bostons who eat too much at mealtime, free feed, or enjoy too many treats end up consuming too many calories, and weight gain ensues. And if exercise isn't a part of their daily lifestyle, those extra calories never have a chance to be burned off.

If your pet is packing on the pounds, you have two choices:

- ✔ **Decrease the amount of food you're feeding your pet.** This means cutting back the size of his regular meals and the number of treats you give him. This lowers the amount of calories he is consuming without changing his diet.

- ✔ **Change the diet to a "light" formula.** Some people feel that this may not be as healthy as simply feeding less. But just as there are formulas for senior dogs, there are formulas for overweight dogs. As always, talk to your veterinarian before changing your Boston's diet.

Supplementing Your Dog's Diet

You take your daily vitamins, but does your dog need them, too? *Supplements* add nutrition to your Boston Terrier's diet. They provide vitamins and minerals that are missing from his daily food intake. If your Boston is eating a well-balanced commercial diet, he probably doesn't need supplements.

Pregnant or lactating bitches, however, require supplements to provide adequate nutrition. Senior Bostons, too, can benefit from formulas, such as chondroitin and glucosamine, that address joint function. And if you're making your dog's food from scratch, you'll certainly need to supplement his diet with added vitamins and minerals found in herbs, eggs, and Brewer's yeast.

 If you feed your dog supplements, do so under the watchful eye of your veterinarian or veterinary nutritionist, and never exceed the recommended dosage or substitute supplements for a well-balanced diet. Oversupplementing your Boston can make him sick.

Treating Your Boston

Treats come in all sorts of sizes and flavors, from fresh-baked biscuits and human treat-inspired cookies to freeze-dried lamb and beef jerky. You can find the treats in pet stores and trendy dog bakeries throughout the country, or you can give your Boston safe human foods, such as hot dog pieces, chunks of cheese, or a slice of raw beef.

You can feed your Boston treats to reward him for good behavior or simply to spoil him from time to time.

 Like regular meals, treats contain calories. They should be calculated into your pup's overall intake for the day, accounting for about 10 percent of his calories. If possible, follow the recommended feeding instructions on the treat package. If you feed your Boston dog-safe human foods, like small pieces of luncheon meat or cheese, factor those calories into your pup's overall intake for the day, too.

As tempting as it may be, don't feed your pooch too many goodies, or you'll wind up with an overweight Boston!

Chapter 8

Looking Good

. . . .

In This Chapter

▶ Grooming your Boston at home

▶ Knowing what to look for in a groomer

▶ Treating your dog to a day at the spa — really!

▶ Dressing your dog in duds designed especially for her

. . . .

*B*eing short-haired and single-coated, your Boston Terrier doesn't demand the labor-intensive grooming that some breeds require. She will, however, require regular washing, brushing, and nail trimming, in addition to ear cleaning and tooth brushing, to keep her healthy and smelling fresh.

Keeping that coat — not to mention her nails, eyes, ears, and teeth — looking its best takes routine maintenance. You can expect daily, weekly, and semi-monthly grooming rituals to minimize shedding and keep her coat glossy and clean. After figuring out what tools you need and what to do with them, grooming time will be a pleasurable experience for you and your Boston, resulting in a strong bond you both will enjoy.

Sometimes, you may require the skills of a professional groomer. Choosing one who you're comfortable with requires research, visits, and recommendations from reliable sources. You can find out more about how to select a groomer in this chapter.

You can also get tips on how to dress your dog in practical and fashionable duds, including how to select appropriate clothing for her and how to fit her. A Boston's short coat also demands an extra layer of protection and warmth during the chilly seasons.

Grooming at Home

Just as you bathe, comb your hair, and brush your teeth daily, your Boston will require routine maintenance to keep her coat clean and lustrous, her nails trimmed, and her breath fresh. Likewise, just as you visit the salon or barber every couple of months, your Boston Terrier will require visits to the groomer for deep cleans — and even a little pampering! (The "Visiting the Groomer or Spa" section later in this chapter has the details you need.) For regular upkeep, though, you can easily groom your Boston at home with just a few tools, a little instruction, and a couple of minutes each day.

These grooming rituals also give you the opportunity to handle and inspect your Boston, checking for abnormalities, such as bumps or cuts. You can also check the condition of your dog's paws, ears, eyes, nose, and mouth.

In this section, you find all the information you need to groom your Boston at home. You discover how to set up a grooming area. You can read about all the tools you need and find out how to clean your pup's ears, eyes, nose, and teeth. You also develop a routine for the whole grooming process, scheduling times throughout the day, week, and month to make your pup clean and cuddly.

Getting ready to groom

Many breeders prepare their pups for grooming when they're still very young. They hold them and coddle them, looking at their mouths, their paws, and their eyes and ears. Most likely, by the time your Boston met you, she was used to being handled. You can continue the breeder's or previous owner's work by handling your Boston every day. Your dog needs to feel comfortable with someone touching her body, inspecting her eyes and ears, tickling her toes, and even rubbing her gums.

Before you begin actually grooming your Boston, however, you need to set up a regular space, gather your tools, and acclimate your Boston to the grooming ritual.

Choose a location

To begin your home-based, Boston beauty routine, you must first choose a specific location. Dogs like regular rituals, so choosing one place teaches your dog what to expect and how to behave while you're grooming her.

Some people place their Boston on a countertop when they clean and brush their dog; others use a grooming table, which allows them the flexibility to walk around it while leaving their dog in one place. Whatever surface you choose, always put a nonslip pad on the surface — and never leave your Boston unattended.

When you think about the best place for your grooming station, consider an area near a sink or tub that has a hand-held sprayer. You also want to have access to an electrical outlet.

Gather your tools

Every Boston household should stock the following:

- ✔ **Shampoo and conditioner:** There are many on the market, but choose one formulated for a small dog with a short coat. Avoid the shampoo-conditioner combos. They may cut bath time in half, but the coat won't be as clean.

    You may also consider a shampoo that is designed for dogs with a white coat. These products do wonders for enhancing and whitening a dirty white dog!

- ✔ **Slicker brush:** These are rectangular brushes with fine pins that are designed to reach to your Boston's skin, massaging it and pulling away dead hair and skin.

- ✔ **Bristle brush:** Resembling a human hair brush, these tools whisk away debris and polish your Boston's coat.

- ✔ **Shedding blade:** These tools have bent wire teeth set close together that pull off dead hair.

- ✔ **Soft towel:** Because a Boston's coat is short and smooth, a quick wipe-down with a damp soft towel in between washes will restore the coat's shine and remove any residual dirt.

- ✔ **Scissors:** Small scissors are used for trimming the hair around your Boston's ears, the bottom of the feet, and the anus. Select small-blade scissors that fit your hand comfortably.

- ✔ **Nail clippers:** The two basic types are the scissor cut and the guillotine cut. Purchase whichever you prefer.

- ✔ **Styptic powder:** Styptic powder, which stops the flow of blood, is good to have on hand for unexpected nail-trimming accidents.

- ✔ **Cotton balls:** You'll use these for cleaning out your Boston's ears and around her eyes.

- ✔ **Ear-cleaning solution:** You'll use this harmless cleaning solution on a cotton ball to clean around your pup's ears and inside the folds.

- ✔ **Blow-dryer:** Though your Boston's coat is short, you'll blow-dry her coat after bath time to prevent her from chilling. Choose one that has low- and no-heat settings.

- ✔ **Toothbrush and dog toothpaste:** A child's soft toothbrush with some dog-specific toothpaste will keep your Boston's teeth tartar-free.

You can find all these items at your local pet supply store, online, through mail order, or through your groomer.

Get her used to grooming

You'll have an easier time grooming your Boston if she's familiar with the grooming area and tools you'll be using. Here's how to introduce her to this new routine:

- ✔ **Let your Boston get used to the countertop or grooming table you'll be using.** Allow her to sniff and inspect it.

- ✔ **Run your hands over her entire body.** Gently give your dog a massage, feeling every bone, muscle, and tendon. This action not only prepares your dog for grooming rituals, but it also helps you become more aware of how your dog normally feels. If she develops a lump or injures herself, you'll know right away.

- ✔ **Show your Boston the grooming tools.** You don't need to use them on the dog just yet; have them out and let her inspect these new items. Slowly introduce her to the pin brush, comb, toothbrush, and blow-dryer, rewarding her for good behavior.

As you help your Boston get used to the idea of regular grooming, encourage good behavior by rewarding her with toys and treats. Soon, your Boston will jump for joy when you take her to her grooming area and pull out the grooming toolkit!

Caring for healthy skin and coat

That short and tight Boston coat is beautiful, and to keep it looking its best, expect to do some daily brushing and monthly washing.

The Boston is a *single-coated breed,* which means she has no undercoat to keep her warm. Though she may get chilly during the cold months (flip to the end of this chapter for details on finding the right fit for doggy clothing), her single coat means less grooming for you. You won't need a de-matting tool, de-shedding comb, or undercoat rake. You won't have to tease out mats or knots. You'll only need a slicker brush, bristle brush, and a shedding blade to keep her coat under control — and not all over your couch!

Oils from sebaceous glands under the skin naturally condition the hair and skin. Too much washing can cause dry, flaky skin and chapping, but daily brushing releases the oils, keeping the skin and coat healthy. With regular brushing, you'll only need to wash your Boston's coat once a month or so, unless she meets a skunk or rolls in a mud puddle!

Daily brushing

When brushing your Boston, follow the same routine each time. That way, she'll know what to expect. You can follow these steps:

1. **Place your Boston on her designated grooming spot. Begin by using the bristle brush to smooth out the coat and remove any dirt or debris.**

   Always brush in the same direction that the hair is growing, brushing from the head toward the tail, and down her sides and legs. And don't forget her belly!

2. **While you're brushing her, feel her body for cuts, scrapes, bumps, or irregularities.**

   This is also the time to check for external parasites, like fleas or ticks. (See Chapter 14 for more on these critters.)

3. **Use the shedding blade to pull off dead hair.**

   Gently rake across your Boston's body, being careful not to scrape her skin.

4. **After you've released the majority of the dead hair, use the slicker brush to gather any excess.**

   If the brush fills with fur, clean it out and keep going. Your dog will shed heavily during certain times of year, but if she sheds an excessive amount often, consult your veterinarian for advice.

Don't forget to carefully brush your Boston's face. You can use the tip of the bristle brush to get around her nose, mouth, and ears. Use extreme caution around her prominent eyes.

Monthly bathing

Depending on her activity level, your Boston will require semi-monthly or monthly baths. Any more than that will dry out her skin and cause dandruff and brittle hair. Shampooing your dog's coat not only washes away dirt, but it also washes away the natural oils that keep her coat shiny and, believe it or not, clean. The natural oils form a barrier that repels dirt and odor.

 When you bathe your Boston, use a shampoo and conditioner formulated specifically for a dog. If the white in your pup's coat starts to loose its snowy sheen, clean it with a shampoo made for white-coated breeds.

Using a coat conditioner when you bathe your Boston is optional. The conditioner simply softens your Boston's coat. It's not necessary, but it's a nice way to make your Boston more huggable.

Before bath time, gather all the gear you'll need to wash, dry, and brush out your dog: shampoo, conditioner (optional), cotton balls, your bristle brush, a blow-dryer, and a couple of fluffy towels.

1. **Brush out your Boston's coat thoroughly before bathing it.**

Strip all the dead hair and skin before you soak your pup! (See the previous section for brushing tips.)

2. **Prepare the bathing area. Place a nonslip mat in the sink and place your shampoo, conditioner, and towels nearby.**

   Many Boston owners use the kitchen or bathroom sink to bathe their pets, while others use the bathtub. On warm, sunny days, you can also bathe her outside using a plastic tub and the hose with an adjustable nozzle.

3. **Gently plug your Boston's ears with cotton balls and put her in the sink.**

4. **With lukewarm water, rinse your dog's head and body, being careful not to get water in her ears. After she's thoroughly wet, turn off the water.**

   A pull-out nozzle or hand sprayer attached to the faucet or hose makes this job easy. You can also use a pitcher or bowl filled with water to wet down and rinse her coat.

5. **Using a silver dollar–size drop of shampoo, wash and massage your dog's coat and skin, including her ears, belly, and rear.**

   Do not get the shampoo near her eyes. Repeat if necessary.

6. **Rinse the soap out completely, working from her head down her back and underneath her body.**

7. **Apply the conditioner according to the manufacturer's instructions. Let it soak in, and then rinse thoroughly.**

8. **Let her shake off the excess water, and then wrap your clean dog in a big fluffy towel to soak up the rest.**

9. **Finish drying her coat with the blow-dryer using a low- or no-heat setting. Being cautious around her face, start by drying her neck area and work down toward her tail.**

   Because your Boston's coat is so short, blow drying her isn't a necessity, particularly during warmer weather. A dry coat, though, prevents your pup from getting chilled in the wintertime.

Trimming those nails: A paw-dicure

Nail trimming is a grooming ritual that you should do monthly at least. You know your Boston's nails have grown too long if you hear click-clicking when she walks across the floor! An ideal time to trim her nails is after her bath when her nails are softened from the warm water, but anytime will do.

Like all dogs, your Boston's toenails grow continually and need to be trimmed to keep them at a healthy length. If they grow too long past the pads of the feet, they can curve inward and cut into the pad. Long nails can also cause the dog to lose traction, because they may prevent her pads from hitting the ground. They can tear upholstery, snag clothing, and cause scratches, too.

Not only does regular trimming keep the nails at a healthy length, but it also gives you the opportunity to inspect your dog's pads for cracks and her toes for splinters or thorns. Your Boston's pads should be soft yet calloused, depending on her age and activity level. There should be no tender or swollen areas on the paw. If there is, consult your veterinarian for advice.

Watch the quick

Most Boston toenails are black. This color makes it difficult to see the *quick,* which is the vein inside the nail. Clipping the quick is painful and can cause your Boston's nail to bleed.

To find the quick, use a flashlight or look at your dog's nails outdoors. You should be able to see the opaque portion in the center base of the nail — that's the quick.

Whenever you trim your dog's nails, keep a container of styptic powder nearby. If you clip the quick, pour or pack a tiny bit of powder on the nail. It will stop the quick from bleeding.

Cutting and grinding

You can choose from several types of nail trimmers at your local pet store. Whichever style you choose, select the size that's most appropriate for your Boston's nails.

When you trim your dog's nails the first few times, enlist the help of another person to steady your Boston and distract her with a spoonful of peanut butter or a quick ear massage. Having an extra set of hands will be very helpful when your dog starts squirming!

To cut your Boston's nails:

1. **Get you and your dog into a position that's comfortable for both of you.**

   You can position your Boston several ways: held against your chest, standing on a table or other nonskid spot, or laying on her back.

2. **With the dog held securely in place by you or your assistant, hold the trimmers with your dominant hand and the dog's paw with the other.**

3. **Gently press your index finger and your thumb on one toe, which extends the nail and prevents it from retracting.**

4. **Clip off the portion of the nail that's curving downward (see Figure 8-1).**

5. **Repeat with the other 19 toes.**

With time, trimming your Boston's nails will become second nature to you both.

The first few times you clip your pup's nails, be extra cautious about not clipping her quick. Some dogs have very long memories, and a negative nail-clipping experience may make it very difficult the next time you try to trim her!

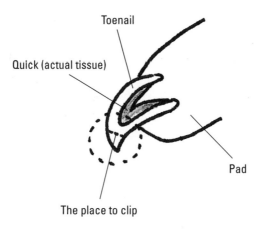

Toenail

Quick (actual tissue)

Pad

The place to clip

Figure 8-1: When trimming your Boston's nails, avoid the quick.

You can also invest in an electric or battery-operated nail grinder. Easy to use, these devices help avoid accidentally cutting the quick and allow you to grind down sharp areas on the nail. If you purchase a grinder, introduce it to your Boston when she's a puppy. The device makes a whining sound and vibrates when applied to the nail, both of which take some getting used to.

Here's to clean ears

A Boston's ears stand erect, which leaves them prone to dirt, grime, and even ear mites. When Bostons play in the yard or meet friends at the dog park, their ears are vulnerable to all sorts of debris. Cleaning your dog's ears several times a week keeps them healthy.

Ear care takes some getting used to. She may not like to have her ears handled at first. Work with your Boston until she is comfortable with you touching her ears, looking in them, and cleaning them.

Follow these steps to wipe out your Boston's ears:

1. **Inspect your Boston's ears. Gently hold the edge of her ear and check for wax, discharge, odor, or signs of ear mites.**

   A moderate amount of wax is normal, but any discharge or odor may signal other problems, such as an infection. Monitor the situation and consult your veterinarian if it persists.

2. **Using a cotton ball moistened with ear-cleaning solution, wipe the inside of the ear, getting inside all the folds and creases (see Figure 8-2).**

   If you see some dark brown or black debris on the cotton ball, your Boston may have ear mites, which thrive on ear wax and other debris in the ear canal. Continue to wipe until the cotton ball comes out clean, and do it daily. (For more on ear mites and their effects, see Chapter 14.)

3. **Use a fresh cotton ball for the other ear.**

4. **Make sure to thoroughly dry both ears with a clean cotton ball.**

If possible, cotton swabs should be avoided because they can damage the inner ear if used incorrectly.

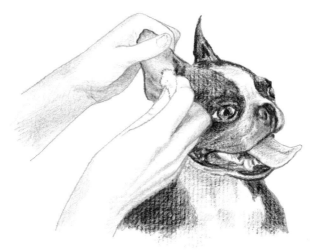

Figure 8-2: Use a cotton ball moistened with ear-cleaning solution to wipe the inside of your dog's ear.

Keeping the eyes bright and nose wiped

Boston Terriers' eyes are prominent features on their expressive faces. Protruding like they do, their eyes are vulnerable to ocular irritation or injury. You should check your Boston's eyes daily for redness or unusual discharge. If you see anything unusual, bring it to your veterinarian's attention immediately. He should check out any eye problems within 24 hours.

Because they have a short coat, you don't need to worry about trimming the hair around your Boston's eyes, but you will need to make sure you clean them as often as needed with a soft, damp cloth. Use extreme caution when brushing your dog's face, paying special attention to the area around her eyes.

Your Boston's nose is normally cool and moist. It should not appear red or irritated; if it does, that could be a result of an injury, illness, or sensitivity. Any secretions from her nose should be clear and watery, not cloudy, yellow, or green, which indicates a sinus or respiratory infection and requires a visit to your veterinarian.

To clean her nose, simply use a damp cloth and wipe off any dirt that may be present. Your dog's nose is sensitive, so be extra gentle with it!

Tending to those pearly whites

Dental hygiene is an extremely important part of your Boston's grooming routine. Bacteria buildup from poor oral health has been linked to infection and disease in dogs' major organs, including their hearts, livers, and kidneys.

Oral health is especially important for Bostons. Tartar builds up quickly, resulting in plaque, gingivitis, and bad breath. The dog's gums become swollen and irritated, and in extreme instances, bleed and fill with pus. If left untreated, periodontal disease can set in, and the dog may need to have her teeth pulled. All of this can be prevented by establishing and maintaining good dental habits.

Your Boston's teeth should be brushed at least once a week (though once a day would be ideal) with a child's soft toothbrush and toothpaste designed especially for dogs, not for humans. The brushing removes the tartar and breaks up the plaque. If your Boston doesn't like the toothbrush, try massaging her teeth and gums with dog toothpaste on your finger to get her used to the procedure.

Get your Boston used to the teeth-cleaning routine when she's a puppy. With the pup on your lap, gently use your pinky finger to massage her gums and feel her teeth — including the back ones. After her adult teeth come in, introduce the toothbrush and toothpaste.

Follow these steps when polishing your Boston's teeth:

1. **Put a dime-size dollop of doggy toothpaste on the tooth-brush, and get your pup into position.**

   Don't use human toothpaste when you brush your Boston's teeth. It's not safe for your Boston, and she probably won't like the taste.

   At first, this tooth-brushing ritual can be done with your Boston sitting in your lap. When she grows accustomed to the routine, brush her teeth while she's on the designated grooming table.

2. **Let your pup sniff and taste the toothpaste.**

   Doggy toothpaste tastes good to dogs, so as soon as she tastes it on the toothbrush, she'll let you lift her lip so you can start brushing. If your dog resists, consider using a finger toothbrush. A small, plastic brush that fits on your finger like a thimble, it lets you get inside your dog's mouth, especially if you trained her as a puppy.

3. **Use a circular motion when brushing your dog's teeth, just as you use on your own teeth (see Figure 8-3).**

   Clean the outside and the inside of the teeth, and don't miss those teeth in the back of the mouth — plaque and tartar tend to accumulate there the most.

4. **Give her some water to wash down the toothpaste.**

   Dogs don't need to rinse and spit (so to speak); the dog toothpaste is okay for them to swallow. But have some clean, fresh water nearby to allow your pup to take a drink after you brush her teeth.

In addition to brushing, offer your Boston treats designed to break down tartar and plaque. Several are available from pet supply stores; ask your retailer or veterinarian for recommendations. Feeding your Boston dry food or a special tartar-control diet can also break down plaque that builds up on the teeth, but there's no substitute for actually brushing her pearly whites.

No matter how often you brush your Boston's teeth, you should plan to have your dog's teeth professionally cleaned at your veterinarian's discretion.

Figure 8-3: Massage your Boston's teeth and gums with the toothbrush, using a circular motion to break down the plaque and tartar.

Bostons who aren't eating, drinking, or playing with their favorite chew toys may be suffering from gum disease. Look at your dog's teeth and gums, and if her gums look red and swollen, are sensitive, or are bleeding, call your veterinarian.

Visiting the Groomer or Spa

Some Boston Terrier owners choose to take their pet to the groomer for regular shampooing, nail trimming, tooth brushing, and ear cleaning. Others visit the groomer only occasionally for deep cleanings or if their pooch gets herself into something that requires a groomer's expertise.

Groomers specialize in keeping your dog looking and smelling good. Some take classes to perfect cutting techniques, and some compete in grooming shows. These "dog hairdressers" can be found in strip malls, pet stores, boarding facilities, and veterinarian's offices. Often, you can find a groomer through references from your breeder, veterinarian, friend, or colleague.

Dog spas are another stylish option that have enjoyed growth in the past five years. Often doubling as a doggy daycare facility, dog spas encourage Boston owners to drop their dog off at the spa for a day of aromatherapy, hair styling, grooming, massage, and more. Your pup can also play with other dogs in a controlled and supervised environment or enjoy a day of training and exercise. The spas also allow you to leave your dog in the hands of a capable guardian while you enjoy a day of shopping or pampering yourself!

Before you drop off your Boston for her grooming session or spa day, you should examine the shop and meet the handler who will be working with your dog. Just as you wouldn't leave your child with a stranger at an unfamiliar daycare facility, you shouldn't leave your Boston without first doing some homework.

Inspecting the facility

Safety is extremely important in any grooming facility. The life of your Boston is at stake, so you'll want to examine everything — from the washing area, the grooming tables, and dryers to the outdoor play area and common areas. Check for the following:

- ✔ **Ask if the facility requires proof of vaccination and whether a current *bordetella* vaccination (a highly contagious respiratory disease commonly known as "kennel cough") is required.** Dogs with communicable diseases should never be allowed in the shop.

- ✔ **Take note of the facility's atmosphere.** Dogs sense and respond to mood, so the atmosphere should be relaxed and calm, with groomers showing no signs of stress or exhaustion.

- ✔ **Inspect the shop itself.** Both the washing and the grooming areas should be neat and clean. The shop should be relatively odor-free and a comfortable temperature.

- ✔ **Assess the space dedicated to grooming.** Is there enough room for multiple grooming tables? Are there enough crates in all sizes to house clients' dogs? Is there an area dedicated to potty breaks, and is that area safe and clean?

- ✔ **Look closely at the free-standing or cage dryers and how they're used.** Ask the groomer how she dries the dogs, and whether the dryers turn off if they get too hot. You don't want your Boston getting burned!

Evaluating the staff

When you leave your Boston with a groomer or handler, you want to feel confident that your dog is in capable and loving hands. The best groomers and handlers have years of experience managing many different types dog breeds, personalities, and temperaments. They continue to learn about their trade, honing their skills through workshops and competitions.

Keep in mind the following points about groomers and handlers when you visit the facility:

- ✔ **Observe how the staff interacts with the animals.** Do they show genuine love and compassion to the dogs? Do they leave them unattended on the grooming tables? Do they work with more than one animal at a time?

- ✔ **Find out how much experience the groomers have.** Ask the shop manager or owner what types of dogs frequent the facility. Are the groomers adept at handling all types of dogs, including Boston Terriers? How long have they been grooming?

- ✔ **Talk to the groomer herself.** Do you feel comfortable with her and her co-workers? You should be able to bring questions or concerns to her without hesitation. If you like the groomer, your dog will like the groomer and enjoy the experience.

If you like the staff and the facility (see the previous section), ask the groomer for some references of recent clients she's worked with. Ask these pet owners for honest reviews and anecdotes.

Considering certification

Whether to use a certified groomer is up for debate. As of press time, there are no legal requirements that a groomer be certified, but the ones who are have documented proof that they passed a practical skills assessment test and a written exam.

These tests require the individuals to demonstrate their grooming expertise on one breed from each AKC-recognized group. They also quiz the groomers on subjects like anatomy, breed standards, breed identification, canine terms, general canine health, and pesticides.

When groomers pass the exams with an 85 percent or above average, they earn the title of National Certified Master Groomer. Though no database of certified groomers currently exists, you can find a certified groomer through referrals from your veterinarian, pet store, breeder, or breed club.

Handling sticky situations

Because Bostons are curious dogs, it's inevitable that your pet will get into something she shouldn't. Here are some common grooming problems and some ways to handle them:

✔ **Burrs and stickers:** Those little pieces of nature are sure to cause your Boston some grief. Brush or pick them out as soon as possible. Stubborn pieces can be coaxed out using some conditioning spray.

✔ **Bubble gum:** What a sticky mess! Before pulling out the clippers, rub the gum with ice cubes and try to break it out. If that doesn't work, use some conditioner, vegetable oil, or peanut butter to pull it out. If none of those methods work, turn to the clippers.

✔ **Skunk spray:** Several over-the-counter shampoos are formulated just for this purpose. Brush your dog thoroughly before bathing her, and wash according to the package instructions.

✔ **Paint:** All paint is toxic, so you'll need to remove it immediately and not let your Boston ingest any of it. Latex paint is water soluble, so it will rinse out with water. Oil-based paint will necessitate a trim. Never use turpentine or any solvent on your Boston's coat.

Even if your groomer is not certified, ask her if she continues to educate herself with regard to pet hygiene and care. Hands-on seminars and competitions keep groomers current on the latest wisdom in this field, so if she is continually seeking to improve her skills, she's a good groomer to have.

Clothes and Accessories for Your Boston

The quintessential Boston look doesn't typically include a bow or booties, but with your dog's short coat, she'll appreciate a jacket or sweater to keep her warm when the weather turns cold. If your Boston Terrier spends a lot of time outside during chilly days, invest in some outerwear to keep her toasty and dry.

In most pet specialty stores today, you can find a range of clothing designed especially for dogs. From T-shirts and jackets to booties and hats, you can choose from all sorts of fashionable accessories.

Sizing clothes for your dog

When choosing clothes for your Boston, measure around her chest, and from the nape of her neck to the base of her tail to determine the correct size.

Typically, Bostons wear a size small or medium, depending on the cut of the clothing and the size of your dog. When you're considering a piece of clothing for your dog, take a look at its cut. It should look like it would fit a dog, not like a dog-size human garment. The arm holes should be in the front for a proper fit.

When you try the outfit on your dog, take a look at how it fits. It should be adjustable and have some give in areas around the neck and legs. Make sure there are no tight areas that could cut off your pup's circulation. And make sure that the garment isn't too big because she could get tangled up in it.

Dressing your Boston

Some dog clothing is functional. These pieces keep your dog warm, dry, and protected. Here are some garments to consider:

- ✔ Sweater or sweat shirt
- ✔ Waterproof slicker
- ✔ Wool or leather jacket
- ✔ Long-sleeve T-shirt

Some clothing, however, is purely for the dog owner's benefit. A crystal-encrusted tiara, froufrou dress, and patent-leather Mary Janes look adorable, but they're mainly for show. These fashionable pieces make a statement about you and your Boston's personalities. Haute couture or trendy outfits are fun to put on your dog, but don't make a habit out of it. Your dog is a dog, after all, and you wouldn't want her dirtying up her favorite outfit.

Along with the clothing, your Boston may also appreciate some dog-size shoes. Though your dog shouldn't wear shoes all the time, she'll like them when it's icy outside or when it's too hot for bare pads. Measure one of your dog's paws (from the tips of her toes to the back edge of her rear pad) to size the shoe correctly.

Hats are another accessory you can use to keep your Boston warm and dry or fashionably trendy. Water-repellant rain hats, for instance, will keep your pup dry, while an adorable dog-size sombrero would be perfect for that Cinco de Mayo party!

Part III
Stepping Out

"That's actually the dog's wee wee pad, Doug. I don't want to confuse him, so you should either do something on it or step off."

In this part . . .

Still having a bit of terrier spunk in his blood, there's no doubt that your Boston loves to get out and explore his world. Before he does, however, he needs to learn how to behave like his "American Gentleman" nickname.

This section essentially explores dog training and behavior. You get pointers on how to teach your dog to hold his bladder and use the bathroom area. You discover the importance of proper socialization at all stages of his life. And you get an introduction to basic training, including schooling your Boston on how to sit, stay, and heel.

This section discusses ways to get out with your dog, too. From competition and trial events, like obedience and agility, to sporting challenges, like flyball and freestyle dancing, you have plenty of reasons to head outdoors with your Boston. And if you have vacation plans on your calendar, you can find travel tips for you and your Boston in this section as well.

Chapter 9

Housetraining for Bostons

- -

In This Chapter

▶ Teaching your puppy about bathroom breaks

▶ Correcting mistakes

▶ Introducing alternative potty spots

- -

*L*ike an infant child, your Boston Terrier puppy has yet to develop bladder control or learn what areas in the home he can hang out in. He relies completely on you for guidance and to care for his basic needs, from feeding to eliminating and every-thing in between. Even if you adopt an adult dog, he needs to know when and where he can eliminate. With your patient leadership and instruction, however, your Boston will learn his household manners from day one.

Housetraining instructs your dog when and where he can relieve himself. Because he typically won't eliminate in the same space where he eats and sleeps, keeping your dog in his crate or in a restricted space trains him to hold his business until it's time to visit the designated bathroom area.

This chapter explores methods for housetraining your Boston, from using crates and X-pens to housetraining pads and litter boxes.

Each dog is different, but generally, Bostons can be considered housetrained by 6 to 8 months old, as long as they're not required to hold it too long. Because they're intelligent dogs, Bostons are relatively easy to housetrain (compared to other dogs, like Yorkshire Terriers). Keep in mind the process takes time. Be patient, stick to a schedule, and remember to praise your pup for doing the right thing!

Setting the Stage for Success: Housetraining Basics

Housetraining involves training your dog to let you know when he needs to eliminate, where he should go, and how to do it on command. At first, he won't be able to tell you that he needs to use the bathroom; you'll tell him when to go. In time, however, he'll learn to hold his bladder and bowels, let you know that he needs to go outside, and go to the bathroom in a designated area.

The best time to start housetraining is when your puppy is between 7 and 9 weeks old and his physical coordination has been refined. A reputable breeder will start your Boston's housetraining before you bring him home. Plan to continue housetraining until your dog is 6 months old, and plan to limit his freedom until he's 1 year old. By the end of this training period, you'll be confident that your pup knows when and where to do his business.

In this section, you find out what you can do to help your Boston succeed at housetraining. You get the lowdown on how to reward your Boston for going to the bathroom at the right time in the right place, how to set up and introduce his designated bathroom area, and how to limit the areas he's allowed to explore.

Reinforcing positive behavior

One of the best ways to train your Boston is through positive reinforcement. *Positive reinforcement* rewards good behavior with treats, praise, and lots of love. (You can read about this approach in detail in Chapter 11.)

When using positive reinforcement to housetrain your Boston, keep the following points in mind:

- ✔ **Reward him for doing the right thing:** When your Boston goes potty when you tell him to, reward him immediately with treats, praise, playtime, and other positive motivators.

- ✔ **Correct him in the act and redirect him:** When your Boston makes a mistake (and he will!) correct him by saying, "No," and then pick him up and take him to the bathroom area, praising him when he goes in the right spot. (See the "Mistakes Will Happen" section for tips on correcting behavior.)

- ✔ **Timing is critical:** Dogs have short memories; when you praise or correct your dog, he associates it with the action he just performed. Any positive reinforcement or correction needs to be done during or immediately after he does something.

Your Boston wants nothing but to please you. When you reward his correct behavior with praise and love, he knows that he did the right thing, and he'll want to keep doing that to reap the reward.

Making the trip to the bathroom area

Dogs are creatures of habit. Housetraining will be much easier for you and your Boston if you designate a particular bathroom area and take your Boston there frequently. Here are some points to consider when setting up your pup's potty spot:

- ✔ **Designate a space:** Choose a bathroom area outside and always take your pup on leash to that area. It could be a patch of grass or dirt, a curb, or even a litter box on your patio. When he eliminates, use a voice command, such as "Go potty," to help him associate a command with eliminating.

  Immediately after your Boston eliminates outdoors in the bathroom area, praise him lavishly and give him a treat. Don't wait until he comes inside — by then it's too late, and he won't associate the reward with relieving himself. Immediately giving the dog positive reinforcement lets him know what's expected.

- ✔ **Plan frequent visits to the bathroom area:** Your pup's small bladder doesn't hold much, so you need to take him outside frequently: after every meal, after playing, when waking up from one of his many naps, and about every half-hour to two hours in between, depending on his development. After sleeping all night, carry your puppy outside because he may need to relieve himself right away. (See the "Training Your Boston" section later in this chapter for more about taking him to the bathroom at regular intervals.)

- ✔ **Go out with him:** You need to accompany your pup outside, using the "Go potty" command. Going with him is the only way you know that he's going to the bathroom and not sniffing and playing instead. You also need to continue praising and rewarding him for eliminating outside. Eventually, your Boston will be able to go on command, which is very useful in the middle of the night or when you're traveling.

  Your puppy may want to play as soon as he gets outside, but command him go to the bathroom first. Doing so reinforces that he should do what you say first — take care of business — and then enjoy the reward of playing with you.

✔ **Show him the other "living areas" in the home:** Besides learning where he *can* go to the bathroom, your Boston also needs to learn where he *can't* go to the bathroom. Introduce your dog to other living areas, like the bedrooms, guest room, dining room, and den, besides the frequented areas of your home. After he recognizes these rooms as places where the family lives, he'll be less likely to use them as alternative bathroom spots.

✔ **Clean up accidents:** When your pup goes potty someplace he shouldn't, clean it up with an enzyme-based cleanser and deodorizer. Dogs have a keen sense of smell: They'll sniff out a spot they've used before and use it again. Remove all traces of the accident so he doesn't think it's another bathroom area.

Restricting his freedom

When your Boston comes home, you probably won't know his housetraining habits. He may have been living on sheets of newspaper and allowed to relieve himself anywhere he wanted, or he may understand the concept of going outside. Until you know his habits (and he learns how to control his bladder and bowels), you need to limit his access to a certain area of the house.

You can restrict his freedom in several ways:

✔ **Use his crate:** Because your pup's instincts tell him not to eliminate where he eats and sleeps, you can use his crate to teach him bladder and bowel control. Limit his time in the crate to two hours at a time during the day, letting him periodically stretch his legs and play in his X-pen; at night, he'll stay in his crate until you let him out to go to the bathroom.

Young pups who were kept in kennels and allowed to eliminate where they slept (like at a disreputable breeder facility or pet store) will be harder to housetrain using a crate. Because they are already used to eliminating where they eat and sleep, you'll have to work diligently to untrain and retrain these dogs.

✔ **Use an X-pen or playpen:** These devices keep your Boston contained to one area that you can easily monitor. Because X-pens and playpens give your Boston more space, your pup may choose a corner for a bathroom area. Line the entire area with several layers of newspaper or some absorbent housetraining pads to sop up accidents, and clean the area thoroughly if (and when) accidents happen.

> ✔ **Give him supervised "freedom:"** Of course you'll want to let
> your pup romp and play while you're watching television or
> hanging out in the living room. It's perfectly okay to do this —
> as long as you (or a responsible family member) are there to
> keep a constant eye on him. Take him potty regularly (see the
> next section, "Training Your Boston," for specifics) and lay
> down some absorbent pads, just in case.

As your Boston becomes housetrained, you can slowly expand his
area to include part of a room, then an entire room, and eventually
the entire house. But his success in going when and where he's supposed to hinges on you setting and following a bathroom schedule.

Training Your Boston

Teaching your puppy to go to the bathroom on command and in
the right place will challenge both of you. Don't worry: It's not difficult. But you (and your family) need to be committed to consistent
training, following these same steps every time you take your
Boston to the bathroom. You can tweak the routine as your pup
starts to get the hang of housetraining.

Plan to follow this routine until your pup is at least 6 months old,
depending on the dog's maturity level. Even then, restrict his free
access to the entire house until he's 1 year old. You want to be able
to trust your Boston completely, and even though 6 months or a
year sounds like a long time, it's really not when you compare it to
a lifetime of no accidents!

Assuming that you've introduced your pup to the house, all the
rooms, and his bathroom area, use these step-by-step instructions
to guide you through the housetraining process. Remember:
Follow these steps each and every time you (or your family
member) take your pup to the bathroom.

1. **When it's time to go outside, say, "Outside" in a happy,
   upbeat tone. Attach your Boston's leash to his collar and
   lead him to the bathroom area.**

   You need to let him do his business at regular times
   throughout the day, including:

   • **As soon as he wakes up in the morning and after
     every nap:** Those small Boston bladders don't hold
     much, and after a full night's sleep or a relaxing nap,
     he'll be ready to relieve himself. When your pup is
     very young, carry him to his bathroom area after he
     wakes; when he gets older and develops bladder con-
     trol, you can walk him outside.

- **Right after he eats:** Most dogs need to do their business shortly after they eat. Take your puppy outside no more than 15 minutes after he finishes his meal. Older dogs can wait a bit longer.

- **Right after he plays:** When puppies get excited, sometimes they lose control of their bladders. (Think of when you were young and somebody tickled you until you almost wet your pants.) Right after a fun play session, take your pup to his bathroom area. As he gets older and learns to control his bladder, you can taper off this trip.

- **Right after you give him a bath:** That warm sudsy water can trigger the urge to go potty, so take him outside as soon as he's bathed — and try to keep him out of the dirt!

- **Every two hours (or so):** At first, you'll take your pup outside every one to two hours to relieve himself (which includes the occasions I've listed above). Your Boston will gradually develop bladder and bowel control as he gets older, so you can adjust this rule as he matures.

- **Right before he goes to bed:** To help him have an accident-free night, take your puppy to the bathroom right before you put him in his kennel at night.

2. **As soon as he starts going to the bathroom, say, "Go potty."**

   He knows what he's doing, and by giving him a verbal command, he links his action with your cue. Teaching him to go on command is particularly useful when it's raining or snowing outside, when you're late for work, or when you're on a road trip and don't have a lot of time to spare.

3. **Immediately after he's done, say "Good boy to go potty," or whatever phrase or word you choose, and give him a treat.**

   He'll begin to associate three things: the command ("Go potty") with the action (going potty), the action with the reward (treat), and the reward with your praise. You're teaching him that by going potty on command, he will earn a reward. That reward will ultimately be your praise.

Slowly, your Boston will show signs of getting the housetraining concept. He'll wait by the door when he has to go, or come up with some other way to say, "I have to go!" He'll be able to hold his bladder through the night without whimpering. He'll head to the bathroom spot first thing when you let him outside. It will take time — at least six months — before he gets the hang of it, but he will.

Prevention is key to housetraining. Don't give your pup the opportunity to make a mistake. Keep him in your sight at all times by attaching his leash to your chair or waist, or using a baby gate to keep him confined. If you see him start to sniff around or walk in circles, immediately grab the lead and take him outside to his bathroom spot, saying, "Go potty." Then praise and give him a treat.

Mistakes Will Happen

You've been taking your Boston puppy to his bathroom area regularly, and letting him relieve himself after every meal, playtime, and nap. Your dog is becoming housetrained. But then, he makes a mistake. What do you do?

✔ **Correct him in the act and redirect him:** The act of going to the bathroom isn't the mistake; it's going in the wrong place. So if you catch your pup in the act, say in a corrective tone, "Pete, no," and immediately take him to his bathroom area and let him finish his business there. Then praise your Boston and celebrate that he's going outside.

Don't correct the dog *after* he makes a mistake — he can't understand the connection between the correction and the mistake he made hours (even minutes) ago. Also, *never* rub your dog's face in the mess. It's not only an unnecessarily harsh punishment, but your dog will think that you're mad because he defecated, not because he went in the wrong place. Instead, encourage and praise your dog even more when he does go in his correct bathroom area. Reinforcing the positive behavior is the best way to discourage house-soiling.

If your Boston seems to be having more accidents than usual, it may be a sign of stress or illness. Sometimes dogs react to pain or discomfort by soiling in areas where they normally don't. Talk to your veterinarian if you see any changes in your Boston's urinating habits.

✔ **Clean it well:** Clean the soiled area with white vinegar or an enzyme-based pet stain cleaner. Dogs tend to continue soiling in areas that smell like feces or urine, so removing all traces of the accident prevents your dog from using that area again.

✔ **Watch him:** You also want to keep a close eye on your Boston. If you know where your dog is, he can't make a mistake. A circling and sniffing dog means he's searching for a bathroom, so ask him in an upbeat happy voice, "Pete, do you have to go potty?" When he runs to the door, take him out and praise him after he goes.

The scoop on pooper scoopers

Let's face it: Cleaning up after your pooch is dirty business. He may be the love of your life, but bagging his little presents can be a smelly job. And if it's raining or snowing, that makes the task all the more, err, delightful! (I'm being sarcastic, of course!)

Innovative inventors realize this, so they have designed all sorts of devices to make this task mess-free. No longer is the old plastic grocery bag the receptacle of choice. Now you can choose from scoops, claws, and shovels for minimal handling. You can purchase waste bags in bulk to attach to your lead, toss in your purse, and pack in your Boston's carrier. With so many options, cleaning up has never been easier!

For Boston owners who want nothing to do with cleaning up their dog's droppings, however, pooper scooper services can do your dirty business. A pet sitter, dog walker, or someone who is in this line of work (really!) comes to your home a number of times during the week and cleans up your Boston's feces for a fee. It's certainly a convenience to consider.

Okay Ways to Go Inside

If you live in an urban area or work long hours, you may need to leave your Boston inside for the majority of the day. That's a long time for your Boston to control his bladder and bowels! You can enlist the help of your local dog sitter or take him to doggy day care (Chapter 13 has more on these options). Or you can train your pup to go in certain areas inside your home.

In this section, I offer two additional options to using an outdoor bathroom area. They're not meant to replace traditional house-training methods, because your Boston should learn how to hold his bladder and go to the bathroom in a designated outdoor spot. These options are intended to give you more choices for allowing your pup to relieve himself.

Teaching your Boston both traditional housetraining and an alternative method may confuse him at first. Be patient while he's learning, and continue to be diligent with his training. If he just doesn't seem to get it after a couple of weeks, forgo the alternative method and focus on the traditional method. You can always teach your pup the new bathroom trick after he learns the first routine.

Read all about it: Paper training

Typically used during the beginning stages of housetraining, *paper training* teaches your Boston to eliminate on sheets of newspaper rather than wherever he pleases. This method is useful when you can't supervise him or take him to his bathroom area during the day. It's also useful for pups who have developed a habit of going in their crates.

1. **Before your pup is allowed free reign of the house, erect an X-pen to confine him to one area.**

   Choose a place such as the kitchen, living room, or other high-traffic area where he feels like he's part of the family pack.

2. **Lay down three or four sheets of newspaper inside the entire pen.**

   He will develop a habit of eliminating on the newspaper, eventually preferring a specific spot to do his business.

3. **When you know the spot that your Boston prefers to eliminate in and the rest of the papers remain clean, gradually reduce the area that is papered.**

   Remove the sheets that are farthest away from his preferred spot. Eventually, you'll only need to leave a few sheets in that area.

4. **After your pup is reliably going on the papers that you've left, slowly start to move the paper to a location that's more to your liking (that is to say, not in the middle of the floor or under the kitchen table).**

   Don't move the papers too far too soon: An inch or two a day is far enough.

Don't be discouraged if your pup misses the paper or makes remarkable progress and then regresses. Lay down a larger area of newspaper and start again. It's normal to make mistakes. Just stay determined, and your Boston will eventually get the hang of it.

A litter box of his own

Yes, your Boston can be trained to use the litter box! Just as you'd train your dog to use newspaper or a bathroom area outside, you can teach your dog to use a bathroom area inside or on your porch.

Litter boxes are well-suited for dogs who live in apartments or condos, for families who work long hours and can't let their dogs outside during the day, or for older invalid or housebound dogs.

Litter boxes for dogs look just like large litter boxes for cats. You can find them in most pet supply stores or through online vendors, or you can construct your own using a plastic bin with an entry point cut into the side and sanded down so there are no sharp edges. The litter is typically compressed wood, newspaper pellets, or cat litter, depending on the style of litter box you choose.

When your dog is a puppy, take him by his lead to the bathroom area just as you would take him outside. Reward and praise the pup when he goes in the right spot. As always with housetraining, keep a vigilant eye on your Boston, and if he shows any signs of sniffing and circling, take him to the bathroom area immediately.

If your Boston is already paper trained (see the previous section), transitioning to a litter box can be relatively easy. Gradually move the newspaper to the area where the litter box is. Instead of filling the box with litter, line it with newspaper. Replace the paper with litter as your pup gets used to the box.

As with any housetraining method, mistakes will happen, and you'll need to clean any messes. While your Boston is learning how to use his litter box, lay newspaper or absorbent pads on the floor around the box. Clean up mistakes with a commercial cleaner that removes all traces of odor. And be patient and diligent with your training! Bostons are intelligent dogs, and before long, your dog will be doing his business in his box!

Though Bostons' ancestors were once fighters, the dog's "American Gentleman" nickname tells a different tale, as you can read about in Chapter 1. The Boston Terrier is an intelligent, playful, affectionate breed that thrives on companionship.

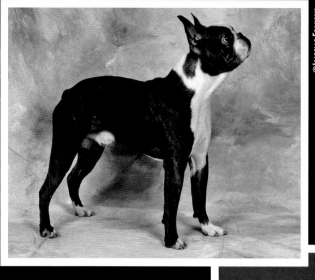

When you look at a Boston Terrier, the first thing you'll notice is his square, compact build and tough-guy stance. His square-looking head, shortened snout, and erect ears give him an alert and kind expression.

Through years of careful breeding, the Boston Terrier's tuxedo-like coat pattern — a white muzzle band, white blaze between his large eyes, white chest, and white boots on a black or brindle body — has become a hallmark of the breed. You can read about the Boston's breed standards in Chapter 2.

Boston Terriers are a healthy breed, but they are susceptible to several medical conditions related to their conformation. Your Boston may snort and wheeze because of a narrow trachea and elongated soft palate. To learn more about breed-specific ailments, skip to Chapter 15.

When you know a Boston is the breed for you, you have several other decisions to make, including: Do you want a male or a female? Do you want a puppy or an adult? Turn to Chapter 4 for more information about how to choose the right Boston for you.

Who can resist that face? Boston Terriers are known for their amiable personalities and adorable expressions. You and your pup can expect attention wherever you go — whether it's to the pet store, the local bistro, or even at home watching the world pass by.

As ever-attentive companions, Bostons make ideal indoor dogs in virtually any household — from small apartments with one or two people to large homes filled with family members. Chapter 6 describes how you can help your new pup fit into your life.

Boston Terriers get along well with children, particularly those who understand how to act around dogs. When you begin to socialize your Boston (check out Chapter 10), include children in the mix — supervised by you, of course — and make sure that the child understands the ground rules.

Your Boston and your cat (or other family pet) can become friends, but it takes time and planning on your part. Introduce the two slowly and always keep your dog controlled. Find out more about managing multiple-pet households in Chapter 6.

As an ever-eager travel companion, your Boston will need his own suitcase when you take him on a road trip. Make sure to pack portable water and food dishes, a travel first-aid kit, a leash and collar with updated ID tags, and a favorite squeaky toy. Trek to Chapter 13 for more travel tips.

A crate or kennel serves as your Boston's safe and cozy den, his travel carrier in the car or airplane, and his home away from home. As you read in Chapter 9, it also serves as a training tool while you're teaching him bladder control.

To ensure your Boston stays healthy and happy, he'll need regular visits to the veterinarian. Your dog's doctor will give him vaccinations, make sure he's growing up strong, and answer any questions you may have. Chapter 14 describes how to find a veterinarian and what you can expect during your pup's annual visits.

Bostons don't tolerate extreme cold very well, so your pup will need some dandy duds to keep him warm. Choose a coat that is designed for a small dog, is easy to put on and take off, and can be cleaned. Flip to Chapter 5 for more fashion tips for your pup.

Chewing is a normal puppy behavior, but that doesn't mean you have to sacrifice your favorite slippers! Offer your Boston puppy a chew toy designed especially for growing dogs. For more puppy-product know-how, turn to Chapter 5.

Though you'll train your Boston to be a well-behaved gentleman, he'll still get into trouble. Correct him by redirecting his action, and always use positive reinforcement to shape your Boston's behavior. Chapter 11 describes ways to encourage your pup to be a good boy.

To give your Boston gusto, he needs a quality diet packed with digestible protein, carbohydrates, fats, minerals, and vitamins. He also needs access to clean, fresh water all the time. Chapter 7 describes the dietary delights that your pup will savor.

Tapping into their terrier roots, Boston Terriers enjoy active play, whether it be agility challenges, obedience trials, or a fun game of fetch. Here, Kazoo darts through a tunnel during an agility trial, which also includes jumps, weave poles, and maneuvering through obstacles. Chapter 12 has more information about these sports.

It takes practice for a Boston to fly through the air and leap over an obstacle! Boston Terrier clubs can provide information about practice courses and local and regional competitions.

Weaving through poles and leaping over hurdles expends a lot of Boston energy. If it's hot and your dog shows signs of respiratory distress, such as labored breathing or pale gums, calm him down. Wait 5 to 10 minutes, and if your pup's breathing doesn't return to normal, call your veterinarian immediately.

Because your Boston wears a short coat, grooming him is a relatively simple task, as you find out in Chapter 8. Plan to brush him daily, brush his teeth and check his body once a week, and bathe him once a month — unless he decides to roll in the mud, of course!

Chapter 10

Socializing for Life

In This Chapter

▶ Identifying key developmental phases in your Boston's life

▶ Looking at strategies for socializing your pup

▶ Interpreting canine body language

▶ Calming your dog's fears

A well-socialized Boston delights all who cross her path. She plays well with other dogs. She welcomes new faces, smells, sights, and sounds instead of cowering in fear. She enjoys meeting people and exploring unknown territory. In essence, she fits well in any social situation.

A Boston who is protected from the world, however, learns to fear what she doesn't know. Everything becomes frightening, and as a result, the dog will be timid and fearful, cowering from noises, sights, people, and other dogs. A fearful dog also may begin to bite out of fear, a habit that can be difficult to correct.

During the first year of your dog's life — particularly the first four months — she experiences developmental milestones that will warrant your special attention, especially as they pertain to your pup's personality and social behavior. In this chapter, I explore those key phases in your Boston's development and how you can help her through them. I also include tips for introducing your puppy to different people and objects. Finally, I provide you with some guidance on how dogs communicate their feelings and how you can prevent fear in your Boston. Though each dog differs, you can use these pages as a guideline for what to expect as your pup grows into an adult.

Understanding Your Boston's Developmental Timeline

Before delving into ways to socialize your Boston, you need to understand the developmental phases your dog will experience as she grows from puppyhood through adolescence and into adulthood. Each phase contains its own milestones, like bonding with humans or learning social hierarchies, and as a dog owner, you want to foster those behaviors so the pup grows to be a well-adjusted adult.

If you adopt a puppy from a disreputable pet store or backyard breeder, or if you adopt an adult from a rescue organization or shelter, your Boston may have missed some of these developmental milestones. Healthy development requires human and canine contact, and some of these puppies may not have received what they required to socialize properly. They're not hopeless cases, but these puppies require extra-special care and nurturing.

A brand-new world: The first 6 weeks

There's nothing like a brand-new puppy. Still wriggling and yearning for her mother, she's completely dependent on her canine caretaker for nourishment and development. She's also dependent on her littermates for social stimulation.

From about 3 to 6 weeks old, a puppy gets her social stimuli from other dogs, like her mother and siblings. She learns how to act around other dogs, begins to understand *social hierarchies* (who ranks higher than whom in the pack), and shows the first hints of personality.

Dogs at this age should not be away from their mothers. Because reputable breeders don't adopt out dogs at this age, it's unlikely that you'll see this stage of your Boston's development, though you may have some exposure to it when you visit the breeder to pick out your puppy.

Getting to know people: 5 to 12 weeks

When a puppy reaches 5 to 12 weeks of age, she turns her attention to people. She begins to look to her human caretakers for social stimuli and interaction. At this time in her life, positive human bonding is critical for proper socialization.

Most breeders will let you take your pup home at around 10 to 12 weeks old. While the young Boston lives with the breeder, her socialization with humans begins. The breeder will hold the puppy and invite friends and neighbors over to handle her. When you take her home, you'll continue to do the same.

Puppies experience their first *fear phase* when they're around 8 weeks old. At this age, she has become very aware of the world around her, and sometimes it can be very scary. If she's frightened by something at this age, it's likely that she won't get over it. Breeders know this, and they typically won't adopt out a pup who has yet to experience this fear phase.

During these second and third months of life, your Boston should meet people of both genders and as many ages, ethnicities, and backgrounds as possible. They should hold her, talk to her, coddle her, and interact with her so that later in life, she's already familiar with those types of people. The key is to make all of these experiences as positive as possible.

A challenge will surface, however, when your veterinarian recommends that you not take the pup to pet stores, dog parks, or places where other dogs or strays have been until after she's had all of her vaccinations (about 16 weeks old). So what do you do? Invite friends over for a cookout. Have an intimate get-together with neighbors. Think of ways to welcome as many individuals as possible to your home. Some trainers recommend that your pup meet 100 or more people during these first months of her life! You'll have to get creative.

Though your puppy has already endured her first fear phase, ask your friends not to move too quickly or wear distracting items, like a big floppy hat or dark sunglasses, when they come to visit. Quick movements or colorful disguises can frighten a young Boston!

Interacting with her environment: 12 to 20 weeks

After getting used to all sorts of people, your pup will begin getting used to different surroundings. From 12 weeks to 20 weeks old, a puppy is the most receptive to learning how to handle new sights, sounds, and smells. This is the best time to begin to socialize her to different environments.

Puppy kindergarten offers an excellent opportunity to get your pup out of the house and into new environments. Often held at training centers, pet stores, and dog parks, puppy kindergarten introduces a dog to a new place, new people, and new dogs — a perfect social situation for a developing dog! See Chapter 11 for more information about the benefits of puppy kindergarten.

At 16 weeks old, some dogs experience another fear phase. As with her first fear phase (see the "Getting to know people: 5 to 12 weeks" section), if a dog is frightened by something, it's likely that she'll carry that fear with her for her entire life. Use caution when exposing your Boston to scary things at this age. I discuss handling fear in the "Preventing Fear" section later in this chapter. Just remember to stay upbeat, and avoid reinforcing the fear by coddling her when something scares her.

Fourteen weeks marks an important milestone in a pup's development: If she is kenneled and not handled before this period, she will develop some serious social problems, often acting out toward things she doesn't understand. It's absolutely critical that the dog is handled as much as possible during these first few months.

Approaching adulthood: 4 months to 3 years

After a puppy makes it through her first four months of life — her puppyhood — she enters her teenage years. She continues to explore her surroundings, sniffing things, tasting things, and getting to know the world around her. She also experiences three major milestones in her life:

- **Another fear period:** As with the fear periods at 8 and 16 weeks old, some dogs may go through another one at 14 months old that's not as critical as the first two. During this fear period, you may notice your pup being apprehensive toward things she already knows. Help her through this by encouraging her and reassuring her, revisiting some training techniques, if necessary.

- **Sexual maturity:** This inevitable teenage experience occurs in both male and female dogs between 6 months and 1 year of age. Female dogs should be spayed before their first heat cycle, reducing their chances of developing reproductive system cancers and unwanted pregnancies. Male dogs should also be neutered around this same time. Doing so reduces unwanted behaviors such as aggression, urine marking, mounting, and wandering in search of a mate. (Chapter 14 has more specifics on spaying and neutering your Boston.)

✔ **Social maturity:** From 1 year to 3 years old, a dog continues to mature socially. She's still considered a puppy during this time, despite her adult appearance! She continues to develop her personality, she refines her behavior, and she experiences more new sights, sounds, people, and places as her world continues to expand.

Though the dog has passed her prime for growing accustomed to various environmental stimuli, you should still expose your Boston to as many social situations as possible. By the time she reaches her third birthday, she's ready for just about anything.

Socializing Your Puppy

You know you need to introduce your pup to as many social situations as possible. So how do you do it? The process begins as soon as your puppy is born. When a Boston first enters the world, she begins to develop her senses of smell and taste. She learns to interact with her mother and littermates. Then she begins to explore the human world, bonding with people and expanding the world around her.

You can help her through these phases so she becomes a dog who adores — and depends upon — people. The key is to introduce your Boston to the world without frightening her. That means your tone of voice should be happy and upbeat. It takes some work and a lot of patience, but when your adorable puppy develops into a well-adjusted and demonstrative adult, all your efforts will be worth it.

Keeping her safe, yet social

After your puppy comes home, you'll want to introduce her to as many people as possible. You're a proud new puppy parent, after all, and you want to show her off! Exposure to people helps your dog learn who belongs to the pack and who doesn't.

Trainers recommend that your pup meet and be handled by at least 100 people of all different ages, sizes, and ethnicities during the first few months of life! She should meet people who wear glasses or hats. She should also be exposed to people who use a wheelchair or cane. She should meet the children down the street, the teenagers next door, and the retired seniors across the way. The more variety she experiences, the better.

Your veterinarian will probably tell you not to take your dog out until she has been fully vaccinated. That's easier said than done! You know you need to expose her to a variety of people, but you also want to keep her healthy.

Here are some ways to both keep her safe and allow her to meet a variety of people. Start slowly; stick to your house the first week or two and expand from there.

- ✔ **Take her with you wherever you go.** Dress her in a fancy pup-size collar with an ID tag, attach a matching leash, put her in colorful carrier, and let her shadow you as you go to the market, the coffee shop, or a friend's house.

- ✔ **Expose her to as many different people as possible.** Let her meet your neighbors, the postal carrier, and the pet store cashier. Wherever you go, you and your adorable Boston will create a stir. Let people pet and fawn over your pup. The more people she meets, the better she'll adjust.

- ✔ **Invite friends and relatives to your house and ask each person to hold your pup.** By meeting people on her own turf, your Boston develops confidence as well as social skills. And as each person handles your Boston, she gets used to being touched by different humans — all with different smells and appearances.

- ✔ **Host play dates with other dog owners and their dogs who have already had their vaccinations.** If you know that they're up to date on their shots, you can have other dogs over to meet your puppy. Always supervise them, of course, especially if the dogs are older or larger than your pup.

- ✔ **Avoid places where strange dogs have been.** Let your Boston explore as much as she can, but steer clear of areas with potentially parasite-ridden animal feces, like public parks, beaches, or unfamiliar neighborhoods.

Introducing children — slowly

Puppies and children — responsible children, that is — go together like cookies and milk. When the two pair up, they often develop an uncanny bond, much to the chagrin of adults! They'll play together, the dog will obey the child's commands, and the two will become inseparable (and mischievous!) in no time at all.

The key to a successful child-pup relationship, however, is the child's maturity level. A child who is too young may play too rough with a puppy, or a child who is too immature or inexperienced with dogs may become frightened by a pup's playful postures. Without parental supervision and ground rules, the experience can be a negative one for both the dog and the child.

Before you let any child play with your Boston puppy, first determine how comfortable the child is with dogs. If he's your child, you'll know his comfort level. If he's your child's friend or a neighbor, ask his parents how much experience he has had with puppies. If they give you a green light, let them play together — always supervised, of course.

You can set up some ground rules to make playtime a positive one for everyone. Here are some suggestions:

- ✔ **Sniff first, play later.** Ask the child to approach the pup slowly and offer an outstretched hand for her to smell. If your Boston sniffs and wags her little tail, the child can pet and play with her.

- ✔ **Move slowly.** Don't allow children to run or move erratically around the puppy. Doing so can be frightening or overwhelming, or the pup may accidentally be trampled. Instead, require deliberate, cautious movements, especially when the pup is very young.

- ✔ **Use an inside voice.** Don't let kids scream or yell while playing with the puppy. Again, this can be overstimulating or scary to a young dog.

- ✔ **Give the puppy some space.** Though a Boston pup may look like an adorable stuffed animal, don't let kids grab the pup and hug her. Instead, allow the child to pet the puppy while she's on the ground, in her bed, or in an adult's lap. Watch the dog's body language. If she looks frightened, ask the child to back off a little.

- ✔ **No wrestling!** Part of that child-dog bond includes wrestling and playing with the pup. Some physical play is fine, but don't let kids throw themselves on the puppy. Not only can that endanger the dog, but it can also endanger the child if the pup gets scared and nips at him.

- ✔ **Limit face time.** Don't allow kids to grab your Boston's face, put their face to hers, blow in her face, or stare at her. Those are all intimidating postures that can lead to nipping and biting later on. Let the kids pet the pup's head, neck, back, and belly, but keep her face off-limits.

After the puppy has grown, you can relax some of these house rules. You'll know instinctively when it's okay for your child to play more exuberantly with your Boston. Use common sense and good judgment, always supervising the new best friends.

Interacting with four-legged friends

Dogs bond with other dogs when they're first born. Right out of the womb, they learn to share — or battle for — their mother's milk. When playing and wrestling, they learn how rough is too rough. Natural leaders and followers emerge. They develop the canine social skills required to live and interact in a dog pack.

When a puppy leaves the litter and moves into her new home, she'll use her learned pack behavior to interact with her new family — which may contain dogs, cats, hamsters, reptiles, or even a goat. Similarly, when a puppy comes across new four-legged friends at dog parks or puppy kindergarten, she uses those same learned behaviors to meet and greet her new friends.

Just as your dog needs to be exposed to different types of adults and children, your dog should also be exposed to other animals and learn how to interact with them appropriately. Below, I've listed some strategies to make those introductions a little easier.

At home

Whether you have a tank full of bearded dragons, a pair of finicky felines, or a cow and a couple of goats, you need to introduce your Boston puppy to each one. Flip to Chapter 6 for more tips on introductions, but here are some things to keep in mind:

- ✔ **Talk to your veterinarian.** Because your vet likely cares for the other critters in your menagerie, ask him if there are any dangers to watch for, especially when your puppy is young. A grumpy 12-year-old cat may bear his claws and take a swipe at the new pup. Reptile feces can contain salmonella. Give your vet a call, just to be safe.

- ✔ **Introduce them slowly.** For most animals, you can create a safe environment in your kitchen or living room. Place your Boston in her carrier or kennel and allow the other animal to sniff and inspect the new puppy. After the two learn to recognize each other, give them more freedom. But don't rush the introductions. You'll have plenty of time!

- ✔ **Always supervise.** Keep an eye on your pets, especially in the beginning when they're getting to know each other. Cats may be territorial, while other dogs may play too rough.

- ✔ **Guard smaller pets.** Keep pets such as reptiles and small mammals caged or in your care. Those little critters may look like prey to your puppy! Rather than risk losing a hamster or gecko, keep them locked up and safe, just in case.

Out and about

A few weeks after you bring your puppy home, when she's 14 weeks old or so, you'll begin to expose her to new environments. She'll see new sights, smell new smells, and meet new people. She'll also come across other dogs. Make it a positive experience by taking the following actions:

- ✔ **Verify vaccinations.** If you meet a fellow dog owner walking his dog, for example, ask whether the other dog is up to date on his vaccinations. Most responsible dog owners will be current with their pup's inoculations, and they won't be offended if you ask.

- ✔ **Encourage encounters with friendly dogs.** When a familiar dog approaches your Boston and you know that he is current on his shots, let them sniff each other and get to know one another. Dog parks, puppy kindergarten and other organized socialization classes, and planned play dates are great opportunities for dog-dog bonding and socializing.

- ✔ **Be wary of unknown dogs.** They may harbor disease or be aggressive, so steer clear of strange animals, especially those that aren't leashed. If you see one in the distance, turn around and walk away.

- ✔ **Stay away from animal feces.** Parasites and diseases hide in animal excrement (see Chapter 14 for details), so keep your Boston far from dog, cat, and other animal feces. She'll likely want to investigate little piles left behind, but pull her away and redirect her.

- ✔ **Get involved in dog social activities.** Puppy kindergarten offers a safe place for your Boston to meet other dogs and interact with other humans. Dog owners must show proof of their dog's vaccinations before they can register, so you can be assured that your pup won't be exposed to any disease. And you'll meet other dog owners with pups the same age as yours, so you can talk about your pup-raising experiences — the good and bad!

Socializing Your Adult Dog

If you raise your Boston from puppyhood and socialize her properly, she already knows how to act around other animals, dogs, and humans, and she's been exposed to a variety of environmental situations. Essentially, her brain has been programmed for how to properly behave in many different scenarios.

But what if you adopt an older dog who hasn't been socialized? Is all hope lost? Not necessarily. It will take a lot of patience and training, but she can be socialized.

Here are some ways to teach your older dog new socialization tricks:

- **Enroll in a dog obedience class.** Besides learning how to obey your commands, your Boston will meet many different people and dogs, and be exposed to a new environment. By introducing her to so many new things at once, you'll kick-start her socialization process.

- **Progress to agility or other competitive sport.** As soon as your dog learns some basic obedience and social skills, try her paw (or your hand) at agility or tracking (jump to Chapter 12 to learn more about these sports). These are challenging and energy-expending competitions that give your dog the opportunity to interact with many different people, dogs, and situations.

- **Introduce her to new environments.** As you would with a puppy, take your adult Boston with you wherever you go. Let her meet your friends and neighbors. Ask your child to invite his friends over to meet your dog. Go to a dog park. Do everything you can to expose your Boston to as many situations as possible.

- **Reward her for a job well done.** *Positive reinforcement,* or rewarding your dog for good behavior, teaches your Boston that she'll be praised when she greets new people with a lick and a wag, or meets new dogs with a friendly sniff and *play bow* (see more about this posture in the "Reading Your Boston's Body Language" section).

- **Keep working at it.** Dogs who have not been socialized as puppies require continuous training about how to behave among other dogs and humans. Luckily, Bostons are intelligent, and a little reminding goes a long way.

Reading Your Boston's Body Language

Dogs don't use words to communicate with humans, but they do use postures and body language to convey their mood. Canine *body postures* refer to the way a dog positions her body when she comes into contact with another dog or animal (including humans). It signals to the other animal whether she is fearful, playful, submissive, or aggressive.

When you can identify these various postures, you can better understand your Boston's behavior and mood, taking appropriate action when needed. If your dog displays an aggressive posture, for example, you can take hold of her leash, walk away calmly, and redirect her attention so she doesn't attack. Likewise, if another dog strikes an aggressive posture, you and your dog can walk away to prevent problems. In the following sections, I list the most common postures and their telltale signs.

Neutral relaxed

When your Boston is *neutral relaxed* (see Figure 10-1), she's simply hanging out, enjoying the day. Her head is erect, her ears are up, her tail is relaxed and wagging, her mouth is slightly open, and her weight is evenly distributed over all four of her feet.

Figure 10-1: A neutral relaxed posture means your Boston is content.

Greeting

Dogs who are saying hello to other dogs (shown in Figure 10-2) approach each other cautiously. The more dominant dog has her ears and tail up. The submissive dog has her ears back and her tail down, and her eyes are semi-closed.

The two sniff each other's genital region. This may seem rather strange to humans, but to dogs, it's completely natural. Dogs have scent glands on either side of their anus. These anal glands contain a scent that's unique to each dog. When they greet each other, dogs sniff at these glands. Talk about getting up close and personal!

Figure 10-2: When dogs meet, they'll slowly approach and sniff each other.

Play bow

When your Boston wants to play, you'll know immediately when she strikes a *play bow* (see Figure 10-3). She lowers her front end, including her head and shoulders, and leaves her hips high. She happily wags her tail, her ears are up, her eyes are soft, she relaxes her mouth, and her tongue is out. This posture lets everyone know that she's ready to have some fun.

If you want to play with your Boston, you can strike the same pose. Lift your hands high, and then bring them down in front of you, mimicking her bowing motion. Use an upbeat, positive voice, and get ready to toss the ball!

Figure 10-3: A play bow means one thing: Let's play!

Arousal

A Boston who has been stimulated by something (shown in Figure 10-4) — whether it be a sound, a sight, or a smell — will hold the *arousal posture*. Her ears are up and forward, her eyes are wide open, her tail is up, and her weight is over her front legs. Her muzzle may appear tense, with her lips lifted to expose her teeth, and her *hackles* (the hairs on her neck and back that stand up) may be raised, especially if she's responding to an unfamiliar stimulus.

If she's responding to something pleasurable, however, like when her best dog friend comes to the door, she wags her tail loosely and relaxes her muzzle, and her hackles are down. She knows something fun is about to happen, and she's ready for it.

Figure 10-4: An arousal pose means that something has piqued your Boston's interest.

Defensive aggression

If a dog feels threatened, she strikes a *defensive aggression posture* (see Figure 10-5), warning the other dog (or animal) that she doesn't want to be approached.

Her hackles may be up. Her tail is down and tensed, and her ears are back. Her weight falls over her rear legs. Her muzzle is tense, and she may snarl and expose her teeth. A Boston in this type of posture may attack or bite if the offending animal doesn't back down.

Aggressive attack

A posture that no one likes to see, an *aggressive attack pose* (see Figure 10-6) means your Boston is in fight mode. It's a threatening posture intended to frighten, chase away, or attack intruders. Poorly socialized or highly protective Bostons may take this pose when they feel their home is being invaded or their human is threatened.

When she's in this posture, you see a raised tail and hackles. Her ears are erect, tilting forward, and her eyes seem to shoot darts at her adversary. She curls her lips, revealing her teeth. Her weight is on her front paws, and she'll likely be charging and barking.

Figure 10-5: A threatened Boston will strike a defensive aggressive pose.

Figure 10-6: When a Boston takes the aggressive attack pose, she's defending her territory, chasing away any threatening intruders.

Submission

The opposite of aggression, *submission* (shown in Figure 10-7) is when a dog acknowledges the dominant animal by surrendering. Behaviorists identify two types of submission:

✔ **Active submission:** The dog tilts her head down, lowers her tail, cocks her ears back, and half-closes her eyes. She may raise her paw, and her mouth may be partly closed with her tongue tip darting in and out.

✔ **Passive submission:** The dog lies on her back, exposing her belly. She's essentially surrendering to the other animal. She cocks her ears back, turns her head away, and tucks her tail. This is the position your pup should take when you tell her to settle. (See Chapter 11 for more about training your pup.)

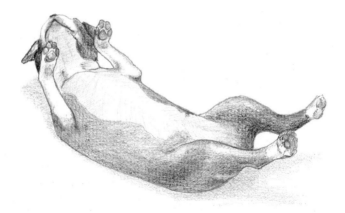

Figure 10-7: Your Boston will strike a submissive pose when she acknowledges a dominant animal or person.

Preventing Fear

During your Boston's 8th week, 16th week, and 14th month of life, she'll go through fear periods when she's more apt to view things around her as frightening. It's important at this age that you try to prevent scary things from happening, but if your Boston does experience something scary, don't reinforce that fear by coddling and comforting her. If you do, the puppy will remember that acting fearful yields a reward — your attention — and that fear response will stay with her.

Fear periods last anywhere from several weeks to several months, depending on the puppy's temperament and ability to cope with frightening situations. If your Boston shows excessive fear or doesn't seem to be coming out of a fear phase, talk to your veterinarian for advice.

Being proactive

Part of preventing fear is to expose your Boston to as many people and situations as possible. As I explain in the "Socializing Your Puppy" section earlier in this chapter, dogs need to meet people of different races, ethnicities, ages, and appearances. They should also experience a range of different activities and scenarios. By helping them become familiar with these things, they will be less likely to fear them later on.

Coping with fear

Boston puppies show they are in a fear period in many different ways. Some become cautious about everything, approaching objects and situations — even familiar ones — tentatively. Other pups are more selective, being bold about some things and timid with others.

When you think your puppy is in a fear phase, you can do several things to handle her fear:

- ✔ **Watch your tone of voice.** When your Boston seems fearful of something, speak to her in a calm, matter-of-fact tone, or speak to her in a higher-pitched, fun tone. Tell her that it's okay, that there's nothing to fear. Resist the urge to use a soothing tone that she could mistake as sympathy. That only reinforces her fears.

- ✔ **Distract her.** Another approach is to distract your Boston by turning her away from what scared her. When you redirect her attention, give her a treat or a toy, saying, "What's this? Here's your ball!" The key is to make her think about something else.

- ✔ **Investigate the fearful item.** If the scary item is accessible, walk up to, touch it, and show her that it's not as frightening as she thought. Approach the item and hold it, pat it, and tell her, "Look! It's not scary." If a cookie sheet falls to the floor, for example, walk up to it, pick it up, investigate it, and show it to your Boston. When she starts to approach and sniff it, praise her and tell her how brave she is.

- ✔ **Don't force her.** Sometimes your Boston may just want to hang back and look at the scary item. That's okay. When she's ready, then let her approach it on her own. If you force her, you may just make the fear that much worse.

If your pup still is afraid or starts to show signs of aggression at things she fears, you may want to talk to your vet or enlist the help of a trainer who can help you through the phase.

Chapter 11

Training and Behavior

In This Chapter

▶ Taking your Boston to school

▶ Mastering basic obedience commands

▶ Using humane methods to correct problem behavior

▶ Deciding when to call a behavior expert

*E*very year, pet owners relinquish millions of dogs to shelters because of their pets' bad behavior. Well-meaning families purchase puppies with every intention of training them to be well-behaved adults. They take them to puppy kindergarten and practice their lessons at home with hopes that the adorable puppies will obey their commands and behave as good dogs should.

Unfortunately, many times those good intentions fall by the wayside. Puppy kindergarten, for example, may meet the same day as their child's soccer team plays its matches. It becomes hard to find time to practice the Sit, Stay, and Leave It commands at home.

Before too long, the dog has asserted his dominance over the home, greeting houseguests with a bark, jumping up for attention, and digging dozens of holes in the perfectly manicured lawn. The owner throws up her hands in frustration and sequesters her beloved Boston to the basement or patio, then banishes him to the backyard, and eventually drops him off at the pound or humane society.

But it doesn't have to be this way. You can raise a well-behaved Boston who obeys commands. *Behavior training* is about teaching your Boston what actions are allowed and which ones are forbidden. It also means that you, the owner, have to be decisive about what you permit and prohibit.

School Days

Puppy kindergarten and obedience classes teach you how to handle your dog, and they teach your dog how to listen to you. Often organized through humane societies, veterinary offices, and pet stores, these courses are led by trained instructors who have particular expertise in teaching dog owners how to handle their pets.

Although you can skip puppy kindergarten and train your Boston at home, you and your dog achieve much greater success when you're taught by a dog trainer. In the structured environment, the trainer lays down fundamentals that you build upon throughout your Boston's life. It may seem like a hassle to take your pup to these classes, but they pay off later on.

Why classes are a good idea

Unless you're a dog trainer or an experienced dog owner, you probably don't know too much about training a dog. A dog isn't a little human; you can't reason with him, you can't talk him into behaving a certain way, and you can't ground him for bad behavior. The only thing he understands is how to act like a dog, so as his owner, you need to communicate with him in a way that he understands. You can learn these communication skills in a puppy kindergarten or obedience class.

Here are some more reasons to enroll your dog in classes:

- ✔ **Safety:** One of the most important reasons to train your Boston to obey your commands is to keep him safe. If you're outside and he starts to chase a bird, a trained dog will stay and come at your command. The untrained Boston will keep running and can hurt himself, lose his way home, or worse.

- ✔ **Manners:** You also want to train your Boston so you can take him on outings. A well-behaved Boston will sit and lay down at your side without barking, nipping, or trying to run away.

- ✔ **Harmony:** A well-behaved dog will be a pleasure to be around. If he starts to act rambunctious, he'll settle when told, or he'll lie down in his bed when the family wants to enjoy a movie.

Though more and more people think of their dogs as their "children," it's important to remember that dogs are dogs, and they need to be treated as such. Treating your pet like a miniature human only confuses him. He wants to be part of the pack, not your daughter's younger brother.

Your Boston wants nothing more than to find his place in the pack. If you don't assert yourself as leader, he'll assume that role — which is not what you want. You are the pack leader, and your job is to communicate clearly and firmly what you want him to do through humane training techniques, such as positive reinforcement.

Obedience classes can help you master these training skills and show your dog that you are the leader of the household. The end result will be a happy dog and a happy owner.

The right ages to learn new lessons

Though the old adage "You can't teach an old dog new tricks" may be true in some cases, dogs of any age can learn how to obey basic commands. Puppies pick up commands much more quickly than adult dogs, but both puppies and adults benefit from organized classes that instruct the dog and the owner.

Puppy kindergarten

The place to start with a puppy is puppy kindergarten. Intended to be an opportunity for your puppy to socialize with other dogs and humans, this course introduces you and your Boston to behavior basics, such as having the dog settle on command and look to you for guidance. It also teaches you how to be pack leader by asserting your dominance in a humane, loving way.

You can enroll your Boston in puppy kindergarten when he's between 10 and 12 weeks old. In most cases, your Boston will have to complete at least two rounds of vaccinations to participate.

Basic training courses

After your Boston graduates from kindergarten, you can take his training a step further by participating in basic and intermediate obedience training. You can also enroll your adult dog in basic and intermediate obedience training.

Your Boston will learn more specific commands, like Sit, Stay, Leave It, Take It, Come, and Heel. You'll get advice on how to handle problem behaviors, such as digging, barking, and chewing. These courses are for dogs who are 4 months of age or older.

You can also hire a private trainer to come to your home. Normally reserved for dogs with severe behavior problems, private training is done one on one to fit you and your Boston's needs.

Advanced obedience challenges

For Bostons and their owners who excel at obedience training, kennel clubs like the American Kennel Club (AKC) offer obedience competitions that require your Boston to perform specific exercises that illustrate how well he obeys his handler's commands. You can also enroll him in the Canine Good Citizen program, which awards certification for passing a ten-step test. Turn to Chapter 12 for more information about these advanced courses.

Finding the right trainer

Taking your Boston to a puppy kindergarten or dog obedience class should be a fun and educational experience for both of you. It gives your pet a chance to socialize with other dogs and learn how to behave. You can usually find trainers who run these classes through your veterinarian's office, through your local pet supply store, online, or in the phone book.

Before you settle on one trainer, however, you'll want to visit her class to observe her in action and make sure you're comfortable with the training methods. Here are some things you should look for when you're choosing a trainer and class for your Boston:

✔ **An interesting, enjoyable atmosphere:** The participants should be enjoying themselves and having a successful learning experience. The instructor should be approachable and encouraging, showing courtesy to the humans and the dogs.

✔ **Informative lessons:** A skilled instructor should explain the day's lesson and provide clear instructions through written handouts or demonstrations, give the students plenty of class time to practice the day's lesson, and assist the students individually with proper techniques.

✔ **Proper training methods:** You should be comfortable with the instructor's training tools and methods. They should always be humane and not harmful to your dog or you. Hitting, kicking, electronic devices, or any other training device that causes harm should not be used.

✔ **Ongoing education:** The trainer should be well-informed about new innovations in dog training and behavior tools and techniques. Ask if the trainer is a member of any educational organizations or associations.

✔ **Vaccination requirements:** Vaccinations should be required before any puppy or dog attends the trainer's class. It protects you and your dog's health.

✔ **Positive references:** Chat with some current clients, if possible, after the class. Find out if they're learning from the instructor and how their dogs are progressing.

✔ **Satisfaction guarantee:** Ask the trainer if she offers some kind of client satisfaction guarantee with the services. Because of variables in dog breeding and temperament, and owner commitment and experience, a trainer cannot and should not guarantee the results of her training, but she should ensure some type of client satisfaction.

Establishing a Commanding Presence

Many different training theories and practices exist today. Trainers use different approaches to teach dogs how to behave. Some use a balanced method that incorporates positive reinforcement and correction. Others use a behavior-driven approach. Successful and humane methods have positive reinforcement in common.

Positive reinforcement rewards good behavior with treats, praise, and lots of love. Timing is critical when using this approach. For example, if you're teaching your dog the basic Sit command, you reward him immediately with a treat when he sits correctly. If he doesn't sit correctly, you *don't* say, "Bad dog," and smack him with a newspaper. Instead, you correct the behavior, gently showing him how to sit correctly, and then ask him to sit again. When he does sit, you reward him with a treat and lots of praise.

You can start boning up on behavior training before your Boston comes home. Educate yourself by reading books dedicated to positive training and dog behavior (check out *Dog Training For Dummies,* 2nd Edition, by Jack and Wendy Volhard [Wiley]). Or if you're a more visual learner, you can choose from all sorts of DVDs and videos to help you with step-by-step training.

When you have your dog at home, you can prepare for puppy kindergarten by familiarizing yourself and your Boston with the elementary commands discussed in this section.

Getting started

Before you begin your training session, gather some treats, such as small chunks of dehydrated meat or cheese. Attach your Boston's collar or harness to a 4-foot leash and lead him to an area where you'll have plenty of room to work. Plan to dedicate about 20 minutes a day to these training sessions, but practice the commands constantly in your day-to-day activities, and encourage your family members to do the same.

Begin by teaching your Boston to respond to his name.

1. **Standing in front of him, say his name in a fun, upbeat voice.**

2. **When he looks at you, reward him with lots of praise, toys, and a small piece of cheese or meat.**

   If he becomes distracted by a butterfly or a child, repeat his name and use a gentle nudge with your hand to remind him to look at you. His eyes should be on you whenever you say his name.

Practice the name game with your Boston for a few days before you begin training, and before long, when your Boston hears his name, he'll look at you and wait for something to happen.

Settle

The Settle command (see Figure 11-1) shows your Boston that you are the alpha dog. It teaches him that when you say, "Pete, settle," he should calm down and submit to you.

Figure 11-1: Commanding your Boston to settle lets him know that you are the alpha dog in the pack.

Here's an easy way to teach your Boston to settle:

1. **Sit in a chair or on the floor, and flip your dog over in your lap so his belly is up, putting him in a submissive position.**

2. **Calmly say, "Pete, settle."**

3. **When he relaxes in your arms, say, "Good boy to settle," and give him a treat.**

If your dog refuses to settle, use a more direct voice while gently touching his throat area, similar to the behavior a mama dog would do to a misbehaving puppy. Because the throat is a dog's most vulnerable area, he'll instinctively respond.

 This command is very useful when your Boston decides to tear around the house or uncontrollably misbehave. Simply pick up your dog and issue the command. When he calms down, reward him with praise and set him free again.

Sit

The Sit command (see Figure 11-2) teaches your dog to hold still in a sitting position. A very important lesson in self-control, this command is likely the first one your Boston will learn, and it's the cornerstone of many to come.

Figure 11-2: The Sit command requires your dog to hold in a seated position. Most other commands begin with your Boston in the sit posture.

The easiest way to teach this command is to use a treat as a lure — especially because Bostons are motivated by food! Follow these steps:

1. **Stand in front of your dog. Bend down and hold a treat over his nose.**

2. **Say in a firm voice, "Pete, sit." As you say those words, move the treat up over his head toward his tail.**

   The dog will follow the treat with his eyes and head, which will cause his rear to lower to a seated position.

   If he doesn't sit, show him what you want by gently pushing his rump down and saying, "Pete, sit."

3. **Praise him when he does as he's asked (whether on his own or with a little help from you), saying "Good dog," and reward him immediately with a treat.**

   Do this repeatedly until your Boston understands that obeying brings a reward — your praise!

Down

The Down command teaches your Boston to lie down and remain in place. You can use this command when you want your Boston to lie down on his bed and play with a toy or to stay away from the table when you and your family are eating.

1. **Begin by telling your dog to sit.**

2. **Holding a treat in front of his nose, say, "Pete, down," and move the treat down to the floor in front of his paws.**

   As his nose follows the treat, he will lie down.

3. **Praise him and give him the treat.**

   Repeat this process until he's got Down down.

Stay

The Stay command (see Figure 11-3), used with both the Sit and the Down commands, trains your Boston to stay in place until you release him. The Sit-Stay command is for shorter periods of time; the Down-Stay command is for longer periods. Here's how to teach your Boston the Stay command:

Figure 11-3: The Stay command trains your Boston to remain in place until you release him.

1. **Start by facing your dog and telling him to sit.**

2. **Hold an open palm facing his nose, and say, "Pete, stay."**

3. **Slowly take one step backward, and stay there.**

4. **If your Boston stays in place, go back to him after a few seconds and reward him with treats and praise.**

If your Boston fidgets and comes toward you, enlist the help of a friend or relative. Have her hold your Boston's leash gently but firmly after you give the command. Repeat the process until your Boston is trained and stays in place for longer periods of time. Be sure to heap plenty of praise on him through these lessons.

5. **Gradually increase the time your Boston must stay put and your distance from him as your Boston gets the hang of this command.**

Come

Teach the Come command after the Stay command — it's one of the most important commands to master. Your Boston should learn to come to you immediately the first time you call him. Learning to obey this command will keep your dog out of danger.

Luckily, this command is easy to teach. Here's how:

1. **Start with your Boston on a fairly short leash. Ask him to sit and stay.**

2. **Using a treat as a lure, say, "Pete, come," and walk backward.**

   This will cause your dog to follow you.

3. **Reward and praise him when he reaches you.**

Continue doing this with a longer and longer leash, even one up to 20 feet long. Before long, your dog will run right to you every time you call him to come, which is exactly what you want.

Leave It and Take It

The Leave It and Take It commands (see Figure 11-4) teach your Boston that you're the boss. You tell him what to play with and what to leave alone. This exercise is particularly useful if he decides to chew your favorite shoes. To teach this command:

a   b

Figure 11-4: Leave It (a) and Take It (b) are commands that show your Boston that you're in charge.

1. **Tell your dog to sit and stay.**

2. **Put a treat in your hand and show it to him, saying, "Pete, leave it." Make him wait for a few seconds.**

3. **Say, "OK, take it," letting your dog have the treat.**

When he has mastered Leave It and Take It with you holding the treats, try the same exercise, but this time place the treat on the ground. Challenge him even more by using a toy instead of a treat.

Heel

Teaching your dog to *heel* (walk nicely by your side; see Figure 11-5) will make walking on a leash a fun and enjoyable experience for both of you.

Figure 11-5: A Boston who can heel is a pleasure to walk with.

Here's how to teach your dog the Heel command:

1. **Connect the leash to your Boston's collar or harness. Put your right hand through the loop and hold the leash with your left hand.**

2. **Bend down and show the dog the treats with your right hand.**

3. **Move the treat slowly in front of him as if you're leading him by the nose, backing up.**

4. **Continue walking backward, all the while holding the treat where your dog can see it. As he follows you, praise and reward him.**

5. **When your dog follows you nicely, turn so that you and your dog are walking side by side, with your dog on your left side.**

Dogs walk on the left side in shows and other competitions.

Correcting Behavior Gone Bad

Part of being a well-mannered and obedient dog includes following the rules of the household, set down by you. You are your dog's pack leader, so it's up to you to teach your Boston the correct way to act in the house and with other people. Occasionally, though, problems can occur.

Some of the behaviors that we perceive as "problems" are natural to dogs. For example, Bostons are terriers, and terriers love to dig. Dogs communicate by barking. When their baby teeth fall out, they want to chew to relieve the discomfort. These are all normal dog behaviors. But when temporary behaviors become habits, or when they're done inappropriately, the action needs to be corrected.

In the previous section, you discovered how to use positive reinforcement to teach your Boston basic commands, such as Sit and Stay. In correction training, you use positive reinforcement, but you also correct your dog when he does something he shouldn't. You'll need to correct the bad behavior and reinforce the good behavior. You can do this in several ways, depending on the particular action that you're trying to correct.

Correction should never include physical punishment. Harming your Boston in any way is inhumane, and it can create an animal that fears people. Correction, instead, involves getting your Boston's attention and stopping the behavior at that moment.

One tool that you'll use is your voice. The tone of your voice communicates emotion or feeling to your dog. An upbeat higher-pitched tone communicates happiness or excitement. A lower-pitched guttural tone communicates anger or sternness. Your Boston will respond to these sounds as he would to his mother or pack leader. When you're praising your dog for obeying the Sit command, for example, you use an upbeat happy tone. Conversely, when you're correcting your dog for barking inappropriately, you use the guttural warning tone. You're not speaking more loudly to the dog, you're using different tones. This means even a soft-spoken person can correct his dog.

Another tool you'll need to master is consistency. When everyone who comes into contact with your Boston requires the same behavior from him, he won't get confused.

Before you begin corrective training, however, check with your veterinarian. Some bad behavior, such as chronic house-soiling or chewing, can be caused by medical conditions. Other troublesome behaviors can be exacerbated by your Boston's diet or lack of exercise. Get a clean bill of health, and then begin training.

Barking

Dogs bark to communicate. From protecting their homes from strangers to trying to get your attention, barking is a natural dog behavior. Guarding the home can be a positive reason to bark, and it's likely that your Boston will vocalize only when he needs to.

Before you begin corrective training, you'll want to determine why your dog is barking:

- ✔ **Do you pick him up every time he barks?** Then your Boston has trained you! If he barks, he'll get your attention.

- ✔ **Does he bark when someone comes to the door?** If so, he's protecting his territory.

- ✔ **Does he bark when nobody's home?** He may be suffering from separation anxiety.

After you've narrowed down some reasons why your dog barks, you can start correcting his behavior.

When your dog barks, don't yell at him. To your Boston, yelling sounds like barking, and he'll think that you're telling him something! Instead, ignore the barking. This may sound difficult, but if your dog realizes that he won't get any attention when he barks, he's more likely to stop the behavior. Reward him for not barking by saying, "Pete, good dog for being quiet."

Enlist a friend to come to your door and ring the doorbell. Wait until your Boston stops barking, say, "Good quiet," and reinforce the quiet behavior by praising and treating your dog. Your Boston will soon learn that staying quiet will earn him praise.

You also want to practice this nonbarking behavior in public. Grab a bag of treats and put your Boston on his leash. Walk to the park or someplace where he barks at people or other dogs. Use the "Pete, quiet" command, and if he obeys, lavish him with praise and treats.

Biting

Many horrifying dog attacks have been reported in the media. Although these reports tend to revolve around bigger dogs, even a small dog needs be trained to never bear his teeth, touch teeth to skin or clothing, or bite. This is one of the most important lessons you can teach your Boston.

Mouthing is normal behavior in puppies. Between 4 to 12 weeks old, your dog learns bite inhibition from his mother and littermates. He learns the amount of mouth pressure he can use without causing pain or harm by playing with his brothers and sisters, skirmishing, and testing how hard he can bite without causing a squeal. If he is removed from his littermates before learning this inhibition, it is up to you to teach him. Start your "no bite" training as soon as possible to ensure your dog doesn't develop his mouthing habit into something dangerous. Your Boston should know not to bite by the time he is 18 weeks old.

 When your puppy nips or bites you, or even just mouths you, say, "Pete, no bite." Stop playing with him and walk away. Do not allow your dog to nip at your heels or chase your feet. This will teach him that biting and nipping result in withdrawal of your attention.

If your Boston continues to use his mouth and bite, even after your consistent training, discuss the situation with your veterinarian. He may be able to recommend a professional trainer or animal behaviorist to help you deal with the problem.

Chewing

Chewing, like digging or barking, is something dogs do. When they're between 3 and 6 months old, puppies begin teething, and with teething comes chewing. They will chew everything and anything. As their baby teeth fall out and their adult teeth erupt, chewing relieves the discomfort. Puppies go through a second chewing phase when they're between 7 and 9 months old as a part of exploring their territory.

Unfortunately, puppies develop a fondness for chewing during these phases. They find out how much fun chewing can be! It relieves tension and anxiety, and it makes their sore gums feel better. For adult dogs, chewing massages their gums, removes *plaque* (clear buildup on the teeth), and occupies their time.

Chewing the wrong things, however, can be destructive and dangerous. Your Boston can swallow something poisonous, or something small can get lodged in his throat.

 Because chewing is just part of being a dog, your Boston should have his own things to chew from the very beginning. Instead of giving your dog old slippers or waiting until the improper behavior starts, give him his own size-appropriate chew toys, such as hard rubber balls stuffed with treats, nylon bones, or a rope tug toy. Limit his toys to a few; you don't want your Boston to think everything is for his chewing pleasure!

To help him resist temptation, put away items you don't want chewed, especially ones that can be harmful to your Boston. Those include children's toys with small removable pieces that can be ingested, household cleaners and personal hygiene items, insect and rodent traps, electrical cords, and hobby supplies.

Praise your Boston often when he chews the right objects. If your dog finds something else to gnaw on, take the object away and give the dog one of his toys, saying, "Pete, good toy."

Digging

Bostons are terriers, and terriers dig. They're bred to hunt vermin, and often those vermin live in holes in the ground. Some dogs dig to create a cool and cozy place to relax, and some dig to get out of a confined area. Instead of trying to teach your Boston not to dig, give him a specific place to dig. It will appease those digging tendencies and burn off some excess energy.

 Choose a section of your yard and designate it his digging area. Loosen the dirt, making sure it has no pesticides, pieces of glass, or other dangers hidden within. Introduce your Boston to the digging area by bringing him over and placing a toy or a treat on the dirt. You can even bury a biscuit or two after he gets used to the area.

When you see your Boston digging in the right area, praise him, saying, "Pete, good dog for digging here." If he digs in other places and you catch him in the act, move him to the right area and praise him when he digs there. Bury the other holes and, if you have to, lay some wire mesh over them to discourage further digging.

Jumping up

In Boston language, jumping up means, "I'm a happy dog," and "Pay attention to me!" Jumping up means your dog wants to be picked up and made the center of attention. Thankfully, Bostons aren't giant beasts who can knock houseguests over, but this behavior should still be prohibited.

It's imperative not to acknowledge your dog when he jumps up. Do not pet him or pick him up, as tempting as it may be! Instead, tell your Boston to sit. Only after he obeys should you pet him. Eventually he'll learn that to receive the attention he wants, he'll have to sit, not jump up.

Your Boston also needs to learn to sit for other people. Use the leash if you must, and when your guests come to the door and your Boston jumps up, say, "Pete, no jumping," followed by, "Pete, sit." When the dog sits for a period of time, allow your guests to praise him and give him the attention he wants.

This correction must be done consistently by your family and friends. Your Boston must learn that the only way he'll get attention is if he sits first. Praise the dog lavishly every time he does it correctly. Soon, your pup will sit before every greeting.

House-soiling

You've been taking your Boston puppy to his bathroom area regularly and letting him relieve himself after every meal, playtime, and nap. Your dog is becoming housetrained (see Chapter 9). But then he makes a mistake. What do you do?

The act of going to the bathroom isn't the mistake; going in the wrong place is the problem. So if you catch your pup in the act, say in a corrective tone, "Pete, no," and immediately take him to his bathroom area and let him finish his business there. Then praise your Boston and celebrate that he is going outside.

Clean the soiled area with white vinegar or an over-the-counter pet stain cleaner. Dogs tend to continue soiling in areas that smell like feces or urine, so removing all traces of the accident will prevent your dog from using that area again.

Don't correct the dog after he makes a mistake — he can't understand the connection between the correction and the mistake. Also, don't rub your dog's face in the mess. It's a needless punishment, and your dog will think that you're mad because he eliminated, not because he relieved himself somewhere he shouldn't. Instead, encourage and praise your Boston even more when he goes where he's supposed to.

You'll also want to keep a close eye on your Boston. If you know where your dog is, he can't make a mistake. A circling and sniffing dog means he's searching for a bathroom, so ask him in an upbeat happy voice, "Pete, do you have to go potty?" When he runs to the door, take him out and praise him after he goes.

You can also use your dog's kennel to teach him to hold his bladder. Because dogs won't soil the area where they sleep, keep your pup in his kennel (no more than two hours at a time) and let him out to use the bathroom. Flip to Chapter 9 for crate-training tips.

Calling in the Professional

Sometimes your Boston's bad habits are just too much for you to handle. You've tried positive reinforcement. You've tried corrective approaches. But your Boston still won't stop barking or jumping up on your houseguests.

When is it time to seek professional help?

- ✔ If your dog is exhibiting aggressive behavior, such as biting or showing teeth
- ✔ If his destructive chewing is out of control
- ✔ If the dog cannot be housetrained
- ✔ If he will not obey basic commands, even after puppy kindergarten and obedience training
- ✔ If, for any reason, you feel like you can't control your Boston, and his safety or the safety of others is at risk

The most effective way to get your misbehaving Boston back on track is to enlist the help of a professional dog trainer.

Professional dog trainers can be found through referrals from your veterinarian, breeder, or Boston Terrier club. You can also find them through organizations, such as the Association of Pet Dog Trainers (www.apdt.com) or the Certification Council for Professional Dog Trainers (www.ccpdt.org), that allow you to search for trainers by area.

To ensure that you and your dog will get the best possible training, select a trainer who has been certified by the CCPDT. To earn the certification, trainers must demonstrate their dog-training knowledge and experience, and they must continue to educate themselves about the latest in training techniques and equipment.

Here's how a trainer can help:

- ✔ **House calls:** A trainer can come to your home and evaluate your dog, watch your interactions, and develop a strategy to correct problem behavior. She can meet with you regularly and offer guidance and assistance when needed.

- ✔ **Training facility:** You can also take your dog to the trainer's facility. Your Boston may respond better to training when he's away from his territory.

- ✔ **Group dynamics:** A trainer will also encourage you to participate in group training exercises, which allows you and your pup to interact with other dogs and their owners.

- ✔ **Skilled experience:** Because a trainer has seen such a range of problem behaviors, she knows how to correct your dog's bad habits. She also knows when to enlist the help of a veterinarian or veterinary specialist who can prescribe helpful drugs.

Chapter 12

Taking Training to the Next Level

In This Chapter

▶ Training your Boston for sport and obedience

▶ Joining a flyball or freestyle club

▶ Becoming a therapy dog

▶ Introducing dog shows and conformation trials

*T*raining your Boston to sit and stay is one thing, but teaching your pup to strut in a show ring, deliver a smile to hospital-bound seniors, or weave in and out of challenging obstacles in an agility course takes her training to the next level.

Being as high-energy as any terrier, Bostons enjoy healthy doses of organized fun and frolic. Participating in one of the many events available to canines and their caretakers keeps her challenged and sharp — and her exuberance in check.

This chapter explores obedience, sport, and agility trials that will challenge you and your pup. You can also find out how your Boston can become a therapy dog and bring her gentlemanly joy to those who need it most. Finally, you discover the ins and outs of *conformation trials* (also known as dog shows). Chances are, your dog won't be able to compete in a conformation trial because competitors can't be spayed or neutered, but you can still gain lots of insight and information by attending the show as a spectator.

Training for Sport

Bostons love to compete in challenges that test their instincts and trained skills. The American Kennel Club offers all sorts of different activities for dogs of all breeds and groups, but the Boston qualifies for five: obedience, Canine Good Citizen, tracking, agility, and

AKC Rally. These competitions center on how well your dog performs based on her natural abilities and your (or your handler's) instruction.

For the well-behaved Boston: Canine Good Citizen program

Begun in 1989, the AKC's *Canine Good Citizen* (CGC) *program* is designed to recognize dogs who demonstrate excellent manners at home and in the community. Often held in conjunction with or after puppy kindergarten and basic obedience training (see Chapter 11), the CGC program tests a dog's ability to pass a series of obedience tests (listed below). Dogs who pass earn a certificate from the AKC and a dog tag inscribed with "Canine Good Citizen."

The CGC program forms the foundation for many other kennel club and service dog activities and programs, including obedience trials, agility, tracking, and serving as a therapy dog. As you and your dog work through the tests and training, you solidify your bond with your Boston. Plus, the satisfaction of achieving a goal like this will likely lead you to continue training your Boston for other sporting events.

Unregistered? No problem!

To participate in obedience, tracking, or agility trials, or to become a Canine Good Citizen, your Boston must be registered with the American Kennel Club. What if you want to compete, but your dog isn't registered?

Sometimes, people adopt purebred dogs who can't be registered with the AKC. The dogs may have unregistered parents, their papers may have been lost, or they may have been abandoned and adopted by new owners from an animal shelter. They're still purebred dogs, but they aren't eligible for registration.

In cases like these, the dog owner can apply for the Indefinite Listing Privilege program. It allows purebred dogs to participate in almost all AKC events, including agility, obedience, tracking, rally, and other group-specific trials. After she is enrolled in the ILP program, the dog is given an ILP number, which can be used in place of an AKC number on entry forms.

Conformation trials, however, are one event in which an unregistered dog can't participate. To compete in a dog show, the dog must be *intact* (not spayed or neutered); to enroll in the ILP program, the applicant must show proof from a veterinarian that the dog has been spayed or neutered.

For more information about the Indefinite Listing Privilege program, go to www.akc.org/reg/ilpex.cfm.

Any dog is eligible to participate in the CGC program, so even mixed breeds can earn their CGC certificate. All ages are welcome to join in the fun, too, though puppies who pass the test are encouraged to take the test again when they're adults.

To qualify to take the test, you must first sign the AKC's Responsible Dog Owners Pledge, which affirms that you agree to care for the dog's health needs, safety, exercise, training, and quality of life. It also affirms that you agree to be responsible to the community by cleaning up after your dog and never letting her infringe on the rights of others.

After you sign the pledge, you're ready to take the test. You'll need to outfit your dog with a well-fitting buckle or slip collar made of leather, fabric, or chain. The test facilitator will provide a 20-foot leash for the test.

To earn her CGC certificate, your Boston has to successfully demonstrate the following ten test items:

- ✔ **Accepting a friendly stranger:** Allows a friendly stranger to approach you and talk to you.

- ✔ **Sitting politely for petting:** Allows a friendly stranger to pet her while she's out with you.

- ✔ **Appearance and grooming:** Allows a stranger, such as a veterinarian or groomer, to examine and handle her. This test also demonstrates your dedication to your dog's care.

- ✔ **Out for a walk:** Showing that you are in control, she walks attentively beside you while you hold a loose leash and make right, left, and about turns.

- ✔ **Walking through a crowd:** Demonstrates her ability to walk through a crowd of pedestrians.

- ✔ **Staying in place:** Shows that she obeys your Sit and Stay commands.

- ✔ **Coming when called:** Shows that she obeys your Come command.

- ✔ **Reacting to another dog:** Demonstrates that she behaves appropriately around other dogs.

- ✔ **Reaction to distraction:** Shows that she reacts confidently to distracting situations.

- ✔ **Supervised separation:** Demonstrates that she can be left alone with another person and maintain good manners.

You can find CGC training and testing programs through your kennel club, trainer, or some pet specialty stores.

Do as I say: Obedience trials

If your Boston excelled in her puppy kindergarten class, basic obedience training course, and Canine Good Citizen test, consider enrolling her in obedience competitions. *Obedience trials,* which were acknowledged by the AKC around 1935, require your Boston to perform specific exercises that show how well she obeys your commands.

AKC-registered dogs who are at least 6 months old can participate. To enter an obedience trial, you must submit an official AKC entry form to the trial secretary. After the entry period closes, you'll receive a judging schedule for each class.

Obedience trials are broken into two categories:

- ✔ **All-breed obedience trials**, the most common trials, are open to all breeds and varieties recognized by the AKC.

- ✔ **Specialty trials** are limited to specific breeds or varieties of one breed.

Both types of trials have three graduating levels of competition: novice, open, and utility. Each level requires the dogs to complete a series of exercises, which become more challenging as they progress. By level, the exercises include:

- ✔ **Novice:** For dogs new to obedience trials, the exercises include heel on leash and figure eight, heel free, stand for examination, recall, long sit (1 minute), and long down (3 minutes).

- ✔ **Open:** This level is comprised of more-complicated exercises that prove the dog can obey verbal and signal commands, including heel free and figure eight, drop on recall, retrieve on flat, retrieve over high jump, broad jump, long sit (3 minutes), and long down (5 minutes).

- ✔ **Utility:** The highest level of competition, these exercises demonstrate obedience at its best, including signal exercise, scent discrimination, directed retrieve, moving stand and examination, and directed jumping.

In each level, the dog earns points when she successfully completes an exercise. She must earn at least half of the possible points in each exercise, earning a total score of at least 170 out of a possible 200. Each time your dog achieves this goal, she earns one leg toward her title in that particular level. After completing three legs in one level, your dog earns an obedience title.

Your Boston can progress through six different obedience titles:

✔ **Companion Dog (CD):** Earned when your dog has received three qualifying scores, or legs, in the Novice class.

✔ **Companion Dog Excellent (CDX):** Earned when your dog has earned three qualifying scores in the Open class.

✔ **Utility Dog (UD):** Earned when your dog has earned three qualifying scores in the Utility class.

✔ **Utility Dog Excellent (UDX):** Earned when dogs with UD titles earn qualifying scores at ten trials in Open B and Utility B.

✔ **Obedience Trial Champion (OTCH):** Earned when dogs with UD titles win 100 points and a first place in Utility B and Open B, plus a third first-place win in either class.

✔ **National Obedience Champion (NOC):** Awarded annually by the AKC to a dog who wins the AKC National Obedience Invitational.

As with the other training competitions, you can learn more through your local Boston Terrier or kennel club.

Follow that scent: Tracking

Tracking, a type of obedience trial, tests the dog's ability to recognize and trace a human's scent, much like dogs do during search-and-rescue operations. Just because your Boston has a short snout doesn't mean she can't track a scent!

The sport, originally called Obedience Test Field Trials, began in 1936 as part of the Obedience Trial's Utility class. Since then, the sport's tests have been refined to include more specific tracking exercises and adjusted to account for the ever-diminishing fields and open spaces.

Tracking tests are typically held in an open field, with the exception of the Variable Surface Tracking exercise that requires dogs to follow a scent through urban and wilderness environments.

Today, three tracking titles are available:

✔ **Tracking Dog (TD):** Dogs earn their TD title by following a 440- to 500-yard track with three to five changes in direction. The track is aged 30 minutes to two hours before the dog begins scenting. The goal is to locate the object that the track-layer left behind.

✔ **Tracking Dog Excellent (TDX):** Upon earning their TD title, dogs earn their TDX title by following a longer (800 to 1,000 yards), older (three to five hours old) track that has five to seven directional changes and human cross tracks.

✔ **Variable Surface Tracking (VST):** A dog who earns her VST title has proved that she can follow a three- to five-hour-old track through an urban or wilderness setting.

✔ **Champion Tracker (CT):** The dog who earns TD, TDX, and VST titles bears the CT title.

Your kennel club can provide more information about training for and participating in these challenging competitions.

Boston be nimble, Boston be quick: Agility trials

What better way for a Boston to expend some energy than to participate in *agility trials!* This fast-growing canine sport challenges your dog's nimble feet as she runs through a series of timed obstacle courses. Your dog responds to your cues as she races through jumps, tunnels, weave poles, and other obstacles.

The sport began in England in 1978. It made its official appearance in the United States when the AKC held its first agility trial in 1994.

Part of the lure of this fun sport is that dogs of all sizes can compete. The judges adjust the obstacles' heights and vary the time allowance depending on the breed. People of all ages can compete, too, making it a sport for just about any fancier.

Rally together

Are you ready for some fun?

If you and your Boston think you want to try your hand — or paw — at agility or obedience trials but you're not sure if you're ready yet, AKC Rally is for you.

Providing a link between the Canine Good Citizen program and agility or obedience trials, *rally* challenges you and your dog to race through a series of obstacles and exercises.

Rally allows you and your Boston to move at your own pace through the course, which typically includes 10 to 20 stations with signs that tell you what to do. Scoring is not as rigorous as in traditional obedience, but communication and teamwork between you and your dog are highly encouraged.

To be eligible to participate in rally, your Boston needs to be registered with the AKC and at least 6 months old. For more information, visit the AKC Web site (www.akc.org) or talk to your Boston club representative.

You and your Boston can compete in two agility classes:

- ✔ **Standard Class:** The Standard class features *contact objects,* such as an A-frame and a seesaw. Each obstacle has an area painted on the object, and the dog must place at least one paw in the area to complete the obstacle.

- ✔ **Jumpers with Weaves:** The Jumpers with Weaves class has only jumps, tunnels, and weave poles.

Both the Standard and Jumpers with Weaves classes have four increasing levels of difficulty: novice, open, excellent, and master. After a dog achieves Standard Master and Jumper Master, she can compete for the Master Agility Championship title.

Practicing for this event can be a challenge because the obstacles take up considerable space. But clubs across the country conduct practice matches, so if this competition interests you, talk to your local kennel club for more information.

Becoming a Therapy Dog

For those Bostons (and their owners) who enjoy giving back to their community, becoming a therapy dog is an opportunity to bring joy to hospital- or nursing home–bound children and seniors.

Well-behaved Bostons who have their Canine Good Citizen certificate are on their way to becoming therapy dogs. Different from *service dogs* that assist blind or otherwise disabled owners, some *therapy dogs* make informal visits to people in nursing homes and hospitals, while others participate in more structured sessions with people who are receiving physical therapy or coordination lessons.

Organizations such as Therapy Dogs International and the Delta Society evaluate potential therapy dogs and train those who show promise. Therapy dogs must

- ✔ Display sound temperament

- ✔ Be patient, confident, and at ease in a variety of situations, from busy hospital wards to sedate retirement homes

- ✔ Thrive on human contact, because one of their main purposes is to allow people to pet and dote on them

The organizations have different requirements for screening, testing, and certifying dogs to be therapy dogs. If you and your Boston are interested in pursuing this altruistic endeavor, talk to representatives from your local kennel club for details.

Making a difference

As Jasmine, a Boston Terrier therapy dog from New Jersey, approached the myriad firefighters, counselors, Red Cross volunteers, and other relief workers after the World Trade Center attacks on September 11, 2001, she knew what she needed to do: offer them comfort, compassion, and a furry shoulder to cry on.

Her owner, Nicole Hanson, recalls the therapy dogs' impact: "Workers, military personnel, Red Cross and Salvation Army volunteers, American Airlines staff, and military chaplains alike seemed to 'recharge' with the dogs."

Bacon, another Boston Terrier therapy dog from Florida, provided the same loving support to Hurricane Katrina survivors in New Orleans in 2005. While children, still in shock from the traumatic events, mourned the loss of their homes and loved ones, Bacon brought a smile to their faces as they poured out their hearts to the canine counselor.

"The way the children were responding to the dogs was so positive. Talking to and touching the dogs was a tremendous help," says Bacon's owner, Janet Morgan. "Bacon was just delighted with all the children."

Jasmine and Bacon approached these disasters with a wag of their short little tails, eager to help in any way possible. If your Boston shows a spark of compassion, behaves well with strangers, and possesses a true gentleman's demeanor, consider applying for a therapy dog program in your area.

Anecdotal and clinical evidence has shown that when people hold or pet an animal, their blood pressure drops, and their stress decreases. Pets can also pull people out of depression. Your Boston brings you joy at home, so why not share that joy with others in need?

Having Some Organized Fun

Outside the AKC or other kennel club circuit, you can engage your dog in organized and spontaneous sporting events. You can bring your Boston along to just about any activity you can imagine. Consider playing a fun game of Frisbee or fetch in the local dog park, hiking some scenic trails, or trolling the beach for shells with your best canine companion. It doesn't get much better!

Two organized sports that you and your Boston may find fun and challenging are flyball, a timed relay race, and freestyle, a dance competition.

Why not try flyball?

Flyball is a timed relay race that pits two teams of four dogs against each other. In this game, at the signal, the first dog must run over a series of hurdles to a box of tennis balls and jump on a lever to send a ball flying. The dog then catches the ball and runs it to her owner. Then the next dog goes. This fun activity can burn a lot of Boston energy!

Your dog can earn ten titles in this fast-action sport, including Flyball Dog (FD), Flyball Dog Excellent (FDX), Flyball Dog Champion (FDCh), Flyball Master (FM), Flyball Master Excellent (FMX), Flyball Master Champion (FMCh), ONYX (named after the first dog to reach 20,000 points), and Flyball Grand Champion (FGDCh-30).

A group of trainers in Southern California invented Flyball in the late 1960s and 1970s. By the 1980s, the sport enjoyed huge popularity, thanks in part to a spot on *The Tonight Show Starring Johnny Carson*. The first flyball organization, the North American Flyball Association (NAFA), formed in 1984 to design uniform competition rules and tout the sport as one that could be enjoyed by virtually every dog.

The sport currently enjoys international representation, with clubs in the United States, South Africa, Australia, and the United Kingdom.

If your Boston loves to catch tennis balls, seek out a flyball club in your area. You can find a list of clubs on the NAFA Web site (www.flyball.org) or on the United Flyball League International Web site (www.u-fli.com).

Dancing with the dogs: Canine freestyle

Canine freestyle is a human-dog choreographed dance that incorporates obedience commands like Sit and Stay. The object of the sport is for you and your dog to display innovative and original dance using movements to showcase teamwork, creativity, costumes, and style while interpreting the theme of the music.

Begun in the late 1980s in Canada, freestyle made its way to the United States in the 1990s, appearing at various demonstrations across the country. By the mid '90s, competitive teams developed, and major sponsors joined in the fun. Two approaches to the sport — and two organizations — began to diverge: the Canine Freestyle Federation (CFF), which emphasized the dogs and their movement; and the Musical Canine Sports International (MCSI), which emphasized the handler's costuming and movement.

Today, several organizations regulate competitive canine freestyle, including the CFF, MCSI, World Canine Freestyle Organization, and Musical Dog Sport Association. Competitions differ from group to group, but generally, titles are awarded to high scores in technical merit and artistic impression.

Attending a Conformation Trial

If you're like most Boston owners, you probably think that your dog looks perfect — or very close to perfect! Her markings make her unique, her temperament is top-notch, and her conformation is in a class by itself.

Conformation trials, or dog shows, give you the opportunity to see and interact firsthand with other beautiful purebred dogs. Because you've most likely had your Boston spayed (or neutered), she is ineligible to compete against the other four-legged beauties. But you can attend dog shows to appreciate the sport and learn more about the various breeds.

One of the most well-known conformation dog shows, the Westminster Kennel Club Dog Show, held annually at Madison Square Garden in New York, has been showcasing the best of the best since 1877. The show, which was initiated by a group of hunters who frequently met at the Westminster Hotel in Manhattan, originated as a sport for hunting dogs. The men formed the Westminster Kennel Club, one of the first kennel clubs in the United States with the purpose of showing dogs.

Bostons who compete in dog shows are judged based on how well they meet the *breed standard,* which is the ideal physical representation of the breed as described by the American Kennel Club-sanctioned Boston Terrier Club of America. You can read more about the Boston breed standard in Chapter 2.

Conformation dog shows are organized three ways:

✔ **All-breed shows:** The type most often televised, these shows offer competitions for more than 150 breeds and varieties of dogs recognized by one of the major dog registries, such as the AKC.

✔ **Specialty shows:** These shows, often hosted by breed clubs, highlight one specific breed or varieties of a breed. For example, Bostons can complete in the Boston Terrier Club of America Specialty.

✔ **Group shows:** These shows are limited to dogs within a particular group, such as the Non-sporting, Hound, or Herding Group. Bostons fall within the Non-sporting Group, so they would compete with the Bichon Frise, Lhasa Apso, and Poodle.

The judges who critique the dogs must be experts in the breeds in which they are judging. During conformation, judges

✔ Examine the dogs from head to toe

✔ Feel their bones, muscles, and coat texture

✔ Examine the dog's teeth, eyes, and ears

✔ View each dog's profile for overall balance

✔ Watch the dogs strut their stuff to check their gait

After the judges have evaluated the dogs, they present awards to the best examples of the breed based on the breed standard. The dogs don't don a tiara and cape, but they do take home points toward their titles and colorful ribbons to decorate their walls.

Being an informed spectator

Usually publicized in the local media and hosted by an area all-breed or breed-specific club, dog shows can introduce you to the world of showing, give you an opportunity to meet with other purebred-dog owners, and allow you to talk to the club's representatives about how you can join.

As a spectator, make the most of attending a show by remembering these tips:

✔ **Go to learn.** Observe the participants' etiquette. Marvel at the different dog varieties. Talk to as many breeders and handlers as possible. Speak with other spectators and swap fun stories about your Boston. Take the opportunity to learn as much as you can about the dog fancy.

✔ **Visit the grooming area.** For grooming suggestions, talk to the professional groomers about how to keep your Boston looking her best.

✔ **Do not touch a dog before speaking with her owner or handler first.** No matter how tempting it may be to wish a pup good luck and stroke her coat, ask for permission. You wouldn't want to muss a dog's coat right before she hits the show floor!

- **Wear comfortable clothing and shoes.** You'll be doing a lot of walking and standing while watching the various matches, and seating may be limited, depending on the venue.

- **If you take your child to the show, keep a constant eye on him.** Do not allow him to grab a dog's tail, reach his hand into a kennel, or approach a dog on her way to the show floor. Instruct him to respect the dogs and their handlers at all times.

- **Chat with vendors.** Dog shows typically host a number of vendors who sell all sorts of merchandise, from Boston-specific gifts, food, and treats to toys, beds, and dog houses. You'll also find representatives from area kennel clubs and sporting clubs. Talk to them about how to get involved.

After attending several dog shows, you'll want to join your local Boston Terrier club (if you haven't already!). Not only is the group an excellent resource for health and care information, but it also provides a wealth of information about other competitions in which you and your spayed Boston can participate.

Understanding the points

In dog shows, a competitor's goal is to rack up points toward his dog's AKC championship or Champion of Record title. After the dog earns her Champion of Record title, she can compete for the Best of Breed title, in the group competition and, ultimately, for the Best in Show award.

To earn a Champion of Record title, a dog must earn 15 points, including two majors (wins of 3, 4, or 5 points) awarded by at least three different judges. The number of points awarded in any match depends on the number of dogs in the competition. The maximum number that can be earned is 5; the minimum is 1.

Here's how a dog show works:

Dogs earning points toward their championships are first separated by breed, and then by gender. For example, Bostons are separated from the other breeds and then divided into male and female groups. The males and females are broken down further into six classes:

- **Puppy:** Dogs between 6 and 12 months old who are not yet champions

- **12 to 18 months:** Dogs between 12 and 18 months old who are not yet champions

✔ **Novice:** Dogs 6 months of age and older who have not won the Novice, Bred by Exhibitor, American Bred, or Open class, and have not earned points toward their championship

✔ **Bred by Exhibitor:** Dogs who are shown by their owner and breeder who are not yet champions

✔ **American Bred:** Dogs who are mated and born in the United States who are not yet champions

✔ **Open:** For any dog at least 6 months old

The first-place winners of the classes then compete against each other to determine which is the best of the winning dogs. The judges award championship points (from 1 to 5, depending on the number of dogs in the competition) to the best male (Winners Dog) and the best female (Winners Bitch).

The Winners Dog and the Winners Bitch then compete with the dogs who have already earned their Champion of Record title. This competition is called *Best of the Breed Competition.*

Typically, three awards are during the Best of Breed Competition:

✔ **Best of Breed:** The dog deemed best in its breed category

✔ **Best of Winners:** The dog judged better between the Winners Dog and the Winners Bitch

✔ **Best of Opposite Sex:** The best dog who is the opposite sex of the Best of Breed

Only the Best of Breed advances to compete in the Group competitions. Group winners then compete against each other for the ultimate prize: Best in Show.

Competition for children and dogs

Junior Showmanship classes, which are open to children ages 9 to 18 years old, offer the opportunity for budding fanciers to develop their handling skills, learn about good sportsmanship, and learn about dogs and dog shows.

Leonard Brumby Sr. and a group of dog handlers conceived Children's Handling in the late 1920s. Today the competition is known as Junior Showmanship, and it allows children to be judged on how well they present their dogs.

Dressing the part

"Coordinating outfits" take on a whole new meaning when it comes to dog shows.

At point shows, the dog handlers — whether it's the dog owner or someone he hires — typically dress to enhance the dog's appearance. They choose solid colors, like black, blue, or brown, which draw attention to the dog's coat.

Careful not to wear something that draws attention away from the dog's beauty, they often don modest outfits, such as a shirt, tie, and sports coat for the men and a dress or two-piece suit for the women. The outfits always have plenty of pockets for treats and brushes, and they are cut for free movement — which is essential when running in the ring or kneeling on the floor.

The competitions include handling and performance events, similar to those offered for adults. Judges evaluate the children's handling methods, not the animals, though the dogs do need to be registered with the AKC.

As with adult shows, several classes and subclasses divide the competitors. The children are broken into Novice and Open classes. Novice classes, which offer the youngsters an opportunity to gain experience in the trials, are for those who have not yet won three first-place awards. Open classes are for those who have three or more first-place wins.

The classes break down further into age groups. Juniors are 9 years old but under 12, Intermediate competitors are children 12 years old but under 15, and Seniors are children 15 years old but under 18.

If your child shows interest in Junior Showmanship, encourage it! Many junior handlers continue with their love of dogs to become professional handlers, veterinarians, breeders, and trainers.

Take your child to the Junior Showmanship classes at a regional dog show and talk with him about the different levels of competition. Check with your Boston Terrier club about handling classes designed especially for young people.

Chapter 13

Traveling with (Or without) Your Boston

In This Chapter

▶ Packing necessary supplies for the journey

▶ Keeping your dog safe while traveling

▶ Choosing a long- or short-term boarding facility

▶ Knowing what to look for in a pet sitter

*W*ith his relatively small size and gentlemanly demeanor, your Boston Terrier makes an ideal travel companion. He'll happily sit shotgun (safely restrained by a seat belt, of course!) as you motor to the store. He'll be your companion during spontaneous weekend getaways. He'll even fly the skies with you, too, content in his travel carrier.

When it comes to traveling with your Boston, you can liken it to traveling with a 3-year-old child: Pack a bag of essentials, bring plenty of distractions, and prepare for just about anything! Planning ahead before any trip — be it a 10-minute car ride or a cross-country vacation — will make the adventure enjoyable for everyone.

Sometimes, though, you can't take your Boston along, so you may want to enlist the help of a dog sitter, doggy day care, or boarding facility. In this chapter, you find out what to bring on the trip, how to get your Boston comfortable with car rides, and what to do if you have to leave your Boston behind.

Preparing for the Journey

Before you hit the road with your Boston, you need to gather a few essentials to keep your dog safe and his needs fulfilled. They include identification, a travel carrier, and day or overnight bag.

Identification, please

Whether you're traveling a block to the pet store or cross-country to a relative's home, identification tags virtually guarantee that someone will return your Boston to you if he goes missing. With your name and home and cellphone numbers inscribed on that little disk, the person who finds your Boston has an immediate and direct line to you.

To ensure that your dog is returned to you, always keep an updated, legible ID tag on your Boston's collar. If you have multiple collars, purchase multiple ID tags and hang one on each collar. The tags are inexpensive and easy to obtain, and they can save you heartache — and expense — if your dog escapes while you're on the road.

 If you're traveling far from home and staying in a hotel or at a relative's house, purchase some inexpensive disposable tags and list the hotel or relative's phone number, as well as your cellphone number. It's good insurance, just in case.

A microchip is an excellent backup to an ID tag, especially if your Boston's collar slips off. A veterinarian or shelter employee can use a scanner to read the code that is unique to your pup's microchip. That code tells the vet which registry has your contact information. The vet or the person who found your dog can call the registry to get your information so she can reconnect you with your dog. (For more about microchips, see Chapter 5.)

 Keep in mind that it can take some time for the person who recovered your dog to find a veterinarian or shelter with a microchip scanner, contact the registry to get your phone number, and call you. And those hours and days when your Boston is missing can seem like a lifetime!

The right carrier for the trip

A carrier protects your Boston while he's traveling. Depending on your mode of transportation — be it car or airplane — you'll need a different carrier to keep him safe and secure.

By car

You may be tempted to let your Boston sit shotgun or even ride on your lap while you're driving, but doing so is extremely dangerous for you, your dog, and other drivers. An unrestrained dog in your car can be more distracting than using a cellphone or eating lunch while driving. Even if he's well-behaved, your Boston may see a dog walking down the street and lunge toward it, jumping in your lap, blocking your view, and potentially causing an accident.

The safest way to travel in a car is with your Boston secured in a crate, carrier, car seat, or seatbelt harness. Because of the public's growing concern about keeping their traveling pets safe, manufacturers have created a wide range of options to restrain dogs in the car. Most of them include seatbelt loops so you can buckle your Boston in. Your options include:

- ✔ **Crates:** Like the hard-sided plastic kennel that you used to housetrain your Boston, a crate keeps your dog safe and confined in case of an accident. With its solid sides, the crate prevents your dog from flying out a window or being crushed. Soft-sided crates often feature steel or aluminum frames that offer some protection, but their greatest asset is that you can fold them down for easy storage.

- ✔ **Travel carriers:** Made rigid with plastic frames, soft-sided carriers make traveling with your Boston relatively easy. They resemble gym bags with ventilated sides, but they are designed to carry your 20-pound pup safely on short journeys to the pet store, veterinarian, or Grandma's house. Some include built-in removable casters for easy wheeling and pockets for storing pickup bags and treats.

- ✔ **Car seats:** Framed with rigid plastic or metal and lined with fleece, faux sheepskin, or canvas, canine car seats keep your pup secure while allowing him to look out the window. Most resemble a miniature dog bed with upright sides that keep your pup both contained and comfortable on the road. If you're thinking about buying one of these, make sure that it has a seatbelt slot and a place to connect a harness or other restraint.

You may have seen dog beds and booster seats designed for use in cars. They look stylish and comfy for your Boston, but avoid them. Many don't restrain your dog in any way, and if you have to stop or turn your car quickly, your pup can be sent flying and possibly get hurt. Instead, invest in a quality travel carrier with a cushy liner or a dog car seat with harness attachment, and buckle him in.

✔ **Seatbelt harness:** Your Boston wears a harness around his torso (see Figure 13-1; check out Chapter 5 for more details about harnesses). You can restrain your Boston in the car by connecting the harness to a seat belt. Some harnesses come with a seatbelt latch built in.

Figure 13-1: Restraining your Boston in your car keeps him, you, and other drivers safe.

By airplane

Airline requirements stipulate what types of carriers you can use to safely transport your Boston. The requirements vary among airlines, so check with the one you're flying well before you get to the airport.

Generally, however, because your Boston will likely be traveling in the cargo area of the plane, you need a hard-plastic crate with absorbent bedding, and food and water dishes secured to the inside of the kennel door. Add your Boston's favorite toy, and he's ready to fly!

Pack your Boston's bags

Any responsible parent keeps a bag of her child's belongings ready to go. Likewise, as a pet parent, you should keep a bag of dog necessities handy when you travel with your Boston. You never know when you'll need a bowl for some water, the first-aid kit in case of a bee sting, or a treat for a well-behaved pup!

For short jaunts to the market, you don't need too many supplies: A leash, pickup bags, a bottle of water, a portable bowl, treats, and a favorite toy, all stashed in a handy tote bag, will do.

For longer journeys, however, you need a lot more. Pack the following items in your Boston's suitcase:

✔ Extra leash and collar with ID tags already attached

✔ Enough food to last for the journey

✔ Bottled water

✔ Treats

✔ Two portable bowls (one for water, one for food)

✔ Grooming supplies, including toothbrush and toothpaste, brush, shampoo, and nail clippers

✔ Extra crate pads

✔ Pickup bags

✔ Medications

✔ Portable first-aid kit

✔ Some favorite chew toys

✔ His favorite bedding

✔ A jacket or sweater if it will be cold

✔ Important veterinary files, including health and vaccination records

Hitting the Road

Before you and your Boston head out on a road trip, you must teach your puppy all about riding in the car. Most dogs are natural-born copilots; a few are more the homebody types. But whether he's an eager passenger or a nervous one, you can teach your Boston to be a well-behaved traveler. And I include some safety pointers so you can keep your pup safe on your journeys.

Introducing the car

Before you even think about taking your Boston on the road, you need to introduce him to the idea of riding in a car. That big metallic beast with the growling motor may intimidate your Boston puppy, and if he's not slowly familiarized with it, he can develop a fear that's hard to shake.

Teaching your Boston about traveling begins with his crate or carrier. If you're crate training him, he already knows that his crate is his den: It's his safe place where he can play with his toys, take a nap, and enjoy some "me" time. (Check out Chapter 9 for more details about crate training.) You can easily carry over that feeling of safety when you put him in his crate to travel in the car. He'll instinctually feel confident in his den, whether it's in your home or in the vehicle.

The first car "ride" should be a brief introduction to the vehicle. By following these steps, you can make your Boston a confident traveling companion:

1. **Place the crate in a secure place in your car, like the back seat, and buckle it in.**

   Make sure the spot has plenty of air circulation.

2. **Load the crate with toys, his blanket, and a crate pad (just in case) — things that will help him feel comfortable.**

3. **Put your Boston on his leash, and walk him to the car. Let him sniff the metallic beast, walk around it, and inspect it.**

   Use positive reinforcement to encourage him and build his confidence.

4. **When you're ready to leave, say "Let's go," and help him into his crate.**

5. **Turn the car on and watch his reaction.**

   If he settles down right away and seems ready for an adventure, take a drive around the block and praise him for a job well done. But if he whines and shakes, calm him down and call it a day. You don't want to overdo it and cause him to fear the car. Next time, however, take his training a step further.

6. **Have him sit in the car while the motor is running, and then back the car out of the garage or driveway and return.**

   As he becomes more comfortable with the car and its sounds and movements, continue to broaden his experience by driving around the block to a dog-friendly park or taking a short trip to Grandma's house.

In time, your Boston will associate driving with a positive experience, and he'll be ready to hit the open road without a backward glance!

Your Boston is an intelligent dog. If you just drive him to the veterinarian for checkups and shots, he'll connect the car with a negative experience. Take your Boston on pleasant trips as often as possible so he associates driving with fun. Excursions to dog parks, lakes, shopping centers, and friends' houses not only give your dog reasons to love to travel, but they also help to socialize him (read more about socializing your pup in Chapter 10).

Driving in style

With his adventurous spirit, there's no doubt that your Boston will love to accompany you everywhere. You'll go to the dog park together, out for coffee with friends, and to doggy play dates.

When you arrive at your destination, don't leave your dog unattended in a closed vehicle, no matter what the weather is. In as little as 15 minutes, the temperature in an automobile can rise to scorching levels, and your dog can suffer a heat stroke that can lead to brain damage or death. If you must leave your pup in the car, designate a responsible family member to stay with your Boston.

Regardless of where you go, your primary goal is to keep your dog safe and secure. Short trips are pretty easy to manage; long trips require a bit more organization.

Short trips

When your Boston feels comfortable riding in the car, you can take him on short car rides around town.

If you're visiting a friend's house or apartment, make sure before you leave that it's okay to bring your dog along. Most likely, your host will welcome your Boston with open arms! Grab your pup's day bag with his toys, water and water bowl, treats, pickup bags, and portable first-aid kit. If you'll be staying longer than a few hours, bring some food along, too. Load him in his carrier and be on your way.

Keeping your dog safe during these short rides is easy: Make sure that he wears his collar and leash inside the car and that he stays in his seatbelt harness or in the carrier while you're driving.

If you use a seatbelt harness and your dog has access to an open window, do not let him stick his head out. His large prominent eyes can be easily scratched or otherwise damaged by dust, rocks, sand, or salt pieces whizzing by.

If possible, don't let your dog ride in a seat with an airbag. The force with which the airbag deploys can injure your dog, just as it would injure a child.

Long trips

Long road trips with overnight stays take a little more planning. Besides grabbing your dog's suitcase and favorite bedding, you also need to check with your veterinarian, find dog-friendly hotels, and map out a course to your destination.

- ✔ **Vet check:** Before you leave, schedule an appointment with your veterinarian to be sure that your dog is healthy and ready for travel. Tell your vet where you're going, and ask him if your pooch will need additional vaccinations or preventive medication before you leave. If you live in a colder climate and you're driving to Florida during the winter, for example, you may need to apply some flea-and-tick repellant to your Boston.

- ✔ **Find dog-friendly lodging:** As you're planning your itinerary, you need to find hotels that accept dogs. Because of the rise in pet popularity, more hotels than ever welcome dogs, but they typically require an additional deposit to cover the cost of cleaning.

When you're at the hotel, treat it as if it were your home: Pick up messes your dog leaves behind, clean up any accidents, and don't let him bark. Keep him off the bed or bring a sheet to put down before he lays on the bed. Many dog-friendly hotels don't allow you to leave the dog unattended in the room, but you can put him in his crate if you go out to dinner or take a shower. Respect the rules so other dog-owning patrons can enjoy bunking with their pets, too.

At campgrounds, follow the same manners with your dog. Just because you're out in the wilderness doesn't mean your dog can run loose! Keep him on his leash at all times and don't let him bark.

- ✔ **Identify appropriate rest areas:** Map out your journey to make sure you can stop at places where your Boston can get out and stretch his legs. As you travel, stop every few hours to let your dog exercise and relieve himself. Though many rest stops have designated pet areas, these patches may be flea infested and frequented by unvaccinated dogs. Old, spoiled food may be laying around, and stagnant water may be disease-ridden. Instead, choose clean areas and pick up your Boston's messes. Offer your Boston water from a portable dish whenever you stop.

If your Boston tends to get motion sickness, avoid feeding him just before and during the car ride. Long trips may require that you feed him, but plan the meals so he has adequate time to digest the food before you hit the road again.

Flying the Skies

Airplane trips with your Boston Terrier require even more preparation than traveling by car (see the "Hitting the Road" section). Use the following tips and begin planning at least 30 days in advance to ensure a turbulence-free journey:

- **Government agency and vet check:** First, check with the necessary government agency (usually the Department of Agriculture) for specifics about what documentation your Boston will need at your destination location. Fill out any paperwork and turn it in well before the deadline.

  A veterinarian will need to examine your Boston and give you a signed health certificate no more than 10 days before your departure. That appointment gives you the opportunity to tell your veterinarian where you're going and ask about any special vaccinations your Boston may require.

- **Talk to an airline representative:** When you make your flight reservation, notify the airline representative that you'll be bringing a live animal onboard. She will ask the dog's size and weight, and tell you what size carrier your Boston will need. If you already have a carrier, have the brand and dimensions available so you can check them with the representative. She will also tell you what documentation you'll need to present to the ticketing agent at the airport. Be prepared and gather these papers well in advance. Ask her, too, where you can pick up your pup at your destination.

  Airlines typically charge for transporting pets; the price varies between companies. When you make your reservations, ask the representative how much they charge and when you will be required to pay. Many times, they collect the fee when you check in your pup at the ticket counter.

- **Prepare your dog's travel crate:** Federal law requires absorbent bedding on the bottom of the crate. You must also provide food and water dishes that are attached to the inside of the crate's wire door.

Fill one of the dishes with water and pop it in the freezer the night before you leave. Just before you head out, place the frozen dish inside the crate. The ice will melt slowly, providing water for your pup and preventing spillage during flight. Tape a small bag of food to the top of the crate with feeding instructions in case of delays.

Also tape all of your contact information on the crate, including your dog's name, your name, cellphone number, destination phone number and address, and flight number.

✔ **Gather your Boston's belongings:** Just as you pack your own bag, pack your Boston's bag, too (see the "Pack your Boston's bags" section earlier in this chapter). Remember any medication, toys, plenty of food, treats, an extra leash, and favorite bedding. Put all your contact info on this bag, too, just as you do for your own suitcase. Make sure that your Boston is wearing a collar with an updated ID tag listing your cellphone number and destination telephone number.

✔ **Before-flight fasting and relieving:** Before you leave for the airport, exercise your Boston as much as possible so he can relieve himself completely before the flight. Do not feed him for six hours before the plane departs; most airlines give specific recommendations for fasting before the flight.

✔ **Arrive early:** Get to the airport at least two hours before your plane is scheduled to leave. At the ticket counter, present the agent with the necessary paperwork and payment for transporting your Boston. She will process the paperwork, put a "live animal" sticker on the crate, sneak a peak at your dog, and check him in. Double-check with her where you'll pick up your Boston when you arrive. After you land at your destination, gather your bags, and then pick up your pup. Have the required documentation handy to show the airline representative.

Airline regulations change constantly, so speak with an airline representative before you leave to be sure you've dotted your i's and crossed your t's. You wouldn't want to have to cancel your flight because of forgotten paperwork!

Leaving Your Boston Behind

You won't always be able to travel with your Boston, no matter how fun it is. Long meetings, business trips, sick relatives, or a range of other circumstances may require you to leave your dog behind for the day, a few days, or longer. In these situations, you'll need to drop your Boston off at doggy day care, board him in a kennel, or hire a dog sitter.

Short- and long-term boarding

Short- and long-term boarding facilities keep your Boston safe and secure when you can't be with him. You can use a doggy daycare facility or a boarding kennel to make sure your dog stays happy and healthy when you can't tend him.

Besides asking your veterinarian, breeder, or dog-owning friends for boarding recommendations, you can visit the American Boarding Kennels Association's Web site (www.abka.com) and search its database for an ABKA-accredited facility.

Doggy day care

Dog daycare centers, which are cropping up in major metropolitan cities and suburbs across the United States, are generally intended for daylong stays. The staff supervises the dogs, feeds them, and plays with them. They lead them through activities, such as fetch, water play, and playground time — yes, playground time! Many dog daycare centers are inspired by children's playgrounds. They often include an outdoor play area that has playground equipment designed for children. Some even have swimming pools for those dog days of summer!

The daily rates for these facilities run from $20 and up, depending on the location and the services provided. For an extra fee, many of these dog daycare facilities offer grooming and training services.

Ask your dog-owning friends and family members, your vet, and members of your local Boston club if they can recommend a doggy daycare center. When you've got a list of places, check out the "Screening the facilities" section later in this chapter to help you make sure you're leaving your Boston in good hands.

The first time you drop off your Boston, you'll need to provide proof of vaccinations, including rabies, distemper, parvo, and bordetella. Different daycare centers have varying rules with regard to bringing your dog's own toys, food, and treats, so talk to the daycare owner or manager before you drop your pup off.

Dog daycare centers provide many benefits to your Boston, including

> ✔ **Focused attention by experienced staff members:** Many daycare employees are skilled in handling and training dogs. Ask the facility manager if you're curious about the employees' credentials.

✔ **Socialization with other humans and dogs:** Meeting and playing with other dogs and humans is essential in your dog's
mental and physical development. Daycare facilities provide a
fantastic opportunity to interact with a range of personalities
and breeds.

✔ **Plenty of free time to run around outside and expend pent-
up energy:** After enjoying the playground equipment, open
fields, and other canine carousers, your Boston will sleep like
a baby when he comes home from doggy day care!

✔ **Opportunities to swim and try agility or other games to
keep his curious mind stimulated:** You may not have room in
your backyard for playground or agility equipment, so visiting
a doggy day care is a great way to introduce your Boston to
these fun activities. Some day cares host agility and behavior
training classes; talk to the facility manger for details.

✔ **Quiet time in a kennel for napping or playing with his
favorite toy:** Most dog daycare facilities have individual kennels or runs for dogs who want to have some space. They're
perfect for naptime or if your Boston needs a timeout.

Long-term kennels

Similar to dog daycare facilities, boarding kennels provide your
Boston a home away from home while you're on longer trips.
Your Boston will be kept in a run or a large kennel, and the facility's
staff will feed your pup, clean up after him, take him for walks, and
give him lots of attention while you're away. Some kennels even
have volunteers who will exercise and play fetch with your dog.

You can find kennels through your veterinarian, your local Boston
club, dog-owning friends, and family members. The best kennels fill
up quickly, especially during holidays and peak vacation weeks
during the summertime, so reserve your space as soon as you
know you're going on vacation.

The facility will require you to provide proof of vaccinations,
including rabies, distemper, parvo, and bordetella. Have your
paperwork handy when you check your pup in. The rates vary,
depending on the facility, the services provided, and your location,
but you can expect to pay a minimum of $25 per day.

It may not be like keeping your Boston at home, but boarding kennels do have their benefits, including

✔ **Assurance that your Boston will be cared for while you're
away:** Knowing that your dog will be fed, cleaned up after,
played with, and safeguarded while you're away assures that
you'll have a pleasant trip — and a happy, healthy dog when
you come home.

✔ **Socialization with other humans and dogs:** Though your pup may not interact with other people or canines as much as he would at a dog daycare facility, he'll be exposed to other dogs during playtime and walks.

✔ **Attention from skilled kennel staff:** Because many kennels are affiliated with a veterinary clinic or hospital, your Boston will get quality care while in the facility. If he falls ill or injures himself, he'll have fast access to veterinary care.

✔ **Access to grooming services:** Many kennels offer grooming services while the dogs are being boarded. Schedule a bath, toenail trim, tooth brushing, and flea bath while he's there, and you'll bring home a dog who smells and looks great — and is delighted to see you!

Screening the facilities

Whether you use a doggy day care or a boarding kennel, you'll want to screen the facility before you drop off your beloved Boston. After getting recommendations from veterinarians, your groomer, Boston club members, and friends, compile your list and schedule meetings with the facility owners or managers. Request a tour of the facility and ask them a few questions about the services they provide. If they're a reputable operation, they won't mind at all.

Prepare a list of expectations and questions in advance, including

✔ **What hours are you open? When can my dog be dropped off and picked up?** Some daycare facilities are open during normal business hours, so you'll have to pick up your pooch at a reasonable hour after work. Likewise, some kennels close at the end of the day and may restrict when you can drop off and pick up your dog.

✔ **Is the kennel supervised 24 hours in case of emergency?** Even if you can't drop off and pick up your dog at just any time of day, you should choose a kennel that has supervision 24 hours a day, seven days a week in case of fire or some other emergency.

✔ **What vaccinations do you require the dogs to have?** Most kennels and daycare facilities require you to provide up-to-date vaccination records to prove that your Boston has been vaccinated against rabies, distemper, and parvo in the past 12 months. Other kennels require a bordetella vaccine within six months of boarding.

✔ **Are incoming dogs screened for fleas, ticks, and other parasites?** Some kennels require that your dog be on a flea-and-tick preventive. If he's not, they may be able to apply one for you.

✔ **Is a veterinarian on call in case of emergency?** Reputable facilities will have a veterinarian on call or even on site. If they don't, ask about their protocol if a medical emergency occurs.

✔ **What experience do you require your staff to have? Do they know dog first aid? CPR?** At least one staff member who has experience administering canine first aid should be on the clock. You want to make sure your Boston is in capable hands if something happens.

✔ **How large are the kennels? Are they cleaned several times a day?** When you tour the facility, make note of the cleanliness of the kennels, the common areas, and the overall grounds. You should see little or no fecal waste and detect very little smell. The kennels should be large enough for your dog to feel comfortable.

✔ **How often are the dogs fed? Watered?** Again, take note of the water bowls in the kennels and common areas as you tour the facility. The dogs should have access to clean, fresh water at all times.

✔ **Can I bring my own food, treats, and toys? Is bedding provided, or can I bring my own?** A change in diet can cause diarrhea in some dogs, so being able to keep your pup on his regular diet is a must. Bringing your dog's favorite toys and bedding will help him feel comfortable in the unfamiliar setting. Some dog daycare facilities, however, do not allow toys from home to avoid dominance conflicts.

✔ **Will someone walk my dog every day? Is there a fee for this service?** Getting out of the kennel will brighten your Boston's day and burn up some extra energy.

✔ **Do you offer any grooming services?** If so, take advantage of them! There's nothing better than picking up a clean dog who's absolutely delighted to see you!

The daycare or kennel representative should take as much time as necessary to answer these questions and give you a thorough tour of the facility. If she is curt or hurried in any way, move on. You don't want to leave your Boston in the care of someone whom you don't trust 100 percent.

After you choose a kennel or dog daycare facility, provide a list of your dog's needs, including any medication he is taking or allergies he may have.

Hiring a pet sitter

Finding someone reliable who is willing to stay with your dog or drop in on him several times during the day while you're away can be a better alternative than boarding your Boston in a kennel. He'll get to stay home with familiar smells and sounds. He'll have access to all his favorite toys and bedding. He won't be exposed to kennel cough or fleas. Plus, he may get some extra attention — and treats — from his favorite auntie or Grandma!

Your neighbor or friend makes an excellent dog sitter during short trips, but if you're going to be away for an extended period of time, you can hire a professional dog sitter to care for your pet. They typically charge between $10 and $30 per day, depending on the services they provide and how many pets you have.

Ask your veterinarian or fellow dog club members for pet sitter recommendations. Often, word of mouth is a good reference. You can also visit the National Association of Professional Pet Sitters Web site (www.petsitters.org) or the Pet Sitters International Web site (www.petsit.com) to search for a pet sitter in your area.

Leaving information behind

Even though the daycare facility, boarding kennel, or dog sitter may have plenty of experience with dogs, the caregiver doesn't know *your* dog and his idiosyncrasies.

A detailed list of instructions gives your dog sitter or care provider a guide to feeding, exercising, and caring for your Boston while you're away. If your dog requires any special needs, jot those down, too, so the person can refer to it if necessary.

As you compose your list, use these suggestions to get started:

✔ Phone number, address, and location of where you can be reached

✔ Your veterinarian's name, address, and office and emergency phone numbers

✔ Written permission for your caregiver to obtain veterinary treatment in your absence

✔ A short list of your pup's medical history, vaccinations, and allergies, if any

✔ Whether your dog is microchipped

✔ Your dog's age and birth date

✔ Feeding amounts and times to feed

✔ Any medication or supplements your dog needs, and instructions on how to administer them

✔ A backup dog sitter or kennel in case of emergency

✔ Your dog's favorite toys, games, and treats

By writing down this information and these instructions, you provide your caregiver with everything she needs to tend to your Boston's every want. It will help you and your dog better deal with the time that you are away.

When you have a list of potential dog sitters, schedule an appointment with each one to visit your home and meet your Boston. You'll know right away if you — and your dog — like her! A good dog sitter will develop a rapport with your pup right away.

Use this list of questions to interview potential dog sitters.

- ✔ **Do you belong to a professional pet-sitting organization, such as the National Association of Professional Pet Sitters?** Your candidate doesn't necessarily have to belong, but members of groups like these have met basic handling standards set by the organization.

- ✔ **Do you have references?** Confident pet sitters will happily provide you a list of satisfied clients. Call the references and ask if they would hire the pet sitter again.

- ✔ **Are you insured and bonded?** Ask to see proof of commercial liability insurance and ask exactly what coverage it provides.

- ✔ **How long have you been working as a pet sitter? Have you ever dog-sat a Boston?** A top candidate should have some experience caring for small dogs, ideally a Boston.

- ✔ **What experience do you have with medical care? Do you know canine CPR? First aid?** If your dog has an emergency, this person should be able to provide or obtain emergency care and treatment.

- ✔ **When will you come to my home? How long will you stay?** Your candidate should come at least twice a day to feed and check on your dog. She should also spend some time with him playing fetch, taking a walk, or just hanging out and watching television.

When you find a quality pet sitter, hold on to her! Notify her well in advance of trips so she can block off the time. Invite her to your home while you're there so she can bond with your Boston before you leave. She will be caring for your baby during your trip, so prepare everything she'll need to make her job easy — and fun!

Part IV
Health and Well-Being

The 5th Wave   By Rich Tennant

"That's the thing with a Boston Terrier. You can get rid of the fleas, you can get rid of the ticks, but you can't get rid of the accent."

In this part . . .

What happens when you discover a skin ulcer or a lump on your dog? How do you treat a bee sting or cut? Do you know what breed-specific ailments your Boston may develop? When she reaches her senior years, how do you keep her comfortable?

Caring for your Boston includes keeping her healthy through all stages of her life. This section introduces you to the world of veterinary care and how to tend to your Boston's medical needs. You find out what to expect during routine veterinary exams, what inoculations your dog needs, how to treat minor emergencies, and when to consult a professional.

You'll likely refer to this part of the book most often during the course of your dog's life. Though you should always consult a veterinarian in emergencies, this section helps you with the basics.

Chapter 14

Your Visit to the Veterinarian

In This Chapter

▶ Choosing a veterinarian

▶ Knowing what to expect during your Boston's veterinary visits

▶ Looking at vaccinations for common diseases

▶ Identifying internal and external parasites

▶ Getting your Boston spayed or neutered

*A*s dapper and determined as they are, Bostons can't take care of themselves, particularly when it comes to their health. One of the first things you need to do as a responsible dog owner is establish a relationship with a veterinarian you trust — someone with whom you feel comfortable asking questions, sharing concerns, and calling if the unthinkable happens. You and your Boston's doctor will work together to ensure a long and healthy life for your beloved dog.

In this chapter, you figure out how to identify a qualified veterinarian. You find out what to expect during your Boston's first veterinary visit, including the host of vaccinations your puppy will need. You also get the lowdown about those unpleasant internal and external parasites, like heartworm and fleas.

Finding a Vet for Your Pet

Your veterinarian's job is to keep your Boston healthy and protected against disease. He will conduct annual screenings and suggest preventive care to ensure your Boston will live a long life. He will also vaccinate your Boston against common diseases, perform treatments as needed, prescribe remedies, and address any questions or concerns you may have. Next to you, the veterinarian will become your dog's best friend.

Start looking for a veterinarian before your Boston becomes a part of your family. You should establish a doctor–patient–pet owner relationship as soon as possible, and that starts with identifying a veterinarian who's right for you.

Getting referrals from trustworthy sources

You can begin your search for a veterinarian by contacting your local Boston Terrier club and asking for a recommendation (search `www.bostonterrierclubofamerica.org` for the club nearest you). Chances are good that veterinarians suggested by club members have cared for many Boston Terriers. They understand the intricacies of the breed and can recommend specific treatments for your dog. Other than your local breed club, you can also get vet referrals from the following sources:

- ✔ **Your breeder:** If she lives in your area, she may be able to recommend a veterinarian; if she lives out of the area, she may know someone who lives in your city.

- ✔ **Family, friends, and other dog owners:** They can give firsthand reports of the vet's bedside manner and expertise — and whether their pets approved of him!

- ✔ **Veterinary associations:** Groups such as the American Animal Hospital Association (AAHA) compile a list of member veterinarians whom they can recommend to you. The medical and management criteria for becoming an AAHA-approved clinic are strict, and a facility that meets these guidelines is often a cut above those that aren't members.

- ✔ **The phonebook and newspaper advertisements:** These resources are helpful if you're new to the area and don't yet know your way around. Focus on those clinics that are near your home.

No matter where you find veterinary recommendations, always check them out before you decide who the best vet for your Boston is. If you find that you don't like the veterinarian or the office staff, or you can't communicate well with them, find another veterinarian. It's okay to try out different doctors until you find one with whom you're comfortable.

Figuring out who's who in the vet world

Like medical doctors for people, veterinarians earn their doctorate degrees and go on to practice as a *general practitioner.* General practitioners maintain your Boston's medical history, perform routine examinations and minor surgeries, and handle emergencies. A general practitioner is your Boston's primary doctor.

Veterinarians can also practice in 1 of 20 American Veterinary Medical Association–recognized specialties, such as dermatology, ophthalmology, and internal medicine. These *veterinary specialists,* to whom your general practitioner will refer you if necessary, have focused their practice on specific areas of medicine.

Here, you can find out the differences between the general practitioners and veterinary specialists.

General practitioners

Veterinarians are licensed through the American Veterinary Medical Association (AVMA). After completing four years in an AVMA–accredited veterinary school with one year dedicated to clinical rotations, they must pass rigorous federal and state board exams to earn their licenses — and the DVM (doctor of veterinary medicine) or VMD (veterinary medical doctor) after their names, depending on the traditions of the veterinary school that they attended.

General practitioners can perform many of the services your Boston will need, including annual checkups, vaccinations, minor surgeries, diagnostics, and prevention. If your Boston is sick, you will first take her to your general practitioner. But if she needs specialized care, your general practitioner will refer you to a specialist.

Veterinarians practice medicine in a variety of settings, from large veterinary hospitals that staff a number of doctors to privately owned clinics that have one or two doctors available. Some doctors work in franchise-like settings, while others practice medicine in teaching hospitals at veterinary schools.

Specialists

Veterinary specialists, such as veterinary behaviorists, surgeons, or dentists, undergo even more training than general practitioners do and choose to focus on a particular area of expertise.

 To earn the title of veterinary specialist, the person must complete a standard veterinary school program and earn her DVM. Then, she must continue her education by completing a one-year internship and a two- to five-year residency program in her chosen discipline. After her educational requirements are complete, she must pass additional examinations to merit certification by a specialty board.

The certification requirements vary, but they are governed by the American Board of Veterinary Specialists, which has established guidelines on how veterinary specialists list their credentials. Veterinarians may not imply that they are specialists when they aren't. If you're seeking a veterinary specialist, look for terms like *board certified* and *diplomate* (often abbreviated as dipl.).

For example, this doctor specializes in veterinary nutrition: Sara Veterinarian, DVM, dipl. ACVN (American College of Veterinary Nutrition), board certified in clinical nutrition.

If your Boston requires the services of a veterinary specialist, your veterinarian will usually give you a referral.

Knowing what you're looking for

Choosing the right veterinarian and clinic or hospital for your Boston depends on many criteria. Just as you would research your own physician, you'll want to do the same with your dog's veterinarian and animal hospital. To get started, ask yourself these questions:

- ✔ Is it important to find a veterinarian near my home?
- ✔ What services do I require from the clinic?
- ✔ What level of doctor–patient–pet owner familiarity do I want?
- ✔ Is a helpful office staff important to me?

The following sections can help you come up with answers that best suit you and your Boston.

Quality over convenience

Choosing a clinic near your home is certainly convenient. It will be much easier for you to show up for routine exams, grooming visits, and booster shots if your vet's office is right down the road.

The clinic's office hours should also be compatible with your schedule. Ask if the doctors have early or late appointments and if they see patients on the weekend.

Don't base your decision solely on convenience, however, because the nearest veterinarian may not be a good fit. You and your dog should feel comfortable with the doctor and his skills, and if you feel hesitant at all, find someone else. (See the upcoming section, "Interviewing your veterinarian," for a list of questions to ask the potential veterinarian.)

Full range of services

Veterinary clinics offer a wide range of services, from grooming and boarding to ultrasounds and cancer treatment. Some practices even stock their shelves with retail products. Talk about one-stop shopping!

Before you select a clinic, jot down what services are important to you. If you plan to groom your own dog, for example, you may not need grooming services. Likewise, if you have a reliable dog sitter, you may not need boarding services.

You should definitely find out how the clinic handles emergencies. Some clinics have a staff veterinarian on call 24 hours a day, while others partner with nearby clinics or animal hospitals for after-hours emergencies.

You may also want to ask whether the clinic has a laboratory in the office or if it sends its lab work out. Talk to the vet or office manager about the length of time it takes to get lab results. You don't want to be waiting for days to find out what exactly is wrong with your beloved Boston.

Also consider whether the clinic has access to specialty practitioners and services, like *oncologists* (vets who treat dogs suffering from cancer), dentists, or behaviorists. Most doctors can refer their clients to specialists, but you may want to have the services on-site.

One doctor versus whoever is available

In some clinics, you can see the same veterinarian each time you visit; in others, you may not have a choice. Practices maintain a history of your dog's visits, including her immunizations, reactions to medications, and behavior traits, so from a treatment standpoint, you don't have to see the same doctor each time.

But a strong doctor–patient–pet owner relationship plays a role in your dog's overall health. By seeing the same vet every time, your Boston will become more comfortable with him, and the vet will really get to know your dog. Plus, seeing the same doctor each time may be important if your Boston has a recurrent or chronic problem.

Alternative treatments

In addition to traditional veterinary care, you can consider complementary and alternative health care for your Boston. Some of these alternatives include acupuncture, acupressure, massage, and chiropractic care.

Acupuncture and *acupressure* are ancient Eastern therapies that consist of stimulating precise points on your dog's body by inserting fine needles or applying pressure. Some veterinarians are specially trained in practicing this type of therapy. *Massage* and *chiropractic therapy* work the animal's muscles and skeletal system to ease pain and speed healing.

Before visiting any of these therapists, consult your traditional veterinarian for recommendations, advice, or further information.

If you choose a sole practitioner for your Boston, be sure that another veterinarian can step in if your vet goes on vacation or is otherwise unavailable.

Helpful office staff

From the receptionist to the veterinary technician, the office staff's attentiveness and quality affects the quality of your Boston's care.

The front office staff should be considerate and helpful. They greet you when you arrive and schedule follow-up appointments when you're done. In smaller practices, they may assist the doctor in the exam room.

Veterinary technicians or veterinary assistants typically take your Boston's temperature, weigh her, and take her vital signs before the vet comes into the exam room. Many times, they will explain the doctor's diagnosis in terms that make sense to you.

Interviewing your veterinarian

After you've narrowed down your selections, you'll want to find out more about the veterinarian. You may need to schedule a consultation or appointment to fit into the doctor's schedule and pay a fee for the visit — but it will give you the opportunity to meet the office staff and talk to the veterinarian.

Ask the veterinarian candidate the following questions:

- How long have you been in practice?
- Have you cared for many Boston Terriers?
- What do you know about the Boston's unique medical needs, temperament, and personality?
- What is your area of expertise? Do you specialize?
- Whom do you consult when presented with a medical problem that you're not familiar with?
- Do you perform your own surgical procedures?
- Who monitors the dogs after surgery? Where are they cared for?
- How much veterinary education do you require your staff to have? Do they attend continuing education courses?
- How often do you attend veterinary conventions to learn about new medical procedures?
- Do you offer any alternative therapies?

Visit several clinics, if possible, and weigh the pros and cons of each. Remove from your list veterinarians who appear rude or use too much medical jargon when you ask questions. If a clinic appears dirty or smells offensive, or if the office staff is inattentive, take it off your list.

Instead, choose a veterinarian with whom you feel comfortable and who has a helpful office staff and top-notch service. When you find someone you think you can work with, schedule a routine physical for your dog as a first visit.

Your Boston's First Vet Visit

Your veterinarian will want to see your Boston within 48 to 72 hours of arriving at her new home. Most breeders and rescue organizations require that you have your dog checked by a veterinarian soon after purchase or adoption to be sure she doesn't have any health problems.

Arrive early to your appointment and bring the documents that came with your Boston. They contain important information the doctor needs, such as any vaccinations and tests already performed on your pet. Plan to fill out some preliminary paperwork that lists your dog's vital statistics, activity level, previous health problems (if any), and other pets you may have. Also plan to bring a fresh stool sample so your veterinarian can check it for internal parasites.

You'll likely be escorted to the exam room by a veterinary technician. These trained professionals will weigh your Boston, take her temperature, and ask questions about the reason for your visit.

During the physical exam, the veterinarian will conduct an overall health screening to look for potential health problems. She will listen to your pup's heart and lungs; feel her abdomen, muscles, and joints; inspect her mouth, teeth, and gums; look into her eyes, ears, and nose; and look at your Boston's coat. The veterinarian will look for anything out of the ordinary and watch the dog's reaction when handled. The vet will also look for *congenital problems,* which are health problems an animal is born with.

After examining your dog and reviewing her medical records, your veterinarian may decide to vaccinate your Boston against a range of viruses and bacteria to which dogs are susceptible (see the next section). If your Boston already started her vaccinations, she may need booster shots.

Dirty business

During your Boston's vet exam, you may need to bring a fresh stool sample so it can be examined for things like internal parasites.

Collecting the sample isn't as difficult — or disgusting — as it sounds. It needs to be fresh, so a few hours before your appointment, follow your dog outside with a sealable sandwich bag and a leftover food container with a tight-fitting lid. Turn the plastic bag inside out over your hand and pick up the fresh feces. The sample doesn't need to be too large: A quarter-size amount of stool will do. Turn the plastic bag back around the sample, seal it, place it in the container, and close the lid.

Label the container with your name, your dog's name, and the date the sample was taken. And try not to get too grossed out!

The veterinarian will ask you questions about the dog's behavior. She will want to know your Boston's eating and defecating habits and activity level. If you have witnessed anything out of the ordinary, be sure to tell the veterinarian.

Now is the time to ask any questions you may have, such as what and how much your Boston should be eating, any special health problems Bostons could have, and when your dog should be spayed or neutered. This is the time to establish a comfortable dialogue with your veterinarian.

Vaccinations: Protecting Your Dog from Deadly Diseases

Dogs face a range of communicable diseases today, but they can be prevented with vaccinations. *Vaccines* are essentially weakened or dead forms of a disease that are given to your Boston to stimulate her immune system, causing her to produce antibodies against that disease. When she's exposed to the real disease, her body recognizes the invader, and her defenses fight it off.

When your Boston is a puppy, she gets antibodies from her mama's milk. But starting at 6 weeks old and continuing every three to four weeks until your pup reaches 16 weeks old, your veterinarian will vaccinate your puppy against a range of diseases, which are detailed in the following section.

Knowing the diseases

Dogs are usually vaccinated against eight diseases. Whether your veterinarian inoculates against all of them depends on where you live and what viruses are prevalent. The rabies vaccine, for example, is mandated by state law, but if coronavirus isn't a problem in your region, your vet won't give your Boston that vaccine. Also, if you travel or are planning to travel with your dog, be sure to let your vet know so he can vaccinate appropriately.

Here are the eight diseases your pup will be vaccinated for, and how they can affect your pup:

- ✔ **Distemper:** Distemper is a contagious viral disease that causes symptoms resembling a bad cold with a fever. It can include runny nose and eyes, and an upset stomach that can lead to vomiting and diarrhea. Many infected animals exhibit neurological symptoms, which may include involuntary twitching, paralysis, and convulsions. An incurable and deadly disease, distemper is passed through exposure to the saliva, urine, and feces of raccoons, foxes, wolves, mink, and other dogs already infected with the virus. Unvaccinated young pups and senior dogs are most vulnerable to distemper. Any pup or dog who has received a distemper vaccination prior to exposure to the virus is unlikely to become infected.

- ✔ **Hepatitis:** Spread through contact with other dogs' saliva, mucus, urine, or feces, hepatitis affects the liver. It causes apathy, vomiting, abdominal pain, fever, and jaundice. The mortality rate is high, but vaccination prevents the disease.

- ✔ **Leptospirosis:** A highly contagious bacteria that is passed through the urine of infected dogs, rats, farm animals, and wildlife, leptospirosis attacks the dog's kidneys, causing kidney failure. Symptoms include fever, appetite loss, possible diarrhea, and jaundice. Vaccinations usually prevent the disease, though the bacteria does appear in different forms, and the vaccine may not protect against all of them. Lepto is a *zoonotic* disease, which means that it can spread to humans.

- ✔ **Parvovirus:** Another deadly virus, parvo is transmitted by direct contact with infected dogs and their feces. The virus attacks the inner lining of a dog's intestines and causes bloody diarrhea. Symptoms also include fever, lethargy, appetite loss, vomiting, and collapse. Because this virus replicates very quickly, your Boston needs prompt medical attention if she exhibits any of these signs. The vaccination is usually effective at preventing the virus if given at proper intervals during the first 6 to 16 weeks of life.

✔ **Kennel cough:** Adenovirus, parainfluenza, and bordetella all refer to a condition known as infectious tracheobronchitis, or kennel cough. They are rarely deadly, but they do cause significant coughing, sneezing, and hacking, sometimes with nasal discharge and fever. Severe cases may progress to pneumonia. Symptoms may last from several days to several weeks. This very contagious virus spreads when the sick dog coughs and expels airborne mucous. Some forms of the virus cannot be vaccinated against. Dogs who frequent kennels, training classes, groomers, dog parks, or other public facilities should be vaccinated routinely.

✔ **Rabies:** Carried in the saliva of infected wildlife and transmitted through bites or cuts, rabies attacks the nerve tissue and causes paralysis and death. It's always fatal to unvaccinated animals and people. In most areas, proof of rabies vaccination is required when you apply for a dog license. Some states require yearly rabies vaccinations, while others allow vaccinations every three years. Rabies is a *zoonotic* disease, which means people can become infected by the saliva of a rabid animal.

✔ **Coronavirus:** Rarely fatal for puppies and adult dogs, coronavirus causes a loose, watery stool and vomiting. Dehydration from the diarrhea and vomiting endangers puppies. The virus is spread through the stool.

✔ **Lyme disease:** Lyme borreliosis, or Lyme disease, is caused by a bacterium that can make animals and humans sick. Spread by hard-bodied ticks that bite an infected animal and then bite another animal, the disease causes a range of symptoms, including lameness, swollen joints, fever, appetite loss, and lethargy. In the United States, it is most common around the Atlantic seaboard, upper Midwest, and Pacific coast, though it does occur throughout the country.

Following the vaccination schedule

If you're intimidated by the diseases that can affect your Boston and the number of vaccines needed to prevent them, rest easy. Your veterinarian can help you schedule all the shots your puppy needs.

Typically, at 6 to 8 weeks old, your vet will vaccinate your puppy for the most common diseases — distemper, hepatitis, leptospirosis, parvovirus, and parainfluenza — in one combined injection, called DHLPP. Your Boston will get another shot at 10 to 12 weeks old, and a third at 14 to 16 weeks old.

Your puppy receives her first rabies vaccine at 12 weeks old and her second vaccine a year later. Depending on the laws in your state, your dog may also require a vaccination later on.

Coronavirus and Lyme disease vaccinations are given only if there is a problem in your area. Your vet will administer these vaccines at the same time as her first two DHLPP injections, at 6 to 8 weeks old, and again at 10 to 12 weeks old.

Depending on the vaccine, your vet will give the injection into a muscle or under the skin. Some vaccines for kennel cough are given through the nose. Most times, your puppy won't be fazed by the vaccinations, and she'll be bounding around your home in no time.

After your puppy has completed her vaccinations, you'll need to take her to the veterinarian for booster shots once a year.

Based on recent research that suggests yearly booster shots may be damaging to dogs' immune systems, booster protocols are changing. Some veterinarians give boosters every 18 months, while some veterinary schools recommend that they can be given every 36 months. Talk to your veterinarian about his suggested booster schedule and whether he is concerned about the frequency of booster shots.

Patrolling for Parasites

Vaccinations prevent certain viruses and bacteria from afflicting your Boston, but she is still susceptible to other medical problems, including internal and external parasites.

Parasites are tiny organisms that live off of another living organism. These little thieves come in all shapes and sizes, from single-celled protozoa and small fleas to long intestinal tapeworms. There are two types of parasites: internal and external. They latch onto the *host animal* and draw nourishment from her without providing any benefit in return. Sometimes, the parasites weaken the host (your dog) so severely that they can cause death.

In most cases, your Boston will pick up parasites from exposure to contaminated environments. For example, your dog may romp through a grassy field and bring home some fleas or ticks, or she may ingest a strange dog's feces and develop an internal parasite.

Generally, you can prevent parasites by limiting your dog's exposure to other animals' urine and feces, giving her a heartworm preventive every month (as prescribed by your veterinarian), and applying a flea-and-tick repellant to her coat (also available through your veterinarian).

In the sections below, I detail the most common internal and external parasites, and how you can prevent your Boston from bringing home these troublesome hitchhikers.

Internal parasites: The worms

Internal parasites are a part of pet ownership. They aren't pleasant, but you need to address them to keep your pet healthy. Because these pests live inside your Boston, you can't see the damage they're causing! It can take quite some time before your dog exhibits external signs of an internal parasite problem.

Your veterinarian can detect most internal parasites through testing and microscopic examinations. A stool sample often contains the eggs, dead remains of the parasite, or even the larvae. Your vet will prescribe a treatment, and after it runs its course, you will need to bring in another stool sample to be sure the treatment worked.

Several types of internal parasites affect dogs. Some are more destructive than others. The following are the most common.

Hookworm

Hookworms, which can cause fatal anemia in puppies, attach themselves to the small intestine and suck the dog's blood. After detaching and moving to a new location, the wound continues to bleed, causing bloody diarrhea — often a sign of a hookworm infestation. Like other internal parasites, hookworm eggs are passed through the stool, so good sanitation prevents their spread. Humans can also suffer from hookworms.

Hookworm treatment involves feeding the dog an oral deworming tablet or liquid and giving her another dose one month later. The first treatment destroys the adult worms living in dog, and the second treatment destroys the next generation. After the second treatment, your vet will do another fecal exam to be sure the parasites are gone.

Roundworm

Roundworms, which are long white worms that live in the dog's intestines, are fairly common in puppies. They can be seen in feces and vomit, and the eggs are transmitted through the stool. A dog infested with roundworms is thin and may have a dull coat and potbelly. A stool analysis will confirm diagnosis. Good sanitation will prevent the spread of roundworm.

As with hookworm infestations, treatment involves feeding the dog an oral deworming medication and repeating it several times to ensure subsequent generations of the parasite are destroyed.

Roundworms are also a zoonotic disease that can cause neurological damage and blindness in humans. Small children are at high risk for becoming infected.

Whipworm

This internal parasite lives in the large intestine where it feeds on blood. A heavy infestation of whipworms can be fatal to adults and puppies because it can cause severe diarrhea. Dogs infested with whipworm look lethargic and thin. Whipworm eggs are passed in the feces and can live in the soil for years, so dogs who dig or eat grass can pick up eggs.

If caught early, whipworm can be treated with deworming medications that must be administered over extended periods of time. Because of the long maturation cycle of young worms, a second deworming is needed 75 days after the first one. Additional doses may be necessary, as well.

Heartworm

A dangerous yet preventable parasite, heartworms live in an infected dog's upper heart and arteries, damaging its blood vessel walls. Poor circulation ultimately causes heart failure. The parasite is spread by mosquitoes. Adult heartworms produce tiny worms, which circulate throughout the dog's bloodstream. When a mosquito bites a dog, the mosquito picks up the worms and transmits them to another dog.

The first signs of heartworm include breathing difficulty, coughing, and lack of energy, though some dogs show no signs until it's too late. To confirm a diagnosis, your vet will take a blood test to look for worms. He may also do an X-ray. If the test results are positive, your vet will give your dog medication to kill the worms.

Preventive medications, however, are the best remedy. They are easily available, and they're very effective. If heartworm is prevalent in your area, your veterinarian will first do a blood test to determine whether your dog is infected if your dog is over 6 months old. Puppies under 6 months can be started on prevention without testing. After a clean bill of health, your veterinarian will prescribe preventive heartworm medication. Many of these medications also provide a monthly deworming for roundworms, hookworms, and whipworms.

Giardiasis

Commonly passed through wild animals, giardia, an intestinal parasitic protozoon, affects humans and animals and causes diarrhea and lethargy. It's often found in mountain streams, but it can also be found in puddles or stagnant water. Your veterinarian will test for giardiasis and can prescribe treatment, which consists of giving your pet an oral antibiotic.

Tapeworms

Spread by infected fleas or from eating rabbit entrails, tapeworms live in an animal's intestine, attach to the wall, and absorb nutrients. They grow by creating new segments, which can often be seen around the dog's rectum or in her stool as small rice-like pieces.

Your veterinarian can treat the tapeworm by prescribing tablets or giving your dog a series of injections, but a good flea-control program is the best prevention against tapeworm infestation.

External parasites: Pesky critters

Fleas and ticks (and other bothersome bugs) are not fun on your dog — or in your house! These parasites live off your pet's blood. They spread disease, including tapeworms (an internal parasite) and Lyme disease.

Fleas are small, but they're not invisible. If you see just one flea crawling on your Boston or hopping in your carpet, for example, chances are very high that there are many more. You may see your pup scratching and biting to rid herself of the parasites, or you may see her rolling on the floor to ease the discomfort. When combing through your dog's coat, you may also see white flea eggs or their "dirt," which can resemble specks of pepper.

Ticks look like brown or black sesame seeds with eight legs. They won't overrun your home like fleas can, but they will cause misery as they suck your pup's blood. Ticks prefer the area around your dog's head, neck, ears, and feet, and in the warm areas between her legs and body.

If your pup is scratching but you've found no signs of fleas, she may have mange mites. These microscopic marauders like the areas around the elbows, hocks, ears, and face. They will need to be identified by your veterinarian, who will scrape your pup's skin and inspect it under the microscope.

Thankfully, these pests can be controlled so you and your Boston can enjoy the great outdoors together, where these critters are commonly found.

Fleas

Fleas are small, crescent-shaped insects that suck the blood from your Boston (see Figure 14-1). With their six legs and huge abdomen, they can jump surprisingly far in proportion to their size. Their bite causes allergic reactions in dogs and their humans, causing itching, discomfort, and misery!

In large numbers — especially on a little dog like your Boston — fleas can cause anemia and severe allergic reactions that can lead to open sores and possibly a secondary infection.

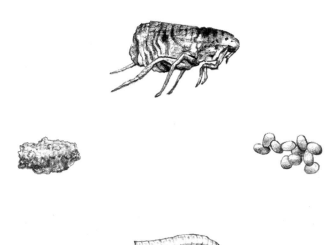

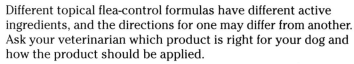

Figure 14-1: Fleas pass through four phases, shown above, as they complete their life cycle. One female flea lays about 20 eggs per day and up to 600 in her lifetime.

Fleas also spread internal parasites, such as tapeworms. When a dog swallows a tapeworm-infected flea, she then becomes infested with tapeworm. In the past, fleas carried bubonic plague. These parasites are a more than a nuisance — they are a real threat.

Luckily for your Boston, more flea-control options exist now than ever before.

✔ **Topical treatments:** These treatments are applied to the pup's skin between the shoulder blades. The product is absorbed through the dog's skin into her system. The flea is killed when it bites the animal or when its reproduction cycle is altered.

Different topical flea-control formulas have different active ingredients, and the directions for one may differ from another. Ask your veterinarian which product is right for your dog and how the product should be applied.

✔ **Systemic treatments:** These treatments include pills that the dog swallows. When the flea bites the dog, the chemical in the pill is transmitted to the flea, which (depending on the product) either prevents the flea's eggs from developing or kills the adult fleas, so the population dies off.

> ✓ **Insect growth regulators (IGRs):** IGRs stop immature fleas from maturing and prevent them from reproducing, so the population ceases to exist. Dispensed as foggers, sprays, and in discs, IGRs can be used in the environment to stop bug populations from thriving.

In addition to treating your Boston, you also need to treat your house and the shady areas of your yard for complete flea eradication. The fleas will return if any one of the three is neglected. Treat both the yard and the house with a spray that contains an IGR.

If you prefer a natural external parasite control, several plant-based flea-control products are available over the counter. Some of the more popular ones include pyrethrins, which are derived from chrysanthemums, and citrus-based derivatives. They both work to knock down the flea population, but they do little to eradicate an infestation.

Ticks

Ticks are eight-legged bloodsuckers that latch on, embed their head into your pet's skin, and suck until they become engorged with blood.

Like fleas, ticks carry blood-transmitted diseases, including Lyme disease and Rocky Mountain spotted fever. Lyme disease is characterized by a lingering fever, joint pain, and neurological problems. Rocky Mountain spotted fever is characterized by muscle pain, high fever, and skin sores.

Some flea-control products also deter ticks, but the best thing to do is check your Boston after romps in tick-infested areas. During the spring and summer, inspect your dog daily, paying close attention to the areas behind her ears, in the armpit area under her front legs, and around her neck.

If you find a tick on your pet, you should remove it. Here's how:

1. **Use tweezers to grab hold of the tick as close to the skin as possible.**
2. **Pull gently but firmly with a twisting motion. Dip the critter in alcohol or flush it down the toilet so it can't crawl back.**
3. **Put a little antibiotic ointment on the wound where the tick was embedded.**

Mange mites

Mange, or microscopic skin mites, causes your dog's skin to swell and form itchy, pus-filled scabs. The disease comes in two varieties: *sarcoptic mange,* which is contagious to people and other pets, and *demodectic mange,* which is not contagious. Your veterinarian will do a skin scraping to determine which variety is plaguing your dog.

Dogs suffering from mange mites may scratch themselves fiercely. Patches of skin look red and scaly, and they may have areas of thinning hair around their eyes, mouth, and the fronts of their legs. In more advanced infestations, crusty sores form and ooze, which may lead to secondary infections. Treatment involves bathing in medicated shampoos, and possibly antibiotics or steroids to relieve the itching symptoms, and ivermectin injections or oral solution. The heartworm prevention Revolution can also be used to treat sarcoptic mange.

Ringworm

Ringworm isn't a parasite at all. It's a contagious fungus that infects the skin and causes a red, ring-shaped, itchy rash. It spreads by contact from other animals. Ringworm responds well to treatment, but because it's so contagious to people and other animals, the plan must be followed diligently to eradicate the fungus.

Treatment for ringworm involves a three-pronged approach:

- ✔ Giving your Boston a pill that stops the fungus from growing
- ✔ Cleaning the affected area thoroughly and frequently with iodine to kill the fungus on your pet
- ✔ Keeping your environment clean using antifungal solutions, such as a 1-to-20 bleach-to-water ratio

To Spay or Neuter

Having your Boston *fixed* means having her spayed (or him neutered), or rendering the dog unable to produce baby Bostons. It may seem cruel and unusual, but the routine procedure is one of the best things you can do for your dog's health and happiness. The surgery prevents certain diseases, like uterine and testicular cancer, and it mellows out your Boston's mood.

Spaying or neutering your Boston doesn't cause personality changes, but it does result in some positive behavioral changes. Dogs who are spayed or neutered

- ✔ Exhibit less aggressive behavior than those who don't have surgery
- ✔ Are less likely to roam in search for a mate
- ✔ Are less likely to mark with urine or soil rugs and furniture

Most importantly, spaying or neutering your pet helps control the pet overpopulation problem plaguing our country today. Countless puppies find themselves relinquished to shelters because their owners couldn't find homes for them.

Growing up fast: Your Boston's sexual maturity

Dogs reach sexual maturity between the ages of 6 to 9 months old, at which time they are capable of reproducing. Their voices don't start to crack, but their hormones begin to activate, and their behavior starts to change.

Most females have their first *estrus,* or heat, cycle when they reach 6 months of age. The cycle, or season, begins with *proestrus,* which is when she bleeds. It can last up to 15 days, and it marks the beginning of the estrus cycle.

During the estrus cycle, the female is the most fertile and will emit a pheromone that makes her more attractive to males. She may even flirt and lift her rear in the air while wagging her tail back and forth! Her behavior may also change. She may seem hyperactive or stressed. The cycle typically lasts 21 to 30 days, though each dog's cycle differs. Female dogs are in season two times per year.

After a male dog reaches maturity, he can breed with a female in heat at any time. If he's not neutered, he'll constantly sniff the air in search of a female in season. He'll also mark his territory by lifting his leg and leaving behind his scent. Male dogs may also grasp pillows or unsuspecting human legs and hump them!

Understanding the surgical procedures

Living with an unspayed female or intact male can certainly be a challenge for you (for specifics, see the previous section). It's no fun for the dogs, either, unless they're allowed to breed freely. But that's where spay or neuter surgery can make life with your Boston pleasurable again.

Your veterinarian can perform a routine operation on your dog under general anesthesia when he or she is about 6 months old, or just before sexual maturity. Your Boston will feel no pain at all during the surgery and a minimal amount after the surgery while he or she recovers:

✔ **Females are spayed.** This process involves an ovariohysterectomy, where the ovaries and uterus are removed surgically. Your Boston will be out of sorts for a few days, but she'll be back to her old self in no time. Not only does this procedure prevent unwanted puppies, but it also protects her from uterine infection, ovarian cancer, and mammary gland cancer, and prevents heat cycles.

✔ **Males are neutered.** Their testicles are removed through a small incision just in front of the scrotum. Like the female, the male will be less social for a few days, but he'll quickly be back to normal. An added benefit of neutering includes protection from testicular cancer and reduced risk of prostate infections.

In some cases, you can take your pup home after he or she has recovered from the surgery. In most cases, however, be prepared to leave your Boston overnight so the staff can make sure that everything went okay.

Making Annual Visits

The first visit to the veterinarian is just the beginning of many regular appointments to come for your Boston. Annual visits, just like annual checkups for you, are a preventive step that ensures your Boston's continued good health. These appointments allow the veterinarian to catch problems early before they turn into life-threatening situations.

During an annual exam, your veterinarian will conduct an exam similar to your Boston's first visit. He will examine your dog's overall health, check for any changes, and ask you questions about her behavior. Your vet will check your dog's vital organs and look at her eyes, ears, nose, and mouth, as well as feeling her body for tumors or sore spots (see Figure 14-2).

Your veterinarian may also ask you questions like these:

✔ How long have you had your Boston Terrier?

✔ When was the last time you took her to the veterinarian?

✔ Are you having any problems with her training?

✔ Do you plan to neuter (or spay) your dog (if it hasn't already been done)?

✔ How many hours a day do you spend with your Boston?

✔ What types of activities do you enjoy doing with your dog?

✔ Do you notice any problems with her eating or eliminating?

✔ Is she drinking more than usual?

✔ Do you use a crate? How is her housetraining coming along?

✔ Have you noticed any signs of illness, such as lethargy, loose stools, poor appetite, excessive sneezing or coughing, or any discharge from her eyes, nose, or ears?

✔ What are you feeding your dog? How much?

✔ Does your dog display any troublesome behavior?

If everything checks out, you won't need to visit the veterinarian again for another year. But if something looks amiss, your vet may recommend laboratory work or X-rays. The office will call with test results as soon as they're available.

With your veterinarian's help, you can keep your Boston Terrier healthy and strong for her lifetime. Disease prevention, annual veterinary exams, and regular checks of your dog for physiological or neurological changes will hopefully catch problems before they become serious.

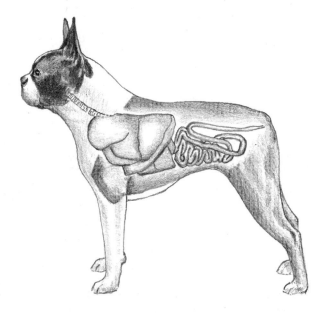

Figure 14-2: A Boston Terrier's anatomy.

Chapter 15

Breed-Specific Ailments

. . . .

In This Chapter

▶ Understanding brachycephalic syndrome

▶ Recognizing respiratory difficulties

▶ Protecting your Boston's ears and eyes

▶ Handling orthopedic problems

. . . .

As a whole, Boston Terriers are healthy dogs with relatively few breed-specific medical ailments. Their strong constitutions are part of what makes them such long-lived companions, often reaching their 11th or 12th birthdays without a hitch.

Your Boston's unique look, however, predisposes him to certain conditions, many of which can be attributed to his adorable flat face and diminutive stature. In this chapter, you can get the lowdown about several breed-specific ailments that Bostons commonly face and discover how you can make your pup's life easier.

With a Snort and Wheeze

When you meet a Boston for the first time, his grunts and snuffles may surprise you. But they're normal. Those sounds characterize the breed and, in time, you'll grow to adore his little vocal oddities — even if his snoring wakes you up every night!

Your Boston, like French Bulldogs, Pugs, and other dogs with flattened faces, are referred to as being *brachycephalic,* which literally means having a short, broad, almost spherical head. The word is derived from Greek roots *brachy* meaning "short" and *cephalic* meaning "head."

Because your Boston has a shortened head, his mouth, nose, windpipe, and larynx are shaped differently than other dogs'. This can cause those quirky noises, but his head shape can also cause high risk for heat stroke and breathing difficulties that can increase stress on the heart. Most brachycephalic symptoms, however, are not life threatening, but you need to make yourself aware of the challenges your pup may face.

Challenged chompers

With their flat faces, brachycephalic dogs don't have a lot of space for their jaws and teeth. As a result, their jaws may develop abnormally, and their mouths tend to be crowded, causing misaligned teeth and bite problems.

The technical terms for these conditions are *prognathia* and *teeth crowding:*

- ✔ **Prognathia:** Common among brachycephalic breeds, prognathism is when the dog's *mandible,* or lower part of the jaw, is longer than his *maxilla,* or the upper jaw. This *malocclusion,* or abnormal bite, is considered normal in dogs like your Boston.

- ✔ **Teeth crowding:** Crowding occurs when there is inadequate space for the teeth in the lower or upper jaw, resulting in tooth contact or overlap. Because your Boston must fit 42 teeth in his shortened mouth, it's likely that his teeth will be misaligned.

A Boston with prognathia or crowded teeth requires you to be diligent about his oral hygiene. A secondary effect of teeth crowding is increased plaque with resulting *gingivitis,* or inflammation of the gums, and a predisposition to periodontal disease, the most common cause of tooth loss in dogs (and humans).

Brush your Boston's teeth regularly to rid his mouth of plaque buildup and bacteria that can lead to *halitosis* (bad breath), behavior changes linked to oral pain, and gum infection. (Flip to Chapter 8 for details about how to brush your Boston's teeth.)

If your Boston develops halitosis, chews his toys less frequently, paws at his mouth, changes his eating habits, stops grooming himself, or shows any other signs of oral pain, contact your veterinarian. She won't recommend braces to straighten his teeth, but she may inspect his mouth, give it a thorough cleaning, and treat any localized infections.

Upper-airway syndrome

Brachycephalic breeds can be born with abnormally small openings to the nose or nasal cavity and relatively long soft *palates*
(the roof of the mouth). Dogs generally breathe through their
noses, so those affected by this upper-airway syndrome find it
difficult to inhale through the narrow openings. As a result, they
must work harder to breathe, even at rest, and doing so results in
exaggerated breathing efforts.

Dogs who still can't get enough oxygen often resort to breathing
out of their mouth, resulting in that wheezing and snorting so char-
acteristic of Bostons. In time, a lack of pressure within the airway
causes swelling of the soft palate — which is already long — further
obstructing airflow.

Telltale signs of upper-airway syndrome include

✔ Avoiding exercise

✔ Becoming short of breath after any mild exertion or stress

✔ Abnormal or noisy breathing when the dog becomes excited,
   such as when you return home from work

✔ Refusing to walk in hot weather because of the dog's inability
   to release body heat through panting

✔ *Cyanotic* (blue) gums from lack of oxygen

✔ Snoring loudly while asleep

This condition can be quite debilitating. Upper-airway syndrome
may be life-threatening if your dog plays too exuberantly in hot
weather. If your pup shows strained breathing after excitement or
overexertion, and his breathing doesn't return to normal within
5 to 10 minutes, call your veterinarian immediately and transport
your Boston to the nearest hospital for treatment.

You can, however, minimize difficulties for your Boston by

✔ Keeping his weight down. Obesity can further complicate
   breathing problems.

✔ Exercising before the sun rises or after it sets during warm
   weather, and keeping him inside on hot, humid days.

✔ Never leaving your Boston outside or alone on a hot day with
   no shade or protection.

✔ Using a harness rather than a collar when going on walks.

✔ Closely monitoring your pup's breathing.

Some Bostons benefit from surgical procedures that enlarge the nostril openings and shorten the long and swollen soft palate. This operation should be performed while the pup is under a year of age.

Tracheal hypoplasia

Brachycephalic breeds can be born with *tracheal hypoplasia,* or an underdeveloped or narrow trachea. Dogs with this anatomical disorder experience insufficient airflow through their *trachea,* or windpipe, even during normal breathing at rest.

No treatments exist to correct this problem, but you can help your Boston live with the condition. As with upper-airway syndrome (see the previous section), make it a habit not to exercise your Boston too forcibly or allow him to get overexcited. Doing so can lead to increased fatigue or even collapse after strenuous tasks or excitement. Clinical signs of respiratory difficulty, including cyanotic gums or collapse, warrant an emergency call to your veterinarian.

As a preventive measure, outfit your Boston in a harness rather than a collar for long treks. Pulling on the leash while walking can aggravate his breathing difficulties. You should also avoid using Martingale-style or choke collars if possible.

Dystocia: Birthing difficulties

Flat-faced breeds like your Boston typically have a narrow or small pelvis. This anatomical feature causes *dystocia,* or difficult birth or the inability to pass the fetus from the uterus through the birth canal. To further complicate matters, brachycephalic fetuses also have unusually large heads and wide shoulders, which further hinder normal birthing activities.

It's not uncommon for a pregnant Boston to have a Caesarian section rather than a vaginal birth, especially if other females in the family have required one.

Because you've likely had your female Boston spayed (or you're planning to do so!), this breed-specific challenge won't affect your dog. If you plan to breed your Boston, however, consult your veterinarian for advice.

What Big Eyes You Have!

Boston Terriers' eyes are set wide apart, square in the skull, with the outside corners in line with the dog's cheeks as viewed from the front. It's an endearing look, but because those eyes are so prominent, they can be prone to external injury, cataracts, and congenital defects.

If your Boston injures his eye or develops an eye problem, contact your veterinarian immediately for an examination. Because eye problems can worsen quickly, have them checked within 24 hours.

This section covers a few of the more common ocular problems.

Corneal ulcers

One of the most common ocular problems Boston Terriers experience is corneal ulcers, which are typically caused by trauma to the eye. Because those Boston eyes protrude from their skulls, they are more prone to scratches, scrapes, and pokes than other breeds' eyes. Superficial injuries to the *cornea,* or the transparent outer tissue of the eye, can lead to infections or other more serious problems.

Some common causes of corneal ulcers include

- ✔ Allergies to dander, dust, or dirt, which can cause your Boston to paw at his eyes, scratching them.

- ✔ Foreign objects, such as sand, plant material, thorns, eyelashes, or flying debris, hitting the eye and scratching it.

- ✔ Getting too close to objects at eye level. Bostons who have had their whiskers removed (typically for conformation trials) lack sensory feelers and can misjudge the distance between their face and an external object, like a plant, causing them to rub against it.

- ✔ Other dogs accidentally scraping or bumping into your Boston's eyes.

If your Boston's eyes appear red or irritated, if he keeps the eyelid partially closed to avoid light, or if you see an abnormal discharge coming from his eye, contact your veterinarian immediately.

Here are some things you can do to protect your Boston's orbs:

- ✔ Avoid prolonged sun exposure. Invest in a dog-size sun visor or some Doggles, which are available at most pet supply stores.

- ✔ Do not allow your Boston to ride in a car with his head out the window. Even when you take your Boston on a bike ride and let him sit in the basket or in a carrier, guard his eyes by making him wear eye protection of some kind.

- ✔ Avoid long hikes on dusty trails. If at all possible, limit your treks to grassy areas or paved roads. When you do hit the trail, protect his eyes and carry dog eye wash with you so you can rinse his eyes before he starts to scratch them.

- ✔ Keep dog eye wash in your travel and home first-aid kits.

- ✔ Landscape your yard with plants with minimal thorns, branches, or other growths at your Boston's eye height. If you do have rose bushes, cacti, or bougainvillea, section those areas off with fencing so your dog steers clear of them.

Cataracts

Another very common problem in Boston Terriers is cataracts, both adult and juvenile varieties. A *cataract* is a spot, or *opacity,* of any size in the lens of the eye. The opacity is usually white, creating a milky appearance over the lens. The degree of vision impairment depends on the size of the cataract and its location within the lens.

Cataracts can be inherited, caused by trauma to the eye, or the result of other diseases, such as diabetes, or nutritional disorders during puppyhood. In adults, they can appear at any age. In juveniles, they begin to show between 8 weeks and 12 months of age. Most times, congenital cataracts don't cause blindness, but they can be a handicap, especially to young dogs.

Watch for these signs that may indicate your Boston is developing cataracts:

- ✔ A bluish, white, or milky substance on his eye

- ✔ Acting surprised when you approach him from the side with the cataract

- ✔ Tendency to bump into things, to hesitate before jumping up or down, or to avoid unfamiliar environments

- ✔ Redness, inflammation, or drainage around the eye

If your Boston develops cataracts, here are some ways to make his life a little easier:

- ✔ Keep objects in the house in consistent places.

- ✔ When outside, confine your dog to a fenced yard and always walk your pup on a leash.

- ✔ If he shows signs of discomfort, this can indicate an underlying cause. Talk to your veterinarian about your dog's symptoms and ask about ways to ease his suffering.

 Though you can't stop cataracts from growing or reverse their damage, they can be surgically corrected. Talk to your veterinarian for more information about treating cataracts and getting a referral to a veterinary ophthalmologist.

Bulging eyeballs

Normally, the eyelids cover and protect the eyeball so only a small portion of the *sclera,* or white portion of the eye, is visible. With Boston Terriers and other brachycephalic breeds, however, the shortened facial bones and shallow bony orbit cause the eyeballs to protrude, exposing more of the sclera — and the eyeball — to the environment.

This abnormality, known as *macroblepharon,* or excessively long eyelids around their bulging eyeballs, can lead to a *macropalpebral fissure,* or an enlarged eyelid opening.

This condition is not life threatening, but it can look strange, especially to people who aren't familiar with brachycephalic breeds. Dogs with macroblepharon and macropalpebral fissures can have red eyes due to excessive exposure to the environment. Other complications include chronic tears or mucus, *corneal melanosis* (black or brown pigmentation of the cornea), and defective eyelid position or movement.

 In severe cases of macroblepharon, the eyeball is susceptible to *proptosis,* or forward protrusion of the eye, where the eyeball can roll forward and pop out of the orbital socket. This trauma most commonly occurs after a blunt blow to the head, pressure to the neck, or a bite wound to the eye area. If this happens, it's a medical emergency and requires immediate medical care to save the eyeball and the dog's vision.

Other eye problems

Those big, beautiful eyes are prone to a host of other ocular disorders, too. Here are some of them:

Cherry eye

This ailment involves the tear gland that normally sits at the base of the dog's third eyelid. It can enlarge and protrude beyond the leading edge of the displaced third eyelid, appearing as a round, red mass (*cherry eye*).

Under veterinary supervision, the disorder can be treated with topical anti-inflammatory medication to return the tear gland to its normal size and prevent further irritation, but cherry eye almost always requires surgical intervention to return the eye to its normal appearance.

Abnormally growing eyelashes

Some Bostons suffer from *distichiasis,* a condition in which eyelashes grow from abnormal locations along the eyelid, damaging the cornea and conjunctiva. The irritation can cause excessive tearing with inflammation.

This conformation defect can be corrected by a veterinary ophthalmologist, who can remove the stray hairs by surgical excision or by *cryosurgery,* a procedure that uses extreme cold (freezing) to destroy unwanted tissue.

Glaucoma

Typically occurring in older dogs, *glaucoma* is a buildup of fluid, causing pressure inside the eye. The pressure causes pain and eventually destroys the *retina* (the light-sensitive layer of cells at the back of the eye), which can lead to blindness.

An eye affected by glaucoma often appears bloodshot, or the cornea may look cloudy. By the time the eye begins to enlarge or swell, it's likely that the dog is experiencing vision loss. If glaucoma occurs in one eye, it's likely that the other eye will develop it, too.

After glaucoma is diagnosed by your veterinarian, the disorder can be treated through medical therapy, such as eye drops or pills that decrease fluid production in the eye, or surgical procedures that involve draining the excess fluid. Talk to your veterinarian about the different options that are available.

If you suspect that your Boston has glaucoma, consider it an emergency and contact your veterinarian immediately for an examination.

Rolled eyelids

Some Bostons experience *entropion,* where their eyelid rolls inward so that the eyelashes and eyelid hairs rub against the cornea, resulting in eyeball irritation or injury. Severe cases require surgical correction.

Dry-eye syndrome

Keratoconjunctivitis sicca (KCS), or dry-eye syndrome, is when a Boston's tear glands don't produce enough tears. This results in irritated eyes, corneal ulceration, and possible scarring. With veterinary supervision, KCS can be treated with various topical therapies, including artificial tear solutions and ointments. In chronic cases, surgery may be required.

Say What?

Boston Terriers exhibit a relatively high incidence of both *unilateral* (one ear) and *bilateral* (both ears) deafness, especially among those who have blue eyes or a high percentage of white in their coats. Some geneticists link this congenital deafness to the *piebald gene,* the gene for a white color, which can cause deafness in animals with blue eyes and white coats.

Some breeders perform a hearing test on their puppies, called a *brainstem auditory evoked response* (BAER) *test,* which detects electrical activity in the *cochlea* (an area of the inner ear) and auditory pathways in the brain. Bostons who test positive for deafness are usually not bred, but they still make wonderful pets.

In unilaterally deaf dogs, most owners won't even notice a problem. But with dogs who are deaf in both ears, the defect poses a challenge because it eliminates the major line of communication between you and the Boston. Most owners resort to training their deaf dog with hand signals and other specialized techniques.

Here are some other ear problems that your Boston may develop:

- **Outer-ear infection:** *Otitis externa,* an infection of the outer ear, occurs when wax, dirt, debris, and infectious material falls down into the dog's *ear canal,* or the outer ear. The material collects and causes the canal to swell, trapping moisture and creating an ideal environment for infection.

- **External parasites:** *Ear mites,* which are tiny arachnids related to ticks and spiders, infest the ear canal of dogs and cats. They cause a dry, reddish-brown wax that can block the ear canal in some cases, which sets up an environment for infection.

You can recognize signs of ear disease before they develop into more serious problems, which could result in permanent damage. Watch for these signs, and contact your veterinarian immediately if you suspect your Boston is suffering.

- ✔ Shaking his head and ears

- ✔ Scratching at one or both ears

- ✔ A foul odor from one ear

- ✔ A yellow, brown, or black discharge from an ear

- ✔ Inflammation, redness, or swelling of the ear flap or opening to his ear canal

- ✔ Pain when you touch on or around his ears

- ✔ Tilting his head to one side, or stumbling or circling to one side

- ✔ Tiredness or obvious loss of hearing

Trick Knees

In some Bostons, the bones, muscles, and ligaments surrounding the kneecaps of their hind legs, or *patellas,* are too narrow, weak, or shallow to keep the kneecaps in place. When a dog has a *luxated patella,* the kneecaps slip in and out of position when the dog exercises or jumps off the furniture. The dog hops and skips around until his kneecap pops back into place. The knee can slip inward toward the body or outward. Though this problem can be caused by trauma, often it's a genetic disorder.

You can provide ramps or steps down from high places to prevent your Boston from leaping off the furniture and dislocating his patella. Surgery can help correct the problem in chronic cases, but your veterinarian can also prescribe anti-inflammatory drugs to help with the pain.

Chapter 16

First Aid

In This Chapter

▶ Collecting items to include in your canine first-aid kit

▶ Handling common first-aid emergencies

▶ Deciding when to call for help

***Y**ou can handle some of your Boston Terrier's medical emergencies; for more serious matters, you'll need to seek immediate veterinary attention. Used appropriately, first aid can spare your Boston further injury and pain as you transport her to a medical facility. Most importantly, first aid can save your dog's life.

Your home should have a first-aid kit that contains a variety of commonly used tools and supplies. You should also know how to perform some basic tasks that allow you to stabilize your dog until you can get her to the veterinarian. You can find out more about these essentials in this chapter.

In addition to having the tools and the knowledge to care for your Boston during her time of need, you also need to have ready access to your vet's office and after-hours emergency numbers. Having these numbers handy will save you time when you need it most.

First-Aid Kit Essentials

Just as you have a human first-aid kit ready for handling common emergencies, you should also have a canine first-aid kit available for when your Boston cuts herself, gets into a skirmish, or heaven forbid, breaks a bone or goes into shock.

You can find prepackaged first-aid kits at your pet specialty store, or you can gather these items yourself and keep them in a prominently labeled, water-tight container in an accessible spot or alongside your human first-aid kit. Let your family — and your pet sitter — know where it is and what it contains, and make sure everyone knows how to use each item.

Your first-aid kit should include:

- Tweezers
- Scissors
- Small nail clippers for small dogs or cats
- Rectal thermometer
- Tape
- Bandages (butterfly and standard)
- Elastic bandages
- Rolls of gauze
- Gauze pads of varying sizes, including eye pads
- Cotton balls or cotton swabs
- Instant cold compress or plastic bag for ice pack
- Antiseptic cleansing wipes
- Alcohol pads
- Saline eye wash
- Hydrogen peroxide, 3 percent (to disinfect wounds)
- Styptic powder (to stop bleeding)
- Benadryl tablets (to stop an allergic reaction)
- Syrup of ipecac (to induce vomiting)
- Kaopectate tablets or liquid (to treat diarrhea)
- Iodine (to sterilize wounds)
- Antibiotic ointment
- Bottle of water
- Pen and paper
- Old blanket or sheet
- An extra leash and collar
- Pen light
- Pet first-aid book, such as the American Red Cross's *Pet First Aid: Cats and Dogs,* by Bobbie Mammato, DVM, MPH (C.V. Mosby)

Check this kit often and replace supplies that have been used or medications that have expired. If you don't know how to use these items, enroll in a basic first-aid course. The Red Cross offers a first-aid course for dog owners. If that's not available in your area, ask your veterinarian for advice.

If you travel with your dog, carry a portable first-aid kit with you in your car or suitcase, as well. Find out more about traveling with your dog in Chapter 13.

Knowing Normal Vitals

In emergencies, you'll need to check your Boston's vital signs, which include her pulse, temperature, mucous membrane color, and breathing rate. In the upcoming sections, I outline how to check these vital signs and what your dog's normal ranges should be.

Take time while your Boston is healthy to familiarize yourself with her typical vital signs. Then if an emergency arises, you'll know how to take her vital signs and how far from the norm they are.

Pulse

A dog's normal heart rate can range from 60 to 140 beats per minute. The *pulse,* or heart beat, should be strong and robust. An abnormally low heart rate, which can cause the dog to faint or lose consciousness, should always be evaluated by a veterinarian. An abnormally high heart rate may indicate that your dog is sick, in pain, or under stress, and should be evaluated by a veterinarian.

Your Boston's heart rate can be determined by *palpating* (feeling with your hands and fingers) the lower chest wall behind the shoulder or by feeling the pulse in the *femoral artery,* which is located high on the inside of each thigh.

Temperature

Normal body temperature for dogs ranges from 100 degrees Fahrenheit to 102.5 degrees Fahrenheit. It doesn't begin to reach dangerous levels until it exceeds 106 degrees Fahrenheit. Your dog's temperature will rise when she has a *fever* (an increase in body temperature due to disease) or if she is *hyperthermic* (unable to release heat as fast as she gains it).

Dogs with a fever will try to conserve heat by seeking a warm environment or by sleeping in a curled-up position; dogs who are hyperthermic will pant excessively and seek a cool environment.

You can check your Boston's temperature by using a small thermometer well lubricated with petroleum jelly and inserted into the rectum for about one minute.

Mucous membrane color

Mucous membranes line the surface of internal body cavities, such as the gums in the mouth. Blood vessels in the mucous membranes give them a pink hue (for resting dogs) or red hue (for active dogs).

When a dog experiences shock, blood loss, or *anemia* (low red blood cell count), the gums appear pale or white. Gray or blue gums can indicate low blood oxygen levels or other respiratory problems.

Check your dog's gums periodically to see what her normal coloring is. When you exercise your dog or spend time outdoors, keep an eye on her mucous membrane color to be sure she isn't overheating or experiencing breathing difficulties.

Breathing rate

The normal breathing rate for a dog at rest can range from 12 breaths per minute up to about 20 breaths per minute. Your dog's breathing rate indicates how well her respiratory system is functioning.

Pain, fever, fear, excitement, or respiratory disease will cause an increase in her breathing rate. A dog with difficult breathing may refuse to lie down and will often look anxious. If you notice a change in your dog's normal breathing pattern, consult your veterinarian immediately.

Managing First-Aid Emergencies

If your Boston is in trouble, you'll need to think and act quickly. A Boston who is bleeding, going into shock, or overheating will rely on you for emergency care. Your prompt, decisive reactions can make the difference between life and death.

You should seek professional help in life-threatening situations like severe injury or trauma. Do everything you can to stabilize the dog by getting her out of danger, and then contact your veterinarian for advice. You could save your Boston's life.

In an emergency, always call ahead to describe the nature of the problem and to let the staff know that you're on your way. You should keep the telephone numbers of your veterinarian, emergency clinic, and poison control center accessible at all times.

The emergency guidelines in this section should not replace emergency veterinary care. They are intended to assist you in caring for your Boston until you can get her to appropriate emergency care.

Restraining your Boston

An injured Boston is not a happy dog. She'll often panic, thrash, fight restraints, bite, and claw anyone who touches her. Your loving dog will turn into a frightened beast who isn't thinking clearly. She only wants to get away from the pain. In an emergency situation, you'll need to know how to restrain her so you can prevent her from hurting herself further, and so you can protect yourself. A muzzle can help in these situations.

You can make a muzzle out of pantyhose, a cotton bandage, a necktie, or any 2-foot-long piece of fabric. Here's what to do:

1. **Tie a loose knot in the middle of the fabric, leaving a large loop.**

2. **Pass the loop over the dog's muzzle and cinch it tight over the bridge of the dog's nose.**

3. **Bring the ends of the fabric under the chin, tie a knot, and draw the ends behind the ears, and tie again.**

4. **Take one of the ends of the fabric from behind the ears, pass it over the dog's forehead, and slip it under the loop around the nose. Bring it back over the forehead.**

   This step ensures that the restraint won't slip off your Boston's short snout.

5. **Tie the two ends together firmly behind the ears but not so tight that the muzzle interferes with your dog's breathing.**

If possible, practice muzzling your dog in nonemergency situations so you know what to do if the time comes. She won't like it, but you don't want to be fumbling with the fabric during a critical time!

Transporting an injured dog

Your Boston is a small dog, so you'll likely be able to transport her in your arms, in her kennel, or in a sturdy container, like a laundry basket or a cardboard box.

Practice by picking her up and rolling her onto her back so her belly is up and her face is looking at yours. Cradle her in your arms, supporting her hips with your hand and her head in your forearm. Wrap her gently in a towel or blanket. If you need to put her in a box, pick her up and carefully place her in a sturdy box lined with an old blanket or towel.

Administering artificial respiration

If your dog isn't breathing, you must perform mouth-to-nose artificial respiration. Take a deep breath and follow these steps:

1. **Lay your Boston on her right side and clear any obstructions from her mouth. Gently pull her tongue out to the side of her mouth so her airway isn't blocked.**

2. **Clasp both hands around the dog's muzzle, leaving her mouth closed yet allowing access to her nostrils.**

3. **Extend the dog's head (stretch her head and neck forward from the body), inhale, and exhale gently into your Boston's nostrils, making an airtight seal between your lips and your hands.**

   Make sure that the air doesn't leak out and that her chest rises and falls as you exhale.

4. **Repeat every five to six seconds. Continue this process until the dog breathes on her own or you can get her to a clinic.**

Performing heart massage (CPR)

Cardiopulmonary resuscitation (CPR) should be performed if your dog's heart has stopped beating. The signs of cardiac arrest include

- ✔ Unconsciousness
- ✔ Stopped breathing
- ✔ Stopped heartbeat
- ✔ White or blue gums
- ✔ Wide dilation of her pupils

When performed properly, CPR can help restore breathing and cardiac function in an emergency situation. Here's what to do:

1. **Lay your dog down on a flat, hard surface that won't bend when the chest is compressed.**

2. **Apply pressure with the flat part of your hand directly over the heart area (just behind the front legs in the lower half of the chest) with a force that's appropriate for your dog, and press firmly at a rate of about 70 times per minute, being careful not to break her ribs.**

   The compression force should be enough to cause the dog's chest wall to compress about 50 percent.

3. **Release the compression completely for a brief period each time to allow the blood to flow back into the chest.**

4. **Check the color of the dog's gums.**

   If the procedure is producing blood flow, you should see her mucus membrane color turn from white or gray to pink or red. Also check for your dog's femoral arterial pulse, which is located high on the inside of each thigh.

5. **Enlist the help of a second person to perform artificial respiration after every three chest compressions.**

6. **If the heart hasn't begun to beat after 5 to 10 minutes, it's probably not helpful to continue.**

   In the hospital setting, CPR is rarely performed after 30 minutes.

Common canine emergencies

Not all injuries require veterinary treatment. You can often handle scrapes, superficial wounds, insect bites, and bruises at home. You can observe your dog if she is experiencing mild vomiting and diarrhea, monitoring the situation if it worsens.

Some medical emergencies, however, will require veterinary care. Here, I list common medical emergencies that you can stabilize at home before taking your pet to the emergency veterinary clinic.

Bleeding

Bleeding can occur from just about any injury. How you treat it depends on the wound and its severity.

- **A bruise:** Apply an ice pack to the area in 15-minute intervals (15 minutes on, 15 minutes off) until the swelling subsides.

- **Minor cuts and scrapes:** Wipe the wound clean with an alcohol pad and apply pressure with a gauze pad until the bleeding stops. Cover the cut with a bandage to keep it clean, changing it as needed.

- **Severe wounds:** Apply several layers of gauze and bandage snugly, being careful not to secure it too tight. If direct pressure fails to slow the rate of bleeding, you may need to apply a tourniquet. Using a length of gauze or cloth, tie the tourniquet on the limb between the injury and the heart. The tourniquet must be loosened for several minutes approximately every 10 minutes to allow blood flow to the tissue.

   Severe wounds should be evaluated by a veterinarian, so as soon as you control the bleeding, call your vet and take your dog to the closest emergency veterinary clinic.

Shock

Shock occurs after a traumatic injury or during a serious, sudden illness like heat stroke or accidental poisoning. It's characterized by the collapse of the cardiovascular system. Dogs in shock show the following signs:

- ✔ They appear weak and listless.
- ✔ Their pupils may be dilated.
- ✔ Their pulse is weak and rapid.
- ✔ Their gums are pale.
- ✔ Their skin color is slow to return when pressed with a finger.

If you suspect your Boston is in shock, treat any visible injuries. Keep her still, bundled in a blanket, and get her to a veterinarian immediately. Shock is life-threatening, and when combined with a traumatic injury, your dog could be in serious danger of dying.

Fractures

Fractures require immediate attention. A dog with a fractured or broken bone will hold its limb in an unnatural position. Sometimes a broken bone is visible through the skin. Muzzle your dog (see the "Restraining your Boston" section earlier in the chapter for the how-to), moving her as little as possible, and place her in a stable box to transport her to the veterinarian. Try to support the broken limb with a rolled-up magazine or cushion, if possible.

Heat stroke

Common in warm climates, dehydration or heat stroke can occur when dogs are overexercised during hot temperatures. It can also occur when dogs are left in cars on warm days or when kennel areas aren't ventilated properly.

A dog with heat stroke breathes rapidly, has a rapid heartbeat, and has a high body temperature (104 degrees Fahrenheit or higher). Depending on the severity, she may also be in shock. A dangerously overheated dog will likely die without proper veterinary treatment.

Immediately spray your Boston with cool water, and pack ice in the groin and around her head and neck. Wrap the dog in cold, wet towels, and seek professional care immediately.

To prevent heat stroke, never leave your Boston alone inside a closed car or in a poorly ventilated kennel on a hot day. Instead, be sure she has fresh air, fresh water, and sufficient shade.

Vomiting and diarrhea

An indicator of problems with your dog's digestive system, vomiting and diarrhea can be caused by anything from spicy food to poison. Mild cases can be watched; contact a veterinarian if the situation worsens.

Excessive vomiting or diarrhea can cause dehydration, and that can happen quickly in a small dog like your Boston, so make sure she drinks plenty of water. If the condition doesn't seem severe, feed your dog a bland diet of plain cooked chicken and rice for the first 12 hours. If her condition doesn't improve, contact your vet.

Insect stings

If you suspect that your Boston has been stung by a bee or a wasp, first determine where the sting happened and remove the stinger by scraping it out or removing it with tweezers. Shave the area if you need to so you can see the sting. Wash the area thoroughly, bathe it with hydrogen peroxide, and watch for swelling.

Animal bites

Play fighting and wrestling with other dogs can sometimes get out of hand, resulting in a small puncture wound or superficial injury. If this happens, simply clean the wound and keep an eye on it. Check with the owner of the other dog to be sure that the dog is vaccinated. Any signs of infection warrant a call to the veterinarian.

If your Boston is attacked by a larger dog or an unknown dog, however, call your veterinarian right away. Some bites may require special treatment, like antibiotics. The attack may have caused internal injuries or bleeding that needs to be treated immediately.

Attacks by cats or wild animals also necessitate a call to the vet. Cat bites frequently cause infections, and bites from raccoons or other wild creatures can put your Boston at risk for rabies.

Poisoning

Dogs love to explore and taste just about everything they come across, but sometimes their curiosity gets them into trouble. They may ingest something poisonous that they find in the garage, in the yard, or in the house.

Symptoms of poisoning vary and depend on what substance your Boston ate. Common signs include extreme salivation and drooling, vomiting, diarrhea, and muscle tremors. The dog's eyes may be dilated, or she may suffer seizures. Rat poisons and other oral rodenticides can produce internal bleeding, convulsions, and death if not treated immediately.

Common household poisons

Store these and other common household poisons well out of your Boston's reach:

✔ Antifreeze and other car fluids

✔ Bleach and other cleaning fluids

✔ Chocolate

✔ Ibuprofen, acetaminophen, or prescription medications

✔ Insecticides and herbicides

✔ Rat, roach, or snail poison

If you suspect that your dog has ingested a poisonous substance, call the ASPCA's Animal Poison Control Center hotline at 888-426-4435 (you may be charged a $55 consultation fee) and contact your veterinarian immediately. The longer the poison is in her system, the more extensive the damage may be.

Chapter 17

Caring for the Senior Dog

- -

In This Chapter

▶ Understanding what it means to own a senior dog

▶ Identifying age-related health changes

▶ Keeping your Boston comfortable as he ages

▶ Coping with the loss of your dog

- -

*Y*ou and your Boston Terrier have enjoyed a long and fun-filled life together. You watched him mature from puppyhood to adulthood, loving him and training him to be a well-mannered dog. You cared for his every need, from filling his belly to taking him to the veterinarian for regular checkups. In return, he looked up to you as his leader. He has been your best friend.

The time will come when you realize that your Boston isn't as spry as he once was. He doesn't dash to the door when visitors come to visit or leap from his bed when you pull out his favorite toy. He's slowing down and losing the spring in his step. He's getting old.

As he ages, your Boston will require some special treatment. Though you can't stop the aging process, you can do some things that make him comfortable through his senior years. The remaining days with your dog can then be filled with fun, love, and caring until the time comes to say goodbye.

For more information about the topics covered in this chapter, pick up *Senior Dogs For Dummies* by Susan McCullough (Wiley). The book is chockfull of advice to help you care for your aging pet.

Knowing the Signs of Aging

Generally, small dogs live longer than big dogs, and your Boston Terrier is no exception. By the age of 8 years old, your pup has reached his senior years. Though he will likely live until he's 11 or 12 years old, he will begin to show some signs of aging, including

- ✔ A loss of strength and flexibility

- ✔ An intolerance of cold and heat

- ✔ An increased susceptibility to certain diseases

- ✔ A gradual deterioration of organ functions

- ✔ A little gray around the edges — just like his pet parents!

Because of his increasing frailty, you need to protect him from environmental stressors, such as allergies and temperature fluctuations. You need to pay greater attention to his health problems, like coughing and weight gain, and take him to the veterinarian more frequently to screen for abnormal body functions. As he ages, you also need to slowly change his diet, provide a comfortable living environment for him, and give him adequate and appropriate exercise.

Keep a closer eye on your Boston as the years pass. Watch for signs of disease acquired in old age, including sudden weight loss, appetite loss, diarrhea or vomiting, increased thirst without a change in activity or urination level, excessive fatigue, limited mobility, or coughing or excessive panting. If your Boston exhibits any of these symptoms, contact your veterinarian immediately.

Age-Related Disorders

As your Boston's body ages, it begins to break down and show signs of wear and tear. His movements may become more deliberate, he may gain weight, or he may become hard of hearing. You'll notice subtle changes in your pup's personality and behavior as his birthdays pass.

Following are some common age-related afflictions that you can look out for as your Boston ages.

Arthritis

Arthritis is a degenerative joint disease that causes stiffness in the joints, just as it does in humans. Age and wear cause the joints to break down, which can be quite painful when your Boston tries to get up from a nap or walk across the room. As he ages, you may see him walk more slowly or hesitate before he moves. If you suspect arthritis, consult with your veterinarian.

An X-ray of the affected joints will confirm an arthritis diagnosis. Your vet will likely prescribe an anti-inflammatory or pain-relieving medication to ease your dog's stiffness and discomfort. She may also recommend alternative treatments, such as massage, acupuncture, or chiropractic work, to relieve pain or stress. Ask her, too, if dietary supplements will help slow the degenerative process.

Be aware that your Boston may be sore when you pick him up. If he yelps, make note of the painful area and select a different area to hold the next time you lift him. Make sure your vet is aware of any yelping because that can signal more serious problems than arthritis or simple aches and pains.

You can change your Boston's environment to make it more comfortable for him and to ease the pain that arthritis can bring. Buy him a cushy bed that's soft and supportive, keeping it away from cold drafts to keep his joints elastic. Move his food and water bowls closer to his bed so he doesn't have to walk as far for food and drink. If you let him on the bed or couch, help him up by providing a ramp or stairs. Do whatever you can to make his life easier.

Just because he's aging, however, doesn't mean you should stop exercising him. Continue to take your Boston on walks and let him play in the warm sunshine. He may not walk three miles, but moving his body will help him feel better.

Cancer

Just as treatments for human cancer continue to improve, scientists are making advances in treating canine cancer, too. Chemotherapy, radiation, and oncology care can be expensive, but cancer no longer means a death sentence like it once did! Lives are being saved every day, thanks to early detection and therapy.

Cancer can occur at any age, but it frequently presents at an older age. It is one of the most common health problems senior dogs may have. Abnormal cells grow out of control and damage healthy tissue, affecting normal body function. Common canine cancers include tumors of the skin and subcutaneous tissue, mammary glands, bone, lymphoid tissues, blood-forming organs, and mouth, though virtually any site may give rise to tumors.

Every lump and bump does not mean cancer, but it should be evaluated by a veterinarian for proper diagnosis. She will either remove some tissue from the lump with a needle or perform a biopsy to determine whether it is *benign* (not cancerous) or *malignant* (cancerous). If it is malignant, you and your veterinarian can discuss the pros and cons of treating your dog.

Deafness

Older dogs frequently suffer from impaired hearing. As they get older, the sound receptors in their ears degenerate, causing gradual hearing loss. It may seem like your Boston is ignoring you, but he's not! It's likely that he's a little hard of hearing.

If you suspect that your Boston is losing his hearing, take him to your veterinarian to rule out an ear infection or generalized neurological disease. If he's otherwise healthy, you can manage his disability by using signal commands instead of verbal commands. You'll also want to watch him carefully when he's outside because he won't be able to hear approaching cars or other dangers.

Dogs who are going deaf may be easily startled. Depending on your Boston's temperament, he may respond aggressively to surprises.

Diabetes

Diabetes mellitus is an abnormal increase in blood sugar levels that is usually caused by an insulin deficiency. Though it is treatable, diabetes can affect your Boston's health and cause long-term complications if left untreated, including blindness, infections, weight loss, pancreatitis, and death.

The cause of insulin-dependant diabetes is unknown, but many factors contribute to its appearance in dogs. Genes, obesity, infection, and inflammation of the pancreas may all play a role in developing the disease.

Watch your Boston's food and water intake. Clinical signs of diabetes mellitus include increased appetite and water consumption, increased frequency and volume of urination, and weight loss. If these signs go unnoticed, sudden blindness may occur because of cataract formation, or *diabetic ketoacidosis* (ketone buildup in the blood) may develop, resulting in lethargy and vomiting.

If your Boston develops insulin-dependant diabetes, your veterinarian will recommend that you adjust his diet to include food that keeps his blood sugar level constant. You may also need to inject insulin under your dog's skin twice a day. Your veterinarian will develop an individualized plan for you and your dog.

Eye disorders

Older dogs frequently suffer from *cataracts,* a cloudy white spot, or *opacity,* on the lens of the eye that interferes with vision. As a cataract forms, it causes lens protein to leak into the eye, which triggers an immune response and inflammation. A veterinary *ophthalmologist* (eye doctor) can remove the cataract, but most dogs handle gradual vision loss quite well, provided home furnishings are kept stable so they learn how to weave through the room and avoid obstacles.

Nuclear sclerosis, an age-related change in the structure of the lens, also causes a cloudiness of the lens, but it doesn't affect the vision or produce any inflammation. Your veterinarian can determine whether a cloudy eye is from a cataract or nuclear sclerosis.

Glaucoma, a buildup of pressure inside the eye, also comes with age. An eye with glaucoma is often swollen and enlarged, and looks red and weepy. If left untreated, it can cause blindness by destroying the retina. Several medical treatment options are available. Your veterinarian can recommend the right one for your Boston Terrier.

If your dog starts to lose his vision, make his treks though your house easier by getting on your knees and making any necessary accommodations. Avoid moving furniture, placing new objects in his path, and leaving doors open. Remove sharp objects or other dangers that can injure him, and put up a baby gate at the top of the stairs to prevent falls.

Dogs who are going blind may not appreciate surprises, and as a result, they may respond fearfully or aggressively, depending on their temperament.

Heart problems

Your Boston's heart pumps blood through four different chambers. It uses valves that open and close to control blood flow through the heart. All these movements create normal heart sounds.

As your dog ages, his heart valves become so worn that they fail to close completely with the beating of the heart. Blood flows backward through the partially closed valve, creating an abnormal heart sound called a *heart murmur.* Small dogs, like Bostons, frequently suffer from heart murmurs. It doesn't cause death, but it should be closely monitored by your veterinarian.

Poor dental care can cause some heart murmurs. When a dog's teeth aren't brushed and cleaned properly, tartar builds up. Bacteria from the tartar sheds into the bloodstream, and it can attach to the heart valves and cause leaks or murmurs. Good oral hygiene — brushing your dog's teeth daily, and having a veterinarian check and clean his pearly whites regularly — prevents tartar buildup, which lessens the chances of your senior dog developing a heart murmur. (Jump to Chapter 8 for details on how to brush your dog's teeth.)

Kidney disease

Though the kidneys can be injured at any time in the dog's life from infection, injury, shock, or an attack of the immune system, geriatric dogs can suffer from *chronic kidney disease,* which is the gradual deterioration of the kidney function. It is often incurable, but you can manage the disease through veterinary care and diet.

Kidneys eliminate waste products from the dog's blood stream and regulate the body's water content. When the kidneys fail, the entire body shuts down, leading to serious illness and death.

If your senior Boston has unusually bad breath, becomes dehydrated, drinks a lot of water, and urinates frequently, he may have kidney disease. Call your veterinarian, who will examine your Boston and perform blood tests to determine whether your dog's kidneys are functioning properly.

Prescription diets available from your vet will help your dog's kidneys to perform at their best. Monitor the amount of water your Boston drinks, too. Depending on his activity level, 15-pound dogs require 20 ounces (2 ½ cups) of water per day; 20-pound dogs require 24 ounces (3 cups) of water per day. Call your veterinarian if your Boston is drinking a lot more than that.

Obesity

As dogs age, they become less active and generally require fewer calories than they did as puppies. Their *metabolic rate* (the speed at which the body burns calories) slows, and if they continue to eat the same amount, they will gain weight.

Weight gain can lead to a host of adverse health effects, including diabetes, susceptibility to infection, shortened life, increased pressure on vital organs and joints, and decreased energy. Obesity also exacerbates problems brought on by arthritis. As your dog ages, you need to keep his weight in check.

To keep off unwanted pounds, follow the same weight-control principles as for all other animals (including humans): Decrease his food intake and increase his exercise. Talk to your veterinarian before changing his diet or taking him for a run. She may recommend a senior diet for your dog that has fewer calories or encourage you to reduce the amount you feed your dog. She will also recommend an appropriate exercise routine.

Urinary incontinence

Older female dogs often develop a loss of voluntary bladder control, or *urinary incontinence*. As she ages, she loses the ability to hold her urine, so you'll find puddles in her bed, or you'll see urine drip from the vulva with her unaware.

Take your Boston to your veterinarian for a complete examination and diagnosis. In some cases, you can manage your dog's urinary incontinence with oral medication; in others, you'll need to put some doggy diapers on your Boston to keep the mess under control.

Handling Your Senior Boston with Kid Gloves

When your Boston reaches his golden years, you'll want to do whatever you can to keep him comfortable. He may not eat as much or play as much as he did when he was a pup, but he still has a lot of love to give. Keeping him comfortable on a cushy bed, taking him for short walks, and visiting your veterinarian will ensure that he'll be happy and healthy during the sunset of his life.

Veterinary visits

As with elderly people, some senior dogs require more frequent visits to the doctor. New health issues crop up more often, and it's always better to get a professional opinion, even if it seems like a minor ailment. It could be the beginning of a more serious problem.

When you take your Boston to the veterinarian, load him gently into the car, hooking his harness into the carrier or car seat, and making sure that he's safe and comfortable. At the office, remember that his hearing and sight won't be as keen as it once was. Be aware of intimidating dogs who may frighten him.

When your Boston reaches his eighth birthday or so, schedule a veterinary visit for your geriatric dog. Your dog's doctor will perform some screening exams to check your dog's bodily functions, to look for signs of disease, and to establish a baseline to measure against as he ages. Tests may include a urinalysis, blood work, and chest X-rays.

If the doctor gives your elderly Boston a clean bill of health, you won't have to return until the following year (unless you notice something out of the ordinary, of course). But if the veterinarian sees signs of health problems or diagnoses your dog with a particular disease, plan to bring him in more often.

Nutrition

Throughout your Boston's life, nutrition is a key component in his overall health and vitality. Food provides the carbohydrates, fats, protein, vitamins, and minerals that help your dog create enough energy to tackle the world. When your Boston gets older, he doesn't need as much energy anymore. He'll require fewer calories to keep him going. Feeding him the same amount of food you did when he was a teenager or adult will cause him to put on unwanted pounds, which could lead to a variety of health issues.

Talk to your veterinarian about what type of diet your Boston should be eating. She'll most likely recommend one formulated for senior dogs, or one that is lower in calories than an adult diet.

Forgo the treats, too, for more healthy alternatives. Instead of giving her biscuits and goodies from the dog bakery all the time, do so sparingly and intersperse crunchy vegetables among the high-calorie choices. Don't forget: Treats have calories, too, and they pack on the pounds just like his regular diet!

Make sure that your Boston drinks plenty of water. If you notice that he's not drinking enough, add some water to his food bowl, or mix his dry kibble with some canned food. Sometimes older dogs can be fussy about their water bowls, so make sure that your Boston's bowl is clean and full of fresh water at all times. If you see that your dog isn't eating or drinking enough, contact your vet.

Exercise

All physically able dogs need exercise, even the older ones. Getting up and moving helps him strengthen and tone his muscles and tendons. It improves cardiac condition and it keeps his digestive tract functioning as it should. It also keeps his weight in check.

Your Boston may not be able to hike five miles like he once did, but he will enjoy a leisurely saunter around the block once a day to keep his mind and body stimulated. Strap on his harness, attach the lead, grab some pickup bags, and stroll to the park, letting him sniff and investigate all along the way. Even on short walks, bring along some water in case he gets thirsty or needs a break.

As your dog ages, follow his lead when it comes to physical activity. If he wants to lounge around all day, that's okay! If he wants to play fetch for only 20 minutes, that's okay! The point is to keep him moving, even if it's less frequently than before.

Bedding and sleeping area

There's nothing like a cushy bed, especially if you have stiff joints or aching bones. As your Boston ages, he'll enjoy a big, comfortable dog bed with a soft blanket and his favorite plush toy. If you can, place a cushion or bed in all the rooms where your Boston relaxes. Make sure that it's washable, just in case of an accident.

Because dogs with arthritis may not be able to jump on or off beds and couches like they once did, purchase some soft dog stairs or stack pillows from the floor to the bed or a chair for easy access. Sometimes your Boston would rather cuddle with you than curl up in his own bed!

Grooming

In general, Bostons don't require too much grooming, and seniors are no exception. With his short coat, he needs daily brushing with a slicker brush to pull away the dead hair and with a bristle brush to make the coat shine. He needs monthly nail trims and baths to make his coat smell fresh. And he needs regular eye and ear checks to inspect for any infections. Maintain a regular dental-cleaning schedule, too, because you want those pearly whites to stay healthy so he can eat!

Grooming time offers a perfect opportunity to look over your Boston's body for abnormal lumps, growths, or sore spots. As you're brushing him, feel all over his body and watch how he reacts. You'll know if something doesn't seem right.

Bidding Adieu to Your Boston

You've raised your Boston since he was a puppy. You housetrained him, cared for him, taught him how to sit, and saw him through good times and bad. You shared adventures and built wonderful memories together. When he was a puppy, you never imagined the time would come to say goodbye. Suddenly, it's right before you.

One of the hardest things to do is say goodbye to a beloved pet. The thought of losing a companion is very painful, and as your Boston reaches the end of his life, you will have to decide when it's time to let him to go.

How to know when it's time

In some cases, it's easy to know when to let your pet go. If he has a serious medical condition that takes him to emergency room, the decision might be made for you, or if his kidneys fail or he has heart failure, you know it's time to say goodbye.

Other times, the decision isn't so easy. It's really up to you to determine what you can watch your dog endure. Some people can't stand to see their dog lose his eyesight or his ability to climb a flight of stairs. Others don't want to see their pet in pain or suffer through a terminal illness, like cancer. At the same time, some pet owners don't want to let their pet go. They'd rather wait until the dog dies from natural causes. As in life, your Boston will rely on you to make the best choice for him.

If your Boston has lost control of his urinary and bowel functions, refuses to eat, can't walk, or just seems completely disinterested in his surroundings, think about putting him down. Why let him struggle to cope with everyday life? Discuss the situation with your family, and then consult with your veterinarian for advice. She will evaluate your Boston's condition and help you make the ultimate decision: whether to euthanize him.

What to expect

Although the decision to put your dog to sleep can take days or months, the act of *euthanizing* him takes only minutes.

Leaving your pet in your will

If you die before your Boston, who will care for him?

Believe it or not, many people neglect this detail when they're preparing their wills, and their beloved pet winds up in an animal shelter.

Talk with your family and friends, and decide who will be a suitable caretaker if you pass away before your dog. Perhaps your sister or son is willing to adopt your Boston. Maybe you have a friend who already has a brood of Bostons, and she would be happy to welcome another.

After you decide on a person, talk to your lawyer and include your pet in your will. You may also decide to specify that a certain amount of money go to the person caring for your Boston to cover the costs of food, veterinary care, and other pet-related expenses.

At the clinic, you will be shown into an exam room or office-like setting. After you say goodbye and give your Boston one last hug, your veterinarian will inject a large dose of barbiturates into his bloodstream, which causes his brain to stop functioning. He will lose consciousness, his heart will stop beating, and he will stop breathing. Some veterinarians administer a sedative before injecting the barbiturates to calm the dog and reassure the owner that the dog won't suffer or feel afraid.

Euthanasia is a completely painless procedure. Your pup will drift off into a deep, peaceful sleep before his bodily functions cease. One minute, he's looking up at you or the vet, and the next minute, he's gone. He experiences no fear at all.

Talk to your vet about whether she can come to your home to euthanize your Boston. If not, schedule an office appointment early or late in the day to avoid having to face a waiting room full of pets and their parents. Let your vet know your feelings and trepidations about putting your pet to sleep, and she's likely to make the process as easy as possible for you.

Some pet owners want to be with their pet during the procedure, and some don't. No matter what you decide, that choice is yours, and it will be the right one for you. Either way, your veterinarian will handle your dog humanely and with care.

You will feel the loss of your beloved pet, but he will be set free from any suffering that he may be enduring. Sometimes, euthanasia is the only thing you can do to alleviate the pain from a major illnesses or trauma. If your veterinarian's prognosis is that your dog will continue to deteriorate, you have little choice.

Remembering your beloved Boston

Before your dog is put to sleep, talk to your veterinarian about what you can do with his remains. Most clinics cremate deceased animals there or at a remote facility. If you want to keep your Boston's ashes in an urn, or if you'd like to bury him in a pet-sized coffin, let your vet know. She can make arrangements to accommodate your request.

You've likely taken lots of photographs of your Boston throughout his lifetime. As you're grieving, take them out and look at them. Put them in a photo album, jotting down significant memories or funny stories that pop into your mind. Gathering the keepsakes together helps perpetuate your pup's memory.

A tribute to cherished pets

This lovely poem offers hope for pet lovers who lose their furry friends. Grab a tissue before you read it because this one's a tear-jerker!

Rainbow Bridge

Just this side of heaven is a place called Rainbow Bridge.

When an animal dies that has been especially close to someone here, that pet goes to Rainbow Bridge. There are meadows and hills for all of our special friends so they can run and play together. There is plenty of food, water and sunshine, and our friends are warm and comfortable.

All the animals who had been ill and old are restored to health and vigor. Those who were hurt or maimed are made whole and strong again, just as we remember them in our dreams of days and times gone by. The animals are happy and content, except for one small thing; they each miss someone very special to them, who had to be left behind.

They all run and play together, but the day comes when one suddenly stops and looks into the distance. His bright eyes are intent. His eager body quivers. Suddenly he begins to run from the group, flying over the green grass, his legs carrying him faster and faster.

You have been spotted, and when you and your special friend finally meet, you cling together in joyous reunion, never to be parted again. The happy kisses rain upon your face; your hands again caress the beloved head, and you look once more into the trusting eyes of your pet, so long gone from your life but never absent from your heart.

Then you cross Rainbow Bridge together.

— Author unknown

Talk about your pet with family and loved ones while you're grieving. Share memories and celebrate the time you all had together. Let the tears flow; don't be ashamed of your pain. Just because your Boston was a dog doesn't mean he didn't significantly affect your life! He was a part of your family, and you have every right to mourn his passing.

Some people advocate rushing out and replacing your pup right away. This may or may not be the best decision; only you know whether you're ready or if you need more time. No matter how many pets you have in your life, each one occupies a special place in your heart.

Part V
The Part of Tens

DR. DOUG AND HIS BOSTON TERRIER SHARED A UNIQUE COMPANIONSHIP.

C'mon Misty — scissors, scissors! That's a scalpel. You know that!

In this part . . .

If you're like many dog lovers, you search out little bits of trivia to share with friends and family. This section contains three chapters that are chockfull of fun facts about Boston Terriers. You discover ten little-known tidbits about the breed and ten ways to bring even more joy to your pet's life.

Chapter 18

Ten Trivia Tidbits about Bostons

In This Chapter

▶ Interesting historical facts about Boston Terriers

▶ The rise and fall — and rise again — of Boston popularity

▶ Bostons making their mark

*P*art of the fun of owning a Boston Terrier — or any purebred dog, for that matter — is to acquaint yourself with fascinating facts about the breed.

In this chapter, I list ten little-known bits of trivia about Boston Terriers that you can use to impress friends and family members.

The Dogfather

J.P. Barnard, known as the father of the Boston Terrier, used his dogs Tom and Mike at stud more than any other dogs at that time through his kennels on Myrtle Street in Boston. Many consider Mike to be the first to portray the 20th-century Boston Terrier look. He was the *sire* (father) of Punch, one of the first Bostons registered by the American Kennel Club.

An American Original

Boston Terriers join the American Water Spaniel, Toy Fox Terrier, and Chesapeake Bay Retriever as one of the few dog breeds native to the United States. Hailing from Boston, Massachusetts, Bostons are such relative newcomers, in fact, that their ancestry can be traced back to the beginning of the breed.

It all started with Hooper's Judge, a bulldog-terrier blend, imported from England in 1865 by Robert C. Hooper. Judge, with his dark brindle-and-white coat, was bred to Burnett's Gyp, a stockier, blockier dog. They produced Well's Eph, who was bred to Tobin's Kate and resulted in Barnard's Tom, owned by J.P. Barnard. That dog was considered to be the first true representative of the Boston Terrier breed.

What's in a Name?

On February 27, 1893, the Boston Terrier was recognized by the AKC. But the breed wasn't always known by that name. Before 1889, fanciers and breeders of this bulldog-terrier blend referred to their dogs as the "round-headed bulldog," "Boston bulldog," "toy bulldog," and "bullet head." Fitting names, indeed!

In 1889, a group of 40 breeders led by Charles F. Leland gathered and began to keep breeding records of these bulldog-terrier blends. They called themselves the American Bull Terrier Club and actively sought AKC approval of the breed.

In 1891, the group applied for admission into the AKC stud book. Bulldog and Bull Terrier fanciers, however, lobbied against acceptance of the breed, citing concerns about the inconsistent breeding program and the confusing name "American Bull Terrier."

After two years of discussions between the AKC committee and the Boston breeders, they decided that only one cross to a Bulldog or a Bull Terrier would be allowed, and that it could only be in the third generation. They also decided that because the dog originated in Boston, he should be called the Boston Terrier.

Manly Moniker

As dapper and well-mannered as any four-legged companion, Boston Terriers have earned the nickname "American Gentleman" for their polite and amiable personalities. With a subdued terrier temperament, most Bostons are alert, loving, intelligent, and devoted: traits embodied by any true "gentleman."

Top Billing

At the beginning of the 20th century, Boston Terriers' popularity soared. The Boston Terrier Club of America's records show that between 1905 and 1935, Bostons held one of the top two spots among the AKC's registered breeds. Between 1921 and 1934, 90,000 Bostons were listed with the registry.

From 1920 through 1964, Bostons remained among the top-ten most popular dogs registered with the AKC. Today, Bostons still rank relatively high, typically falling within the top-20 registered breeds. They ranked the 15th most popular breed in 2006.

Little Men on Campus

Boston University's Rhett became the college's official mascot on November 15, 1922. Named after a character from *Gone with the Wind,* Rhett attends soccer, basketball, and lacrosse games. He performs on the ice during hockey game intermissions. He even makes special appearances on the BU campus, at area hospitals, and at local schools for holiday events. Rhett has become a national celebrity, being named an All-American mascot in 1996 and placing fourth in the National Mascot Championships in 2002.

Wofford College in Spartanburg, South Carolina, boasts three Boston Terrier mascots in its athletic program. Boss the Terrier has entertained Wofford fans since 2001 at football, basketball, and baseball games. Lil' Ruff, a pint-size version of Boss, entertains kids at sporting events and graces the cover of "Terrier Tales," a reading program started in 2006 at the Spartanburg County Library. Blitz, a real-live Boston Terrier, was named the official mascot of the Wofford Athletic Department in 2003. Owned by Chris and Jean Williams, Blitz patrols the sidelines at every home football game.

Popular beyond Boston

Understandably, Boston Terriers enjoy a huge popularity in Boston, but not as much as they once did. AKC statistics show a steady decline in Boston registration in the city, from ranking 8th in 2004 to 10th in 2005, and slipping to 11th in 2006.

Other cities, however, have embraced the Boston. Portland, Oregon; Sacramento, California; and Seattle, Washington, for example, welcomed the Boston on their lists of top-ten registered dog breeds in 2006.

The Incredible Shrinking Dog

The Boston Terrier's breed standard states that the dog should weigh between 10 and 25 pounds. In the early days, however, Bostons weighed anywhere from a petite 7 pounds to a hefty 35 pounds.

After the AKC acknowledged Bostons as an official breed in 1893, breeders and fanciers began to standardize the dog. Its color markings became symmetrical, its "American Gentleman" demeanor was developed, and its body shape evolved from that of a blocky bulldog to a wiry terrier.

State of the Boston

As a testament to the Boston's popularity in its home state, Massachusetts Boston fanciers started a movement to have the Boston Terrier named the state dog. In 1979, Gov. Edward Joseph King made it official. Boston Terriers now join wild turkeys, the Morgan horse, and the tabby cat as the official dog, bird, horse, and cat of Massachusetts.

Odds 'n' Ends

Boston Terriers have enjoyed their 15 minutes of fame. Here are some celebrity Bostons and their owners:

- In the original book version of L. Frank Baum's *The Wonderful Wizard of Oz,* Toto is believed to be a Yorkshire Terrier, being described as a "little black dog with long silky hair." Most people recognize Toto as a Cairn Terrier from the 1939 film version. But in later books in the *Oz* series, Toto transforms into a Boston Terrier.

- Helen Keller's classmates from Radcliffe College gave her a Boston Terrier named Sir Thomas Belvedere. He became one of her canine companions during her life.

- Badger the Boston Terrier starred in a trilogy of MasterCard commercials in 2004. In the ads, his family accidentally leaves him behind in the Redwoods, but Badger makes it home, encountering various acts of kindness from strangers along the way.

- Hollywood celebrity Joan Rivers shares her life with Lulu, a Boston Terrier. Denise Richards, former Bond girl, also owns two Bostons: Lucy and Stella.

Chapter 19

Ten Ways to Make Your Boston's Day

In This Chapter

▶ Giving your Boston treats and toys

▶ Organizing get-togethers for your dog and his canine friends

▶ Getting out and exploring with your Boston

*W*hat you wouldn't do for your Boston! Being your best friend, a source of entertainment, and all-around great pet, there's no doubt that you want to give him the best things in life.

In this chapter, I've listed some ways to truly bring a smile to your Boston's adorable face. Not only are these activities healthy and fun, but they also strengthen the bond between you and your pet.

Get the Day Off to a Good Start

A healthy breakfast fuels your Boston's fun. What better way to make his day than to give him a bowl full of nutritious kibble or wet food? The protein, carbohydrates, and fats give him the energy to patrol the yard, play fetch, and be your little shadow for the whole day.

He also needs a cool drink to wash his kibble down, so provide a clean bowl of chilled water alongside his food bowl. Keep an eye on it all day, too, to be sure that he has fresh water available whenever he wants it. (Chapter 7 gives you the scoop on feeding your pup.)

Take a Walk

With his adorable snub-nose mug, your Boston is likely to be the most popular pup in the neighborhood. Another way to make your Boston's day is to take him on a stroll to visit his human and canine friends around the block.

Get his gear together and prepare to hit the road. Put on a colorful collar with an ID tag, attach a matching leash, and grab some pickup bags and treats for on-the-road cleanup and rewards. Then it's time to head out!

Stroll to the Park

If you're lucky enough to have a dog park in your neighborhood, it's a perfect destination when walking your Boston. *Dog parks* are generally fenced-in play areas where dog owners let their pets stretch their legs, run free, and romp with their canine friends.

Before you take your pup to a dog park, make sure he's up to date on all his vaccinations, including rabies and bordetella (kennel cough). Check his ID tag, too, and purchase a new one if any of the information is outdated or unreadable.

Throw a Party

You host parties for yourself or your child, so why not throw a bash for your Boston, too! Consider birthday parties, play dates, holiday parties, and so on as fun excuses for bringing together your friends and their pets.

Give Your Boston a Bone

Most dogs love chew toys like bones, knuckles, Kongs, and other hard-plastic toys. These items, which keep tartar and plaque from forming on his teeth, can be found at your local pet-specialty store, and they come in a range of flavors, styles, and sizes. Choose one that's sized appropriately for your pup — and one that he likes!

Take a Spa Day

Though a deep doggy massage should only be done by a trained professional, you can give your Boston a light rubdown during his bath, while you're grooming him, or while you're watching television. Follow these simple steps:

1. Have your dog lay on a soft, firm surface, like a carpeted floor or rug. Starting from his head, gently stroke your fingers down his body to his tail.

2. When your pup begins to relax, rub his cheeks, under his chin, and behind his ears.

3. Move down his neck and shoulders in circular patterns, feeling for any burrs or lumps.

4. Massage his legs and feet, taking a look at his toes and pads.

Bake Your Boston Some Cookies

You can make your Boston's day by whipping up some homemade treats from scratch. This peanut butter cookie recipe given to me by a friend makes the kitchen smell like you're baking tempting goodies for humans!

Puppy Peanut-Buttery Cookies

1 to 1 ½ cups flour

¾ cup oatmeal

¼ cup wheat germ

¼ cup crunchy peanut butter

¼ cup vegetable oil

¼ cup honey

1 tsp baking powder

½ cup water

1. Preheat oven to 325 degrees Fahrenheit.

2. Combine all ingredients and mix on low until blended. The batter should be the consistency of human cookie dough.

3. Form into tablespoon-sized balls and place on an ungreased cookie sheet 3–4 inches apart.

4. Flatten balls to a ¼-inch thickness using the tines of a fork.

5. Bake for 15–20 minutes, or until golden brown.

Yield: About 20 cookies

Toss a Ball

Most Bostons love to play fetch with a flying disc, tennis ball, or squeaky toy. It's great exercise for him and quality bonding time for both of you.

When choosing a toy to toss, make sure that it doesn't have little parts that your Boston may chew off and accidentally swallow. Also make sure the toy is sized appropriately for your dog. A ball that's too small can be a choking hazard, while a ball that's too large can be unwieldy for your small dog.

Do Some Homework

If you and your dog are enrolled in puppy kindergarten or basic obedience class, take some time out of your day to practice his commands with him.

Puppy kindergarten, which introduces you to dog-behavior fundamentals, will require you to practice Settle, Sit, and Stay, three basic commands that teach your dog that you are the pack leader. Basic obedience builds on those commands and adds several others, including Leave It and Heel. (Chapter 11 covers all of these commands.)

Grab some small pieces of cheese or chunks of turkey and go outside on the lawn or driveway to practice what you've learned. After 20 minutes a day of practice, you and your Boston will be earning A's in no time!

Enjoy Each Other's Company

There's no better way to make your dog's day than to spend some quality time together sitting on the porch, under the stars, or in front of a warm fire. It's good for him — and it's good for you, too!

Index

• A •

active submission, 144
acupressure, 201
acupuncture, 201
adolescent dog, 42
adoption
  first night, 82–83
  homecoming overview, 75
  homecoming tour, 76–77
  introduction to pack, 78–82
  needs, 41
  puppy versus adult, 43–44
  shelter dog versus purebred, 11
  social development, 130
adult dog
  food selection, 68
  homecoming overview, 75
  homecoming tour, 76–77
  introduction to pack, 78–82
  versus puppy, 43–44
  selection, 50–52
  serving sizes, 99
  social development, 130
  socialization guidelines, 137–138
advertisement, 49, 198, 254
aggression, 70, 142, 143
aggressive attack pose, 142, 143
agility
  adult socialization, 138
  day care, 190
  definition, 15
  trials, 170–171
  weekly chores, 36
airbag, 186
airplane, 182, 187–188
AKC. *See* American Kennel Club
Alain breed, 19
Alaunt breed, 19
all-breed show, 174
allergy, 211, 221
alternative medicine, 201
American Animal Hospital
    Association, 198

American Boarding Kennels
    Association, 189
American Bull Terrier Club, 21
American Kennel Club (AKC)
  agility trials, 170
  breed history, 21–22, 252
  breed popularity, 10, 22
  breed standards, 23–26
  Canine Good Citizen program,
    166–167
  dog groups, 25
  obedience trials, 168–169
  registration, 59–60
American Society for the Prevention
    of Cruelty to Animals, 58
American Veterinary Medical
    Association, 199
anemia, 230
Animal Poison Control Center, 236
annual checkup, 38, 215–216
antifreeze, 236
arousal posture, 141–142
arthritis, 238–239
artificial respiration, 232
Association of American Feed Control
    Officials, 93
Association of Pet Dog Trainers, 163

• B •

baby gate, 68, 82
backyard breeder, 47
ball, 258
Bandog breed, 20
barking, 28, 159–160
Barnard, J.P. (Barnard's Tom), 21, 251,
    252
basic training, 149
bathing, 105–106
bathroom, 14, 56
Baum, L. Frank (*The Wonderful
    Wizard of Oz*), 254
beans, 90
bedding, 69, 239, 245

bedroom, 14, 57
bedtime. *See* sleep
behavior. *See also specific behaviors*
  adult socialization, 137–138
  body language, 138–144
  Boston's needs, 30–31
  Canine Good Citizen program, 167
  carbohydrates, 91
  challenges, 28
  corrective training, 158–163
  grooming rewards, 104
  housetraining, 120–121
  males versus females, 42–43
  overview, 147
  professional help, 163–164
  puppy selection, 50
  rules, 86–88
  spaying and neutering, 213–214
  tug toys, 70
behavior training. *See* training
benign tumor, 239
Best in Show award, 176
Best of Breed title, 176, 177
bird, 82
biting, 160, 235
Bitter Apple Spray, 74
bleach, 236
bleeding, 233
blow-dryer, 73, 103
boarding, 189–192
boating, 71
body
  breed standard, 26
  postures, 138–144
bone
  fractures, 234
  treats, 256
booster seat, 181
booster shot, 207
bordetella vaccine, 113
Boston Site (Web site), 51
Boston Terrier Club of America
    (BTCA)
  adoption, 51
  breed history, 22
  breeder selection, 45
  shelter dog versus purebred, 11
Boston Terrier Rescue, 11, 51
Boston Terrier Rescue Net, 11, 51

Boston University, 253
bowl, 64–65
brachycephalic breed, 4, 217
brainstem auditory evoked response
    test, 225
breathing, 219, 230
breed standard, 22–27, 174, 254
breeder
  adult adoption, 50, 51
  Boston history, 9–10, 19–21
  pet stores, 47
  selection, 44–47, 51
  shelter dog versus purebred, 11
  vet selection, 198
brindle coat, 21, 26
bristle brush, 103
bruise, 233
brush, 72, 103
brushing tips, 104–105
BTCA. *See* Boston Terrier Club of
    America
bubble gum, 115
bull-baiting, 20
Bulldog, 9, 19–21
bumper pad, 73
bunny, 34, 82
Burnett, Edward (breeder), 21
burr, 115

• **C** •

cage dryer, 113
campground, 186
cancer, 239
canine freestyle, 173–174
Canine Freestyle Federation, 173
Canine Good Citizen program, 149,
    166–167
canned food, 12, 95
car travel
  eye health, 222
  safety, 181–182, 234
  tips for success, 183–187
carbohydrates, 91
cardiopulmonary resuscitation
    (CPR), 232–233
care
  children, 38–39
  chore schedule, 30, 31, 34–37

companionship, 32
essentials, 12–16, 30–31
family dynamics, 32–34
medical needs, 18
overview, 10, 29
patience, 31
carrier, 65–67
cat
bites, 235
family dynamics, 34
pet introductions, 80–81, 82
puppy socialization, 136–137
cataract, 222–223, 240
CD (Companion Dog) title, 169
CDX (Companion Dog Excellent) title, 169
celebrity owners, 254
Center for Veterinary Medicine, 92
ceramic bowl, 64–65
Certification Council for Professional Dog Trainers, 163
certified groomer, 114–115
Champion of Record title, 176, 177
Champion Tracker (CT) title, 170
chemicals, 57
cherry eye, 224
chewing
bedding, 69
corrective training, 160–161
deterrents, 74
dog-proofing tips, 56, 57
owner's patience, 31
puppy toys, 74
children
Boston personality, 10
care schedule, 30, 33, 38–39
dog shows, 176, 177–178
introduction to new dog, 78–80
owner compatibility, 30
puppy socialization, 134–135
puppy versus adult dog, 43
rules, 88
chiropractic therapy, 201
choke collar, 61
chronic kidney disease, 242
cleanup duty
children's chores, 38, 39
equipment, 71–72

first night home, 83
housetraining process, 122, 125, 128, 162
clothing
dog shows, 178
necessary items, 71
overview, 115–116
coat
diet, 91
grooming supplies, 103
home grooming, 104–106
collar, 60–61
color, 26
Come command, 17, 156
command, 151–158. *See also specific commands*
Companion Dog (CD) title, 169
Companion Dog Excellent (CDX) title, 169
companionship, 32
compatibility, 29–32
conditioner, 72, 103
conformation trial, 174–178
congenital problem, 203
consistency, 83–88, 159
cookie, 257
corn, 91
corneal ulcer, 221–222
coronavirus, 206
corrective training, 158–163
cotton swab/ball, 73, 103
CPR (cardiopulmonary resuscitation), 232–233
crate
air travel, 182, 187–188
car travel, 181
children's chores, 39
first night home, 83
homecoming tour, 76–77
housetraining equipment, 14, 69
housetraining tips, 122
location, 77
overview, 13, 65–66
pet dynamics, 34
pet introductions, 81
puppy equipment, 73
cryosurgery, 224
CT (Champion Tracker) title, 170

• D •

daily chore, 35–36, 37
dam, 59
dance, 173–174
day care
  grooming service, 113
  travel tips, 126, 189–190
deafness, 225, 240
death, 245–248
defensive aggression posture, 142
dehydration, 235, 242
Delta Society, 171
demodectic mange, 213
denning animal, 13
development, social, 130–133
diabetes, 240
diarrhea, 235
diet. *See* food
digging, 161–162
diplomate, 199
disease. *See specific diseases*
distemper, 205
distichiasis, 224
distraction, 145, 167
dog license, 58–59
dog park, 15, 256
dog-proofing
  house, 56–57
  overview, 14, 55–56
dog show
  attendance, 174–178
  breeder selection, 45
dog sitter, 126, 192–194
Dog Training For Dummies (Volhard
    and Volhard), 151
dominance issue, 70
Down command, 154
dried kibble, 12, 94–95
dry-eye syndrome, 225
dust, 222
dystocia, 220

• E •

ear canal, 225
ear mites, 225–226

ears
  defensive posture, 142
  dog greeting, 140
  exam, 50
  grooming tools, 103
  health problems, 225–226, 240
  home grooming, 108–109
  submission poses, 144
elderly dog
  bedding, 245
  death, 245–248
  diet, 100
  exercise, 239, 244–245
  food, 242, 244
  grooming, 245
  medical issues, 238–243
  overview, 18, 237
  signs of aging, 237–238
  vet visits, 243–244
emergency
  action, 230–236
  first-aid kit essentials, 228–229
  numbers, 193
  vital signs, 229–230
entropion, 225
estrus, 214
euthanasia, 246–247
exercise
  air travel, 188
  daily chores, 36
  elderly dog, 239, 244–245
  schedules, 85
eyelash, 224
eyes
  exam, 36, 50
  health problems, 221–225, 240–241
  home grooming, 110
  signs of shock, 234

• F •

face, 135
family dynamics, 32–34
fashion, 71, 115–116
fats, 91
fear
  prevention tips, 144–146
  social development, 17, 131, 132

feces, 137
feeding instructions, 92
female dog, 41–43, 88, 214
femoral artery, 229
fever, 229
fiber, 91
finger toothbrush, 111
first-aid kit
  essential items, 227–229
  overview, 18, 227
flea
  overview, 210–212
  preventive, 38, 191, 211–212
floatation device, 71
flyball, 16, 173
food
  air travel, 188
  bowls, 64–65
  car travel, 187
  children's chores, 38
  costs, 89–90
  daily chores, 35
  dog-proofing tips, 56
  elderly dogs, 242, 244
  expenses, 40
  home tour, 76
  kennel boarding, 192
  kidney disease, 242
  labels, 92–93
  obesity, 99
  overview, 12
  requirements, 90–92, 255
  rules, 87
  schedules, 84–85, 98
  selection, 68
  serving sizes, 98–99
  supplements, 100
  types, 12–13, 93–98
Food and Drug Administration, 92
forequarter, 26
fracture, 234
free feeding, 98

• G •

game, 15
garage, 14, 57
gardening equipment, 58
gate, 68, 82

gender, 41–43
general practitioner, 198, 199
giardia, 209
gingivitis, 218
glaucoma, 224, 241
grains, 90, 91
greeting, 140
grinder, nail, 108
groomer, 112–115
grooming
  Canine Good Citizen program, 167
  children's chores, 39
  common problems, 115
  daily chores, 36
  dog shows, 175
  elderly dogs, 245
  equipment, 72–73
  medical issues, 18
  monthly chores, 38
  overview, 101
  professional service, 112–115, 191,
    192
  vet selection, 200–201
grooming, home
  coat care, 104–106
  ear cleaning, 108–109
  nail trimming, 106–108
  overview, 101–102
  preparation, 102–104
  spa treatment, 256–257
  tooth care, 110–112
  treats, 104
group show, 175
guaranteed analysis, 92
guillotine-style clippers, 72
guinea pig, 34, 82
gum, chewing, 115
gums
  disease, 112, 218
  vital signs, 230
Gyp (Boston terrier), 21

• H •

hackles, 141
halitosis, 218
Hanson, Nicole (Boston owner), 172
harness, 62
hat, 116

head, 24
health. *See also* medical issues
  adult dogs, 52
  annual exam, 38, 215-216
  breeder selection, 45, 46
  food selection, 68–69
  guarantees, 49
  insurance, 40
  monthly chores, 38
  overview, 11
  pet sitter information, 193
  pet stores, 48
  puppy selection, 49–50
heart
  massage, 232–233
  problems, 241
  rate, 229
heartworm, 38, 209
heat, 42, 214
heat stroke, 185, 234
Heel command, 17, 157–158
hepatitis, 205
Herding group, 25
hiking, 222
history of breed, 9–10, 19–22
hobby breeder, 47
hock, 26
homemade dog food, 13, 96, 257
hookworm, 208
Hooper, Robert C. (Hooper's Judge),
    9, 21, 251–252
host animal, 207
hot spot, 48, 50
hotel, 186
Hound group, 25
house
  Boston's needs, 30
  companionship, 32
  dog-proofing, 56–57
  flea preventive, 212
  homecoming overview, 75
  homecoming tour, 76–77
  overview, 11
  pet introductions, 82
  requirements, 13–14
  rules, 86–87
housetraining
  access to rooms, 122–123
  accidents, 125, 128
  bedding, 69
  behavior challenges, 28
  cleanup equipment, 71–72, 126, 162
  corrective training, 162–163
  daily chores, 35
  definition, 119
  elderly dogs, 243
  equipment, 14, 69, 73
  first night home, 83
  litter box, 127–128
  location, 121–122
  overview, 119
  owner's patience, 31
  paper training, 126–127
  positive reinforcement, 120–121
  rules, 86
  schedule, 84, 85, 121, 123–124
  supervision, 125
  timing, 120
Hurricane Katrina, 172
hygiene, 72–73
hyperthermic dog, 229
hypoglycemia, 98

• I •

identification, 60, 62–63, 180
incontinence, 243
infection, 225
ingredients list, 92
injury
  emergency action, 230–236
  eye health, 221, 223
insect growth regulator, 212
insect sting, 235
insecticide, 236
insulin-dependant diabetes, 240
insurance, 40, 194

• J •

judge, 175
Jumpers with Weaves (agility class),
    171
jumping, 162
Junior Showmanship class, 177–178

• K •

Keller, Helen (Boston owner), 254
kennel. *See* crate
kennel cough, 113, 206
keratoconjunctivitis sicca, 225
ketone, 240
kibble, 12, 94–95
kidney disease, 242
kitchen, 14, 56
knee problem, 226

• L •

label, food, 92–93
lactating dog, 100
leash, 61–62
Leave It command, 156–157
legs, 26
Leland, Charles F. (club founder), 21, 252
leptospirosis, 205
license, 58–59, 62
life stage, 93
limited registration, 59
Listing Privilege program, 166
litter box, 127–128
litter, puppy, 16, 46
living room, 14
luxated patella, 226
Lyme disease, 206

• M •

macroblepharon, 223
macropalpebral fissure, 223
maintenance diet, 98
male dog, 41–42, 214
malignant tumor, 239
Mammato, Bobbie (*Pet First Aid: Cats and Dogs*), 228
mange, 212–213
manners, 148
manufacturer, food, 93
Massachusetts, 254
massage therapy, 201
Master Agility Championship title, 171

maturity, 132–133
McCullough, Susan (*Senior Dogs For Dummies*), 237
meal. *See* food
meat
 canned food, 95
 homemade diet, 96, 97
 protein sources, 90
 raw diet, 96
medical issues. *See also* health; *specific diseases*
 costs, 40
 death, 246
 diet, 97–98
 elderly dogs, 238–243
 first vet visit, 203–204
 monthly chores, 38
 overview, 18
 vaccines, 205–207
medication, 236
metabolic rate, 242
microchip, 63, 180
minerals, 91–92, 97
miscellaneous group, 25
Molosser breed, 19–20
monthly chore, 37, 38
Morgan, Janet (Boston owner), 172
mouthing, 160
mucous membrane, 230
murmur, heart, 241
Musical Canine Sports International, 173
Musical Dog Sport Association, 174
muzzle, 24, 231

• N •

nails
 clippers, 103
 home grooming, 106–108
name, 151–152, 252
National Association of Professional Pet Sitters, 193
National Certified Master Groomer, 114
National Obedience Champion (NOC) title, 169
Nationwide Boston Terrier Rescue Inc., 11, 51

natural food, 12
neck, 26
neurotic behavior, 28
neutering
  costs, 40
  overview, 213–214
  personality, 42
  procedure, 214–215
  social development, 132
neutral relaxed posture, 139
nickname, 252
NOC (National Obedience Champion)
    title, 169
noise, 135
non-sporting group, 23, 25
North American Flyball Association,
    173
nose, 110
novice level, 168
nuclear sclerosis, 241
nutrition. *See* food
nutritional adequacy statement, 93
nylon collar, 60

• *O* •

obedience
  classes, 138, 147–150, 258
  overview, 17
  trials, 168–169
Obedience Trial Champion (OTCH)
    title, 169
obesity, 99, 100, 242
odor, 71–72
office, 57, 202
oncologist, 201
open level, 168
ophthalmologist, 241
organic food, 12, 94
OTCH (Obedience Trial Champion),
    169
otitis externa, 225
out-cross, 23
outer-ear infection, 225

• *P* •

pack mentality, 88, 136, 148
packing tips, 182–183, 188

paint, 115
palate, 219
palpating, 229
paper training, 127
parasite, 207–213
park, 15, 256
party, 16, 256
parvovirus, 205
passive submission, 144
pastern, 26
patella, 226
patience, 31, 126
personality
  breed standard, 26
  characteristics, 27–28
  family dynamics, 32–34
  male versus female dogs, 41–43
  overview, 10–11
  owner compatibility, 29–30
  pet introductions, 80, 81
pet
  breed personality, 28
  family dynamics, 32, 33–34
  greeting, 140
  health insurance, 40
  introductions, 80–82
  overview, 11
  puppy socialization, 136–137
  purse, 65, 66–67
  sitters, 126, 192–194
  store, 47–49
Pet First Aid: Cats and Dogs
    (Mammato), 228
Pet Sitters International, 193
photo album, 247
pin brush, 72
plants, 57, 58, 222
plaque, 110, 161
plastic bowl, 64
play bow, 138, 140–141
playpen, 68, 122
playtime
  ball toss, 258
  day care, 189–190
  equipment, 69–71
  events, 172–174
  homecoming tour, 77
  new pets, 81
  overview, 15–16

puppy socialization, 134
  schedule, 85
pneumonia, 206
pocket pet, 34
poison
  emergency action, 235–236
  homecoming preparations, 57, 58
pooper scooper, 72, 126
popularity, 10, 22, 252–253
positive reinforcement
  adult socialization, 137
  definition, 17
  housetraining, 120–121
  overview, 151
  trainer selection, 150
posture, 138–144
pregnant dog, 100
premium food, 90
prescription food, 13, 97–98, 242
prognathism, 218
proptosis, 223
protein, 90–91
pulse, 229
punishment, 158
puppy
  versus adult dog, 43–44
  distributors, 47
  fear prevention, 144–146
  first night home, 82–83
  food selection, 68
  homecoming overview, 75
  homecoming tour, 76–77
  introduction to pack, 78–82
  kindergarten, 17, 132, 137, 147–150
  meal schedule, 98
  mills, 47
  necessary equipment, 73–74
  selection, 44–50
  serving sizes, 99
  social development, 130–133
  socializing guidelines, 133–137
  vaccines, 204–207
purebred dog
  expenses, 39
  versus shelter dog, 11
  standards, 23–27
purse, 65, 66–67

• Q •

quick, 107

• R •

rabies, 205, 206
rally, 170
ratter, 20
raw diet, 13, 96
registry, 27, 166
reptile, 82, 136
reputable dog breeder, 45
rescue dog, 51–52, 130
restraint, 231
Rhett (university mascot), 253
rice, 91
Richards, Denise (Boston owner), 254
ringworm, 213
Rivers, Joan (Boston owner), 254
roundworm, 208
rules, 84, 86–88

• S •

safety
  boating, 71
  car travel, 181, 185, 234
  dog-proofing, 14, 55–58
  introduction of new dog, 78–79
  nail trimming, 107, 108
  pet introductions, 81
  puppy socialization, 133–134
  toys, 70
  training classes, 148
salmonella, 82
sarcoptic mange, 212–213
schedule
  basic needs, 30
  chores, 34–38
  consistency, 83–85
  housetraining, 121, 123–124
  meals, 84–85, 98
  vaccines, 206–207
school-age child, 79–80
scissor-style clippers, 72
scissors, 73, 103
sclera, 223

seal coat, 26
seatbelt harness, 182, 185
security, 30
semi-moist food, 12, 95
Senior Dogs For Dummies
    (McCullough), 237
service dog, 171–172
Settle command, 17, 152–153
sexual maturity, 132, 214
shampoo, 72, 74, 103
shedding blade, 103
shelter dog
  adoption, 50–52
  expenses, 39
  versus purebred, 11
  social development, 130
shock, 234
single-coated breed, 104
sire, 59
Sit command, 17, 153–154
size
  breed, 24
  clothing, 116
  crate, 66
  food, 93
  toys, 70
skin, 104–106
skunk spray, 115
sleep
  first night home, 82–83
  rules, 87
  schedule, 85
slicker brush, 103
slip chain, 61
sniffing, 80–81, 135, 140
snorting, 28, 217–220
social hierarchy, 130
socializing
  adult dogs, 137–138
  developmental timeline, 130–133
  doggy day care, 190
  fear prevention, 144–146
  kennel boarding, 191
  milestones, 16–17
  overview, 16, 129
  puppy guidelines, 133–137
  rules, 88
  weekly chores, 36

spa
  home grooming, 256–257
  professional service, 112–115
spaying
  costs, 40
  overview, 213–214
  personality, 42
  procedure, 214–215
  social development, 132
specialty show, 174
Sporting group, 25
sports
  adult socialization, 138
  breed history, 20
  events, 172–174
  overview, 15–16
  training, 165–171
  weekly chores, 36
stainless steel bowl, 65
Standard Class (agility class), 171
Stay command, 17, 154–155
sticker, 115
stifle, 26
stool sample, 204
styptic powder, 107
submission pose, 144
sun exposure, 222
supplements, 100
sweetener, 95

• *T* •

table scrap, 87
tail, 26
Take It command, 156–157
tapeworm, 210
tartar, 110
tattoo, 63
TD (Tracking Dog) title, 169
TDX (Tracking Dog Excellent) title,
    169
technician, veterinary, 202
teen, 80
teeth crowding, 218
temperature, 229
terrier, 9, 19–21
Terrier group, 25
therapy dog, 10, 171–172
Therapy Dogs International, 171

tick
Lyme disease, 206
overview, 210, 212
preventive, 38, 191
removal from pet, 212
toenail clippers, 72
toilet, 56
tools, 58
tooth issues
breed problems, 218
chewing, 161
chores, 36
cleaning equipment, 73
food choices, 12, 95
grooming supplies, 103
heart murmurs, 241
home grooming, 110–112
signs of disease, 112
toothbrush, 73, 103, 110
toothpaste, 110–111
tote, 65, 66–67
tourniquet, 233
towel, 103
toy
balls, 258
overview, 15
puppy equipment, 73–74
selection, 69–71
Toy group, 25
tracheal hypoplasia, 220
tracking
definition, 15–16
trials, 169–170
Tracking Dog Excellent (TDX) title,
169
Tracking Dog (TD) title, 169
trainer, 150, 163–164
training
Boston's needs, 30, 31
children's chores, 39
commands, 151–158
corrective, 158–163
costs, 40
daily chores, 36
method selection, 87
overview, 147
pet dynamics, 34
practice, 258
professional help, 163–164

puppy versus adult dog, 43, 44
sports, 165–171
therapy dogs, 171–172
weekly chores, 36
trash, 56
travel
boarding, 188–192
carrier, 65–67, 180–181
day care, 126, 189–190
emergency action, 232
homemade diet, 96–97
overview, 179
preparation, 180–183
treat
elderly diet, 244
grooming rewards, 104
homemade, 257
housetraining reward, 120
overview, 68–69, 100
rules, 87
tooth care, 111
toy choices, 71
trivia, 251–254
tug toy, 70

• **U** •

unaltered male, 42
United Flyball League International,
173
United Kennel Club (UKC), 27, 59
unspayed female, 42
upper-airway syndrome, 219–220
urinary incontinence, 243
Utility Dog Excellent (UDX) title, 169
Utility Dog (UD) title, 169
utility level, 168

• **V** •

vaccine
boarding, 190, 191
day care, 137
overview, 204
professional groomer, 113
puppy socialization, 137
schedule, 206–207
trainer selection, 150
types, 205–206

Variable Surface Tracking (VST) title, 170
veterinarian
  air travel, 187
  annual chores, 38, 215–216
  car travel, 186
  elderly dogs, 243–244
  emergency action, 230
  euthanasia, 246–247
  expenses, 40, 49
  first visit, 203–204
  kennel boarding, 191
  overview, 18
  puppy socialization, 136
  selection, 197–203
  vaccines, 204–207
veterinary specialist, 199–200
vision loss, 241
vital signs, 229–230
vitamins, 91–92, 97
voice, 145, 159
Volhard, Jack and Wendy (*Dog Training For Dummies*), 151
vomiting, 235
VST (Variable Surface Tracking) title, 170

• *W* •

walking
  breed standard, 26
  Canine Good Citizen program, 167
  care basics, 15
  commands, 17
  daily chores, 36
  importance, 255–256
  kennel boarding, 192
  schedules, 85
water
  air travel, 188
  bowls, 64–65

canned food, 95
children's chores, 38
daily chores, 35
emergency care, 235
importance, 13
weekly chore, 36, 37
Well's Eph (Boston terrier), 21, 252
Westminster Kennel Club Dog Show, 174
wheezing, 28, 217–220
whimpering, 83
whipworm, 209
will, 246
Wofford College, 253
The Wonderful Wizard of Oz (Baum), 254
Working group, 25
World Canine Freestyle Organization, 174
World Canine Organization, 27
World Trade Center attacks, 172
worm, 208–210
wrestling, 135

• *X* •

X-pen, 68, 122

• *Y* •

yard
  Boston's needs, 30
  dog-proofing, 14, 57–58
  housetraining location, 121–122
yelping, 239

• *Z* •

zoonotic disease, 205

BUSINESS, CAREERS & PERSONAL FINANCE

Fundraising For Dummies
0-7645-9847-3

Investing For Dummies
0-7645-2431-3

Also available:

- Business Plans Kit For Dummies 0-7645-9794-9
- Economics For Dummies 0-7645-5726-2
- Grant Writing For Dummies 0-7645-8416-2
- Home Buying For Dummies 0-7645-5331-3
- Managing For Dummies 0-7645-1771-6
- Marketing For Dummies 0-7645-5600-2

- Personal Finance For Dummies 0-7645-2590-5*
- Resumes For Dummies 0-7645-5471-9
- Selling For Dummies 0-7645-5363-1
- Six Sigma For Dummies 0-7645-6798-5
- Small Business Kit For Dummies 0-7645-5984-2
- Starting an eBay Business For Dummies 0-7645-6924-4
- Your Dream Career For Dummies 0-7645-9795-7

HOME & BUSINESS COMPUTER BASICS

Laptops For Dummies
0-470-05432-8

Windows Vista For Dummies
0-471-75421-8

Also available:

- Cleaning Windows Vista For Dummies 0-471-78293-9
- Excel 2007 For Dummies 0-470-03737-7
- Mac OS X Tiger For Dummies 0-7645-7675-5
- MacBook For Dummies 0-470-04859-X
- Macs For Dummies 0-470-04849-2
- Office 2007 For Dummies 0-470-00923-3

- Outlook 2007 For Dummies 0-470-03830-6
- PCs For Dummies 0-7645-8958-X
- Salesforce.com For Dummies 0-470-04893-X
- Upgrading & Fixing Laptops For Dummies 0-7645-8959-8
- Word 2007 For Dummies 0-470-03658-3
- Quicken 2007 For Dummies 0-470-04600-7

FOOD, HOME, GARDEN, HOBBIES, MUSIC & PETS

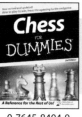

Chess For Dummies
0-7645-8404-9

Guitar For Dummies
0-7645-9904-6

Also available:

- Candy Making For Dummies 0-7645-9734-5
- Card Games For Dummies 0-7645-9910-0
- Crocheting For Dummies 0-7645-4151-X
- Dog Training For Dummies 0-7645-8418-9
- Healthy Carb Cookbook For Dummies 0-7645-8476-6

- Home Maintenance For Dummies 0-7645-5215-5
- Horses For Dummies 0-7645-9797-3
- Jewelry Making & Beading For Dummies 0-7645-2571-9
- Orchids For Dummies 0-7645-6759-4
- Puppies For Dummies 0-7645-5255-4
- Rock Guitar For Dummies 0-7645-5356-9
- Sewing For Dummies 0-7645-6847-7
- Singing For Dummies 0-7645-2475-5

INTERNET & DIGITAL MEDIA

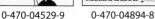

eBay For Dummies
0-470-04529-9

iPod & iTunes For Dummies
0-470-04894-8

Also available:

- Blogging For Dummies 0-471-77084-1
- Digital Photography For Dummies 0-7645-9802-3
- Digital Photography All-in-One Desk Reference For Dummies 0-470-03743-1
- Digital SLR Cameras and Photography For Dummies 0-7645-9803-1
- eBay Business All-in-One Desk Reference For Dummies 0-7645-8438-3

- HDTV For Dummies 0-470-09673-X
- Home Entertainment PCs For Dummies 0-470-05523-5
- MySpace For Dummies 0-470-09529-6
- Search Engine Optimization For Dummies 0-471-97998-8
- Skype For Dummies 0-470-04891-3
- The Internet For Dummies 0-7645-8996-2
- Wiring Your Digital Home For Dummies 0-471-91830-X

Separate Canadian edition also available
Separate U.K. edition also available

Available wherever books are sold. For more information or to order direct: U.S. customers visit www.dummies.com or call 1-877-762-2974. U.K. customers visit www.wileyeurope.com or call 0800 243407. Canadian customers visit www.wiley.ca or call 1-800-567-4797.

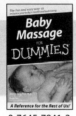